ANGLO-SAXON
POTTERY
AND THE SETTLEMENT
OF ENGLAND

ANGLO-SAXON POTTERY

AND THE SETTLEMENT
OF ENGLAND

BY

J. N. L. MYRES

OXFORD
AT THE CLARENDON PRESS
1969

Oxford University Press, Ely House, London W. 1

GLASGOW NEW YORK TORONTO MELBOURNE WELLINGTON
CAPE TOWN SALISBURY IBADAN NAIROBI LUSAKA ADDIS ABABA
BOMBAY CALCUTTA MADRAS KARACHI LAHORE DACCA
KUALA LUMPUR SINGAPORE HONG KONG TOKYO

PRINTED IN GREAT BRITAIN
AT THE UNIVERSITY PRESS, OXFORD
BY VIVIAN RIDLER
PRINTER TO THE UNIVERSITY

FOREWORD

I WOULD like to express my grateful thanks to all those whose kind co-operation with me in one way or another has made the publication of this book possible. I am indebted first of all to those who have the control of the museums and collections, over sixty in number, where I have worked, who have placed their contents at my disposal with the greatest cordiality. To the following especially I am grateful for permission to publish drawings or photographs of material in their keeping, and for information about it: Ashmolean Museum, Oxford; British Museum; University Museum of Archaeology and Ethnology, and Girton College, Cambridge; Bedford Museum; Moyses Hall Museum, Bury St. Edmunds; Royal Museum, Canterbury; Colchester and Essex Museum, Colchester; Herbert Art Gallery and Museum, Coventry; Borough Museum, Dartford; Grantham Museum; Guildford Museum, and the Surrey Archaeological Society; Hull Museums; Kettering Museum; King's Lynn Museum; the Trustees of the Layton Collection; Leicester Museum; Barbican House, Lewes, and the Sussex Archaeological Society; City and County Museum, Lincoln; London Museum; Society of Antiquaries of London; Luton Museum; Maidstone Museum; Dorman Museum, Middlesbrough; Borough Museum, Newbury; Museum of Antiquities of the University of New-castle upon Tyne and the Society of Antiquaries of Newcastle upon Tyne; Central Museum, Northampton; Castle Museum, Norwich; Castle Museum, Nottingham; Oakham School Museum; Peterborough Museum; Reading Museum; Scunthorpe Museum; Sunbury and Shepperton Local History Society; County Museum, Warwick; Worthing Museum; Yorkshire Museum, York; Mr. G. Wyman Abbott; and the Ministry of Public Building and Works.

I am similarly indebted to the authorities of the many museums in Germany, Holland, Belgium, Denmark, Norway, and Sweden whose collections I have studied and who have kindly answered my questions and supplied me with drawings, photographs, and off-prints. I am particularly grateful to Dr. A. Genrich of Hannover, Dr. P. Schmid of Wilhelmshaven, Professor Dr. H. Roosens of Brussels, Dr. W. A. Van Es of Amersfoort, Dr. H. Norling-Christensen of Copenhagen, Dr. Wencke Slomann of Oslo, Professor Dr. J. Werner of Munich, and to many other scholars associated with the Arbeitsgemeinschaft für Sachsenforschung who have taken part in the annual meetings of the Sachsensymposium. Amongst these I remember with especial gratitude the late Herr K. Waller of Cuxhaven, the late Professor Dr. F. Tischler of Duisburg, and the late Dr. E. Grohne of Bremen. The late Professor Dr. G. Bersu of Frankfurt-am-Main was so good as to make it possible for me to take part in two of the early meetings of the Sachsensymposium which I could not otherwise have attended.

Among English friends I am greatly indebted to those who have supplied me with their own drawings or photographs, or have allowed me to take copies of them, especially to Messrs T. C. Lethbridge, Graham Webster, and K. R. Fennell, the excavators respectively of the great cemeteries at Lackford, South Elkington, and Loveden Hill. Dr. Fennell in particular has not only kept me supplied with copies of all his drawings, but has generously allowed me to use those that I needed as illustrations to this book, in advance of his own definitive publication of Loveden Hill. My former pupil, Mr. John Bartlett, Director of the Hull Museums, has kindly given me similar facilities in connection with the unpublished material from Sancton.

Some twelve years ago the Council for British Archaeology generously undertook to circulate on my behalf a request for information on their holdings of Anglo-Saxon pottery to all the museums in this country which I had not at that time visited. This saved me much correspondence and the expense of fruitless visits to places which had no relevant material, while on the positive side it not only revealed some collections which I might otherwise have missed, but made it possible to form an estimate of the work likely to be involved in the compilation of a complete *Corpus Vasorum Anglo-Saxonicorum*. I am grateful for this welcome help not only to the Council and its Secretary, Miss B. de Cardi, on whom the work mainly fell, but also to all the Museum Curators who put themselves to some trouble in replying to the questionnaire.

I must also record my thanks to all those who have enabled me from time to time to set aside the cares of a busy official life in order to work on the material which I was accumulating. An imaginative and most welcome suggestion by my former tutor, Professor Sir Llewellyn Woodward, secured for me in 1956 an invitation to spend three months in this way at the Institute for Advanced Study at Princeton, the first period of continuous devotion to these matters which had come my way for over twenty years. The Curators of the Bodleian Library generously granted me leave of absence on that occasion and again for three months seven years later to prepare the Rhind Lectures for 1965 on which this book is based. By inviting me to give these lectures the Council of the Society of Antiquaries of Scotland provided me with the ideal opportunity for bringing into publishable form the outcome of many years work which I would not otherwise have found it easy to set in order. I have been privileged also for three years to receive from the British Academy a Research Grant towards the completion of my *Corpus*. This enabled me, amongst other things, to enlist for eleven months the services of Miss Felicity Pearce, M.A., now Mrs. J. P. Wild, as Research Assistant. She not only reduced the mass of my material to order in a systematic arrangement provided with appropriate documentation and indices, but also added substantially to it, and prepared from my originals nearly half the finished drawings from which the illustrations both to my Rhind lectures and to this book have been made. The remainder of the drawings here used have been fair copied by Miss Mary Potter of the Oxford University School of Geography from originals in my collection. The officials of the Clarendon Press have carried out the production of the book with their accustomed skill and accuracy, and I am particularly grateful for their patience and understanding in handling the illustrations and preparing the rather complicated maps.

Since leaving the Bodleian Library at the end of 1965 I have been greatly indebted to my colleagues on the Governing Body of Christ Church not only for renewing the Studentship which, in one form or another, has made me a member of that ample foundation for over forty years, but for the financial provision and encouragement which now enables me to pursue these studies without undue distraction. *Funes ceciderunt mihi in praeclaris; etenim hereditas mea praeclara est mihi.*

J. N. L. MYRES

Christ Church
Oxford

CONTENTS

LIST OF PLATES

(at end)

LIST OF FIGURES

(pp. 148–249)

LIST OF MAPS

ABBREVIATIONS

Abingdon	E. T. Leeds and D. B. Harden, *The Anglo-Saxon Cemetery at Abingdon, Berks.* (1936).
Altenwalde	K. Waller, *Das Gräberfeld von Altenwalde* (1957).
Ant. Journ.	*Antiquaries Journal.*
Ant. Rutup.	J. Battely, *Antiquitates Rutupinae* (1745).
Arch.	*Archaeologia.*
Arch. Belg.	*Archaeologia Belgica.*
Arch. Cant.	*Archaeologia Cantiana.*
Arch. Journ.	*Archaeological Journal.*
Bøe	J. Bøe, *Jernalderens Keramikk i Norge* (1931).
B.M.	British Museum
C.A.S.	*Proceedings of the Cambridge Antiquarian Society.*
Coll. Ant.	C. Roach Smith, *Collectanea Antiqua* I–VI (1848–68).
Duhnen-Wehrberg	K. Waller, *Die Gräberfelder von Hemmoor, Quelkhorn, Gudendorf und Duhnen-Wehrberg* (1959).
E.H.R.	*English Historical Review.*
Fuhlsbüttel	F. Tischler, *Fuhlsbüttel, ein Beitrag zur Sachsenfrage* (1937).
Galgenberg	K. Waller, *Der Galgenberg bei Cuxhaven* (1938).
Genrich (1954)	A. Genrich, *Formenkreise und Stammesgruppen in Schleswig-Holstein* (1954).
Girton	E. J. Hollingworth and M. M. O'Reilly, *The Anglo-Saxon Cemetery at Girton College* (1925).
Gudendorf } *Hemmoor* }	K. Waller, *Die Gräberfelder von Hemmoor, Quelkhorn, Gudendorf und Duhnen-Wehrberg* (1959).
Hist. Britt.	*Historia Brittonum.*
Hist. Eccles.	Bede, *Historia Ecclesiastica Gentis Anglorum.*
Hull Mus. Publns.	*Hull Museum Publications.*
J.R.S.	*Journal of Roman Studies.*
Lackford	T. C. Lethbridge, *A Cemetery at Lackford, Suffolk* (1951).
Mackeprang (1943)	M. B. Mackeprang, *Kulturbeziehungen im nordischen Raum* (1943).
Mahndorf	E. Grohne, *Mahndorf* (1953).
Med. Arch.	*Mediaeval Archaeology.*
M.G.H.	*Monumenta Germaniae Historica.*

Norf. Arch.	*Norfolk Archaeology.*
Not. Dig. Occ.	*Notitia Dignitatum Occidentalis.*
Oberjersdal	F. Tischler, *Das Gräberfeld Oberjersdal* (1955).
Plettke	A. Plettke, *Ursprung und Ausbreitung der Angeln und Sachsen* (1920).
Proc. Hants. F.C.	*Proceedings of the Hampshire Field Club.*
Proc. Soc. Ant.	*Proceedings of the Society of Antiquaries.*
Proc. Suff. Inst. of Arch.	*Proceedings of the Suffolk Institute of Archaeology.*
Quelkhorn	K. Waller, *Die Gräberfelder von Hemmoor, Quelkhorn, Gudendorf und Duhnen-Wehrberg* (1959).
Soc. Ant.	Society of Antiquaries of London
Surr. Arch. Coll.	*Surrey Archaeological Collections.*
Tischler (1956)	F. Tischler, 'Der Stand der Sachsenforschung archäologisch gesehen' (35. *Bericht der Römisch-germanischen Kommission* (1956), 21–215).
Trs. Ess. Arch. Soc.	*Transactions of the Essex Archaeological Society.*
V.C.H.	*Victoria County History.*
Wageningen	W. A. van Es, 'Het Rijengrafveld van Wageningen' (*Palaeohistoria* x (1964), 183–316).
Wehden	K. Waller, *Der Urnenfriedhof in Wehden* (1961).
Westerwanna i	K. Zimmer-Linnfeld, H. Gummel, and K. Waller, *Westerwanna* i (1960).
Wijster	W. A. van Es, *Wijster, a native village beyond the Imperial Frontier, 150–425* A.D., 2 vols. (1967).

I

INTRODUCTION: NATURE AND DISTRIBUTION OF THE MATERIAL

THIS book contains the substance of the Rhind Lectures which I was invited by the Council of the Society of Antiquaries of Scotland to deliver in Edinburgh in March 1965. The text of the lectures has been revised for publication, certain parts being expanded and the whole to some extent rearranged, and provided with the necessary documentation.

The title, which has not been altered, is, I hope, self-explanatory, but my reasons for choosing it require some explanation, and may even justify a few words of reminiscence. It is now over thirty-five years since I first became interested in the studies on which this book forms an interim report. I had been asked early in 1931 to contribute to the Oxford History of England a section covering the Anglo-Saxon settlements, which should serve as a link between the late Professor R. G. Collingwood's volume on Roman Britain and Sir Frank Stenton's account of Anglo-Saxon England. I was urged to include in this all the information that a historian could properly derive from the current state of Anglo-Saxon archaeology, a subject on which neither Professor Collingwood nor Professor Stenton wished to enlarge in their own contributions to the Oxford History. I undertook this commission with the light-hearted enthusiasm of ignorance and youth, expecting that it might provide me for a few years with a congenial research project before passing on to other things. Although my chapters in the Oxford History were published in 1936,[1] it has in fact occupied me ever since. I have never for a moment regretted a commitment which, without any appreciation on my part of its long-term implications, has determined the main course of my archaeological and historical interests for the whole of my working life.

When I came to survey the state of the archaeological evidence for the Anglo-Saxon settlements in 1931 I was impressed at once by the absence of any recent work of consequence on the pottery of the pagan period. Much time and thought

---

[1] R. G. Collingwood and J. N. L. Myres, *Roman Britain and the English Settlements* (1936), 325–461.

B

had been devoted, and was still being devoted, by scholars such as E. T. Leeds, R. A. Smith, T. D. Kendrick, and others, to the brooches and other objects of metal, and in this work English students were assisted by the massive researches of their continental colleagues in Germany, Scandinavia, and the Low Countries. But there was nothing comparable in existence, or in prospect, on the pottery in this country. Even abroad, the pioneer work of A. Plettke, left incomplete on his death in the 1914 war and published posthumously in 1920,[1] could be supplemented only by the studies of F. Roeder on such unusual forms as the window urns and spout-handled urns.[2] These were both published in 1928 and are of comparatively little importance to English students, since these forms are of very rare occurrence in this country. In England the generalized surveys of G. Baldwin Brown in *The Arts in Early England* iv (1915) and R. A. Smith, whose *Guide to the Anglo-Saxon Antiquities in the British Museum* came out in 1923, while they called attention to the great variety and wide distribution of Anglo-Saxon pottery, especially in those parts of England where cremation was a common burial rite, made no serious attempt to classify the types of pottery used, to discuss their bearing on the continental homes of the invaders, or to establish typological, let alone chronological, sequences. As I wrote in 1937, 'we know about as much and about as little about it as was known when Neville published his *Saxon Obsequies* in 1852, or Kemble first drew attention to the continental parallels in a pioneer paper in *Archaeologia* in 1856'.[3]

The extent to which this material had been neglected was indeed extraordinary, especially when it is remembered how significant pottery can be in elucidating the cultures and the chronology of any illiterate age.[4] In such periods it is indeed more normally used to provide type fossils than any other group of human artefacts. But hardly any of the long series of Anglo-Saxon urns in our museums had been properly published: of most of them no illustrations whatever were in print at all. Even when other material from a cemetery was adequately described and illustrated, no attempt was usually made to extend such treatment to the pottery. When, for example, the Girton cemetery

[1] A. Plettke, *Ursprung und Ausbreitung der Angeln und Sachsen* (1920).

[2] F. Roeder, 'Die sächsische Fenstergefässe' (*Röm. germ. Kommission* xviii (1928), 149): 'Die Henkelgussurnen' (*Mannus*, Ergänzungsband vi (1928), 190).

[3] *Antiquity* xi (1937), 389. J. M. Kemble's paper was reprinted in *Horae Ferales* (1863), 221–32.

[4] The two-period map which I compiled for *Roman Britain and the English Settlements* in 1936, (Map X), must have been one of the first to incorporate the evidence of the pottery in an attempt to distinguish cemeteries in use in the fifth century from the rest of the pagan Anglo-Saxon distribution.

at Cambridge, partially explored during the extension of the college in 1881, was written up in 1925,[1] only a dozen out of more than a hundred urns were illustrated, and those by small-scale oblique photographs making accurate measurements impossible: while as late as 1936 the pottery from the Abingdon cemetery near Oxford was published with drawings reduced to 1:9 and photographs to 1:7, so that no detail of the decoration was visible on either.[2] It is hard to imagine such cavalier treatment being tolerated in the publication of any other category of archaeological material. No reduction to a smaller scale than 1:4 should ever be allowed in the publication of Anglo-Saxon pottery.

The situation was the more remarkable in view of the great strides which were being made between the wars in the study of the pottery of other periods in this country. Neolithic wares were being identified for the first time, and their main groups were being distinguished. The urns, food vessels, and beakers of the Bronze Age were being classified anew with illuminating results on our knowledge. The Iron Age was being divided up in time and space, following mainly on a new and intensive study of its pottery. The dating of Roman ceramics was already advancing in precision to the point at which it could make a major contribution to the detailed history of forts, towns, and villas. But no one was paying any systematic attention to Anglo-Saxon pottery, or inquiring seriously whether it could be made to shed light, in any comparable degree, on the dark centuries of the gap between the end of Roman Britain and the emergence of Christian England.

Here then was a major defect in Anglo-Saxon archaeology as I saw it in 1931, and until it was remedied, or at least shown to be irremediable, it seemed unlikely that historians of this period would regard the information supplied by archaeology as either complete or reliable. I accordingly resolved to look into the matter further, and I consulted the leading scholars in Anglo-Saxon archaeology as to the best way to set about it. They were unanimous in agreeing that something ought to be done about the pottery, but they gave me in their different ways the sort of encouragement which one gives to someone bent on pursuing a praiseworthy but forlorn endeavour. I still treasure some scraps of paper which two great scholars presented to me as a symbolic indication that they had once given some thought to the matter themselves, but, having found it unrewarding, were happy to renounce what interest they might have had in it to me. In doing so they wished me luck as one may wish luck

[1] E. J. Hollingworth and M. M. O'Reilly, *The Anglo-Saxon Cemetery at Girton College* (1925).

[2] E. T. Leeds and D. B. Harden, *The Anglo-Saxon Cemetery at Abingdon, Berks.* (1936).

to an explorer setting out upon a wild adventure from which one does not expect him to return. Sir Thomas Kendrick's contribution to my project was a single sheet of paper on which he had set down what turned out to be a very penetrating, if necessarily provisional, scheme for the classification by shape of the main types of Anglo-Saxon cremation urns. Mr. E. T. Leeds gave me some rough sketches of the more interesting stamps used by Anglo-Saxon potters for decorating their wares. It so happens that these two gifts, which, as I say, I still treasure, symbolize two of the lines of inquiry which I have been following ever since. So equipped I sallied forth into the unknown.

Three things had obviously to be done if progress was to be made. It would be necessary in the first place to assemble drawings and photographs of the raw material as it lay neglected in our museums and private collections. And secondly it was extremely desirable to find some highly productive site which could be treated as a type-site, one, that is, from which a really long series of pots had been, or could be, extracted in controlled conditions. Only so would it be possible both to check the range of the material and to form some idea of the relationship which different groups within it might bear to one another. Most of the material in our museums, having been excavated in pre-scientific times, threw little or no light on these groupings and relationships. A third prerequisite to understanding the English pottery was obviously to compare it in detail with the corresponding continental material, as had indeed been pointed out by J. M. Kemble as long ago as 1856. Between 1931 and the out-break of war in 1939 I devoted most of what leisure I had, as a college tutor and university lecturer, to the pursuit of these and other lines of inquiry, and since 1948, when I became Bodley's Librarian, I have done the same. But un-fortunately university librarians, especially when engaged in a continuous series of major building, reconstruction, and reorganization operations, do not have much leisure; nor do they share in the opportunities for personal research that are afforded to their academic colleagues by regular periods of sabbatical leave, or even by the welcome alternation of term and vacation.

A good deal of progress, however slow, has been made in assembling drawings and photographs of the relevant material in our museums and collec-tions. My object was to create a *Corpus*, not of finished drawings, but of measured sketches in pencil, sufficiently accurate to form a finding-list for everything there was to find. At the present moment I have drawings of over 3,500 pots that are sufficiently complete to reveal their form and decoration, and of a great quantity of fragments. This is the material on which this book is based. It is not complete—no *Corpus* ever is—but it is now something more than a random sample and it is continually receiving additions both from old collections and from new discoveries. Its deficiencies, whether those that are remediable, or those that are inherent in the material itself, will become obvious in the course of these chapters, and I shall have frequent occasion later on to refer to them. But without this material at my disposal I could never have written on this subject at all.

The second requirement, to find a site prolific in pottery of this period which could be excavated, or had been excavated, in controlled conditions, was met by the great cremation cemetery at Caistor-by-Norwich. This important site lies close by the south-east corner of the defences of the Roman town of Venta Icenorum, and was dug between 1932 and 1937 by the late Surgeon Commander F. R. Mann, R.N., as a byproduct and sequel to operations conducted in Venta itself by the late Professor Donald Atkinson. The Caistor cemetery was from many points of view almost ideally suited for use as a type-site for Anglo-Saxon pottery of the pagan period. It was the largest cremation cemetery at that time known in this country. On a very conservative estimate it must have contained over a thousand urns, of which some four hundred had been excavated with proper care and were available for study with their individual contents and some indication of their position in relation to each other. The situation of the cemetery, so near the east coast and in immediate proximity to a Roman walled town of some official consequence, made it likely to be of especial significance in throwing light on the early stages of the invasions. The cremation pottery appeared moreover to cover the whole range of the pagan period, for although some fifty-seven inhumations were also found, these could all be shown to belong to the final phase of the cemetery's life before it finally went out of use in the course of the seventh century. It could thus be assumed that the urns formed a continuous chronological series covering the whole period from the settlement of Germanic folk in the vicinity of the Roman town, down to, and perhaps a little after, their conversion to Christianity, a matter of some two hundred years.

This is not the occasion to enter in detail into the conditions under which the Caistor cemetery was excavated, or the tragic circumstances which have deferred its publication for so long. These matters will be fully covered in the report which is now in the final stages of completion, in spite of the delays inevitably caused by the death of all those most closely concerned with the excavations and with the subsequent examination of the finds. I mention it now because of the sense of obligation which I recognize to the late Commander Mann, not only for the meticulous care with which he recorded his discoveries, but for the great assistance which I derived in my own work from being so closely associated with him from 1935 onwards in the examination and discussion of the mass of material which he was revealing. It was of the utmost value to check the views which I was reaching about the typological relationship between different groups of the pottery against his own independent conclusions formed in the course of excavating the cemetery, and to find them so often in harmony. After his death in 1944, and the transference of all the material to the Norwich Castle Museum at the end of the war, I had the same good fortune in being associated with the late Mr. R. R. Clarke, F.S.A., F.M.A., in the plans for publishing the cemetery as a Research Committee Report of the Society of Antiquaries of London. Neither he nor I had the leisure to work continuously on this project, except for brief but intensive spells at all too long intervals spread over more than fifteen years, but the pots had all been drawn and mounted for illustration on some sixty pages of line-blocks and all had been individually described by me, with a general account of the types involved, before his untimely death in the spring of 1963. The Report, when it appears, will owe a very great deal, as I do myself, to his enthusiasm and energy, and to the dynamic qualities of his critical and incisive mind. In this book there will be many occasions to use the Caistor pottery to illustrate stages of the argument, and the knowledge and experience of the material gained from handling and describing every one of this great collection of well-documented vessels constitutes perhaps my main justification in writing on this subject at all.

Caistor-by-Norwich is not of course the only great Anglo-Saxon cremation cemetery whose contents have become available for study during the thirty years in which I have interested myself in these matters. Apart from the continuous stream of smaller discoveries, some of them of very great interest, five substantial collections deserve mention, not only for their intrinsic importance, but because they fill gaps which needed filling in the geographical distribution of the material in eastern England. Two of them are in Lincolnshire, two close together in west Norfolk and west Suffolk, and one in the East Riding of Yorkshire, all areas in which cremation pottery, though by no means lacking, was not available in sufficient quantity to provide a representative series. In west Suffolk, the partial excavation of a great cemetery at Lackford enabled Mr. T. C. Lethbridge, F.S.A., to publish in 1951 sketches of some 160

urns, with a spirited and useful commentary.[1] Lackford conveniently fills the
gap between Caistor-by-Norwich on the east and the cemeteries of the
Cambridge region, such as Girton, St. John's, or Little Wilbraham. This
publication also illustrated a number of products of the so-called Icklingham
(or more accurately, Illington/Lackford) potter, whose existence I had already
postulated in 1937 on the basis of three urns from Lackford and West Stow in
the Ashmolean Museum.[2] Further evidence for the activities of this workshop is provided, on a more massive scale, by the nearby cemetery of Illington
in west Norfolk, from which some 288 urns were excavated in 1949 by Group-
Captain Guy Knocker for the Ministry of Works.[3] Further north in Lincolnshire, Dr. K. R. Fennell's devoted labours in extending the exploration of the
known site of Loveden Hill, near Hough-on-the-Hill (between the Ancaster
gap and the Trent), which had already produced some forty urns many years
ago,[4] have revealed a very large cemetery. Its extent is not yet fully known,
but its contents seem likely to rival, if not surpass, in quantity and quality the
material from Caistor-by-Norwich.[5] Further north and nearer the coast there
is the cemetery of South Elkington, one mile north-west of Louth on the
Lincolnshire Wolds. This site, partially excavated and published by Dr.
Graham Webster, F.S.A., with a brief discussion by myself, produced 204
cremations, of which about half were contained in urns capable of complete
or partial restoration.[6] The cemetery is of importance, not only for its situation
on a part of the east coast from which other evidence of early Anglo-Saxon
settlement is somewhat scanty, but because it provides a valuable link with the
corresponding material beyond the Humber estuary in the East Riding of
Yorkshire.

Here, lying under the western escarpment of the Yorkshire Wolds, and
significantly placed on the Roman road linking Brough-on-Humber and
Malton, is the great burial ground at Sancton. This extensive and important
urnfield was partially excavated by Professor Rolleston in the 1870s and again

---

[1] T. C. Lethbridge, *A Cemetery at Lackford*
(1951). The urns illustrated in this publication comprise less than half of those which were excavated
and can now be studied in the Cambridge Museum
of Archaeology and Ethnology.

[2] *Antiquity* xi (1937), 391 and Pl. I, Fig. 3.

[3] These have not yet been published, but I have
been kindly allowed to use the excellent drawings
of them prepared for the Ministry by Mrs.
Elizabeth Fry-Stone.

[4] *Arch. Journ.* cviii (1952), 97 and Figs. 1, 2, 4, 5,
6, and 8.

[5] This excavation, which is still proceeding,
has not yet been published, but Dr. Fennell has
generously supplied me with photo-copies of his
drawings, which now cover some 350 urns and
their contents, and has kindly allowed me to use
them where their evidence is relevant to my subject.

[6] *Arch. Journ.* cviii (1952), 25–64.

by Messrs. Hall and Wilson shortly after 1900, but its importance has been demonstrated more fully since the end of the war by the renewed explorations of Mr. Southern.[1] Approximately 275 urns are available for study from this site.

These six great urnfields, Caistor and Illington in Norfolk, Lackford in Suffolk, Loveden Hill and South Elkington in Lincolnshire, and Sancton in east Yorkshire, all excavated or re-excavated since I began to work on Anglo-Saxon pottery in 1931, illustrate the enormous increase in the quantity of material that has become available for study in the past thirty years. When to the contents of these large cemeteries are added the numerous smaller or less easily accessible groups that have also come to light, not only from cremations but from inhumation graves and occupation sites, it is true to say that the bulk of the evidence for Anglo-Saxon ceramics in the pagan centuries has at least doubled in that time. Whatever the state of our knowledge had been in 1931, this revolution in the volume of the material at our disposal makes a fresh assessment of its significance most desirable.

The third requirement for an understanding of the English pottery lies in a correct appreciation of its relationship to the corresponding material on the Continent. Here too, much has been done to improve the situation in the past thirty years, and in particular since the end of the war in 1945. Ten years earlier, in 1935 and 1936, I visited most of the relevant museums in Holland, north Germany, Denmark, and Norway, and came back with notebooks filled with sketches of some 350 pots, most of them then unpublished, which have formed the basis of a useful comparative series that subsequent visits have greatly enlarged. But at that time there was little in the way of recent publication carrying on the work begun by Plettke and Roeder; and to form an idea of the range of comparative material it was necessary to work for oneself through the long runs of pots in show-cases and store-cupboards.

After the war the situation greatly changed. The contents of the north German museums had suffered severely between 1939 and 1945. A good deal was actually destroyed in air-raids: more was damaged by hasty evacuation from requisitioned or bombed buildings in conditions which did not permit proper packing or adequate storage. A number of collections were shifted several times with ever increasing risk of breakage and confusion. A great quantity of museum records were lost by fire or by exposure in damaged or

[1] The earlier discoveries, excluding the considerable series in the Ashmolean Museum, Oxford, were partially published in 1909 by T. Sheppard in Hull Museum Publications, LXVI and LXVII. It is hoped that the whole collection will shortly be published in a monograph in the new series of Hull Museum Publications planned by Mr. John Bartlett, F.S.A.

deserted buildings, so that the collections to which they related became difficult to identify or even to locate. Museum staffs were transferred to other duties, and many of them, including some key figures most familiar with the material in their charge, never returned. The late Dr. Hans Gummel, who has recorded the wartime and post-war disasters that overtook the 1,500 pots from Westerwanna in the old Morgenstern Museum at Wesermünde, has described the appalling confusion of what remained in 1950 from the greatest of all Saxon cemeteries.[1] The Westerwanna material was by no means the only great group of Saxon antiquities in Germany to suffer such a fate.

But the lesson had been learnt, and, as conditions returned to something more like normality, a new generation of museum curators and professional archaeologists not only set about the restoration of order, but determined to publish as much as possible of the older collections that had survived, so that some record should remain for posterity. Thus many of the older collections from the north German cemeteries are now in print, including long series of urns from such well-known sites, very relevant to English students, as Altenwalde, Wehden-bei-Lehe, Quelkhorn, Gudendorf, Mahndorf, etc.[2] The crowning achievement was the appearance in 1960 of *Westerwanna I*, which contains all that could be saved of the great Wesermünde collection: it includes drawings, or at least sketches, of 1,576 grave-groups, mostly containing pottery, for many of which, now destroyed, the sole evidence comes from the jottings in a pre-war student's notebook. The publication, even if perforce in so inadequate a form, of so much that seemed as late as 1950 to be irretrievably lost, is an achievement of truly heroic proportions, reflecting the greatest credit on those who have brought it about. The forthcoming appearance of *Westerwanna II*, which will include those parts of the collection which found their way to Hamburg, Hannover, and other museums, is eagerly awaited.

The inspiration behind much of this praiseworthy publishing activity was provided by the late Karl Waller, the energetic and enthusiastic schoolmaster and *Museumsleiter* of Cuxhaven. He had already in 1938 set a high standard of publication with his excavation report on *Der Galgenberg bei Cuxhaven*, which contains, amongst other things, excellent drawings of over 150 pots. After the war he established the so-called *Arbeitsgemeinschaft für Sachsenforschung*, based on his own museum at Cuxhaven, whose main purpose was to act as a

[1] Dr. Gummel writes that when he first began work on what was left in 1950 'ich mich einem heillosen Chaos gegenüber sah'. *Westerwanna* i. 19.
[2] Most of these sites have been published by Karl Waller in the series of Beihefte to the Hamburg *Atlas der Urgeschichte*, edited by H. J. Eggers. *Mahndorf*, ed. by E. Grohne, appeared as a handsome volume issued by the City of Bremen in 1953.

forum for the discussion of problems in Saxon archaeology, not only by German scholars, but by those from all countries bordering on the North Sea who were concerned with archaeological aspects of the migration period in these lands. To this end Waller organized a series of informal annual gatherings meeting for two or three days in some relevant centre, for the exchange of ideas and the discussion of work in progress in these fields. Eighteen meetings of this *Sachsensymposion* have now been held, in eight of which I have been privileged to take part.[1] I have very greatly profited from the opportunities they have provided for meeting German, Dutch, Belgian, and Scandinavian scholars, for studying the local collections in the places visited, and for the exchange of information and publications in the most informal and agreeable surroundings. It is good to know that the death in 1963 of Karl Waller, to whose practical and infectious idealism the whole conception of the *Sachsensymposion* was due, has not brought these meetings to an end, for they are continuing under the direction of Dr. Albert Genrich of the Niedersächsisches Landesmuseum in Hannover who has been actively concerned in their proceedings from the start.

The publication of older museum collections and the activities of the *Sachsensymposion* have not been the only indications of renewed interest on the Continent in the ceramics of the *Völkerwanderungszeit*. Current excavations have revealed much new material, and here the emphasis has perhaps lain rather on the domestic wares produced by the exploration of settlement sites such as Warendorf, Feddersen Wierde, or Tofting, than on the funerary pottery of the cemeteries which had hitherto attracted most attention.[2] In addition there have been some valuable attempts at the synthesis of material in particular regions or surveys of the current state of research in Saxon studies as a whole.[3]

[1] Those held at Bremen (1956), Münster (1957), Amersfoort (1958), Schleswig (1959), Hannover (1960), Oxford (1964), Oldenburg (1965), and Brussels (1966).

[2] Warendorf, first published in *Germania* xxxii (1954), 189–213, is essentially a late seventh- and eighth-century site, but its excavation drew attention to similar kinds of settlement producing pottery of types related to those found in pagan Anglo-Saxon contexts in England, as e.g. at Tofting on the Eider (A. Bantelmann, *Tofting* (1955)), or Feddersen Wierde, north of Bremerhaven on the Weser (W. Haarnagel, *Neue Ausgrabungen in Deutschland* (1958), 215, and subsequent reports in *Germania* 39 (1961) and 41 (1963)).

[3] Such as e.g. M. B. Mackeprang, *Kulturbeziehungen im nordischen Raum* (1943), a valuable survey of the evidence, mainly ceramic, from Schleswig, Denmark, and southern Norway, useful as illustrating the continental background to our Angles and Jutes: A. Genrich, *Formenkreise und Stammesgruppen in Schleswig Holstein* (1954), with its collection of dated burial groups, mostly containing pottery, from the homeland of the continental Angles and their neighbours: F. Tischler, 'Der Stand der Sachsenforschung archaeologisch gesehen' (35 *Bericht der Römisch-Germanischen Kommission* (1956)), a masterly summary of Anglo-Saxon archaeological studies as they stood twelve years ago.

Nor should one omit in any survey of the continental evidence to mention the work that has been proceeding outside Germany, in Denmark and Norway on the one side, and in Holland and Belgium on the other. A great deal has been learnt in recent years about the archaeological evidence for the penetration of the Roman frontiers by Franks and other Germanic peoples in the fourth and fifth centuries, especially from the important researches of Joachim Werner[1] and others, and from the publication of such cemeteries as Haillot and St. Gilles-lez-Termonde in Belgium, and Wageningen in Holland.[2] Some of the graves containing equipment characteristic of German warriors in Roman service around the turn of the fourth and fifth centuries include pots of non-Frankish make. These may provide useful clues in attempting to isolate the ceramic fashions prevalent among the earliest German settlers in this country, where conditions of overlap between Roman and barbarian may for a while, in the years after 400, have resembled those in the frontier provinces of Gaul.

This summary sketch of the evidence now available for the study of early Anglo-Saxon pottery in this country, and of the corresponding situation abroad, will suggest, and rightly suggest, that both here and on the Continent there is plenty of material for study. It should be possible to extract from it some valuable information on the origin and distribution of the settlers, their relationship to the pre-existing population, their social and economic development, and their notions of religion and of decorative art. How far these expectations can be realized it is the purpose of the following chapters to indicate. But first it is necessary to say something about the nature of the evidence itself, its strength and its weakness as raw material for the historian.

The first point to remember is that the overwhelming mass of this pottery, both in England and on the Continent, comes from cemeteries and not from settlements. For whatever purpose they were originally made, most of the pots come to us as funerary equipment: that was the final use to which they were put, and for which they must have been thought appropriate, by those who placed the ashes of their cremated dead in them, or included them among the grave-goods accompanying unburnt burials. When Sir Thomas Browne in his *Hydriotaphia* (1658) gave us the first known description and illustrations of Anglo-Saxon pottery, from a cremation cemetery at Walsingham in Norfolk, he spoke of the pots quite rightly as 'sad sepulchral pitchers'.

---

[1] Especially his paper on the 'Kriegergräber aus der ersten Hälfte des 5. Jahrhunderts' in *Bonner Jahrbücher* clviii (1958), 372.

[2] *Arch. Belg.* xxxiv (1957), xli (1958): *Palaeohistoria* x (1964), 183–316.

A number of consequences flow from this fact. The first is that most of the surviving pottery falls naturally into two main groups. On the one hand there are urns of a suitable size and shape to contain cremated bones, and on the other there are smaller accessory vessels that were used to hold perishable goods, mainly perhaps food and drink, in connection with the ritual of inhumation. This concentration on two types, serving two special purposes only, may give a distorted picture of the range of ceramic forms currently used in an Anglo-Saxon household: dishes and platters, for example, are very uncommon in the cemeteries: so are strainers, or pots, of whatever sort, having handles or spouts. The largest kinds of storage vessels that were treated as fixed furniture and not commonly moved about are similarly absent from the cemeteries. All these types occur among the occupation debris of the comparatively few houses and huts of this period that have been explored in this country; and they are likewise found in quantity in and around the longhouses of north Germany, and in the Frisian *terpen*.

A second consequence is that it is easy to form an exaggerated idea of the extent to which pottery of good quality and finish was available and of the range of decorative techniques that were in everyday use. It is true that decorated pottery of competent manufacture occurs on settlement sites as well as in the cemeteries,[1] but it was proportionately much less used in daily life than it was for the special purpose of honouring the dead. As is normal among primitive peoples, and indeed among more sophisticated ones also, funeral rites, particularly in well-to-do families, called for a special formality and elaboration in the equipment to be used. It was felt to be appropriate to provide the best as a sign of respect for the dead, just because the best differed somewhat from what was in common use. It is not improbable that, then as now, taste in the decoration of funeral paraphernalia was apt to be a bit old-fashioned. This does not mean that all funeral pottery formed a distinct category reserved for ritual employment, or that ordinary household utensils were not frequently used as cremation urns, or as accessory vessels, especially among the poorer classes. But there is undoubtedly a much higher proportion of well-made and carefully decorated pottery to be found in the cemeteries than among the occupation debris of contemporary settlements. The fact that so much of the available evidence comes from cemeteries thus means that we shall be seeing the craftsmanship of Anglo-Saxon potters, not at its day-to-day normal in quality and

[1] The settlement at West Stow Heath, Suffolk, now being excavated by Mr. Stanley West, has produced an unusually high proportion of decorated pottery from hut floors.

technical skill, but rather at its self-conscious best. It is indeed sometimes difficult to believe that folk of the same culture and period were responsible for designing and making the complex and elaborately ornamented funerary *Buckelurnen* on the one hand, and some of the shapeless and incompetent domestic bowls and cookpots on the other. Although they share the characteristic of being all alike hand-made, these two categories seem to present an almost incredible contrast between the extremes of sophistication and crudity possible in ceramic technique.[1]

Further consequences follow from the fact that most of this pottery comes from graves. It is of course an archaeological commonplace that material recovered from cemeteries can be much less satisfactory as historical evidence than that produced from the stratified levels of an occupation site. Except in cases where one burial directly overlies or has disturbed another, stratification is usually absent, and the contents of each interment have to be treated as individual deposits without any indication of their chronological relationship to one another. Even where a later burial can be shown to have disturbed an earlier, the very fact of disturbance may make it difficult to distinguish with certainty the objects accompanying the one from those that had been placed with the other. Moreover, pots which contain cremated remains for the most part lack the evidence of associated objects. While burials by inhumation may be accompanied by well-preserved grave-goods, which at the least provide information for the contemporary use of the objects accompanying each burial, the ritual of cremation itself commonly involves the destruction or distortion of objects such as jewellery or belt-fittings which may have been on the body when it was placed on the funeral pyre. Thus cremated remains are likely to be the least informative to the archaeologist of all the material relics of an ancient culture.

The study of early Anglo-Saxon pottery thus suffers from formidable initial difficulties. They are at their most daunting in the case of the largest and most interesting group of material, the cremation urns themselves. The small accessory vessels sometimes found with inhumation burials do at least occasionally form part of a deposit which includes brooches or other metal or glass objects which can be approximately dated. These clues where they exist are of the highest importance, but they do not occur with sufficient frequency to provide more than an occasional pointer in the search for dates. The vast majority of the cremation pottery on the other hand comes to us with no

[1] Compare e.g. the examples on Figs. 10 and 22.

indication whatever of its date, whether absolute or even relative, at all. Here and there among the burnt bones in an urn may be found the remains of a brooch or a buckle, not distorted completely out of recognition by heat. These occasional clues are of course most precious. But they are of the greatest rarity,[1] and have normally been recognized only in urns excavated in recent times when the importance of keeping the associated objects from a grave group together has been appreciated. In earlier days it was customary for excavators to turn out the contents of cremation urns unmindful of this essential principle, and to mix up all the objects found in them without regard to their individual origin. This was done, unfortunately, even in some nineteenth-century excavations, such as those at Little Wilbraham or Girton (Cambridge), which in other respects were conducted with some attempt to produce a reasonable archaeological record.[2] It goes without saying that the older excavation reports very rarely mention instances of one cremation burial disturbing another in a way that could provide evidence of relative date: and when such an occurrence is recorded the chances are that one or both of the urns will have been thrown away as being too much damaged to be thought worth keeping.

This is, of course, only one illustration of the almost universal contempt with which broken pottery was treated by the earlier excavators even when they were recording and carefully preserving all other objects from their cemeteries. Complete urns, or those recovered in pieces sufficiently large to make a rough restoration comparatively simple, might be preserved, but all the rest would be thrown away.

The fragility and poor firing of most Anglo-Saxon hand-made pots, and the fact that both cremations and inhumations were usually very shallow, have contributed to the tale of destruction. Indeed, under average soil conditions, normal modern ploughing, the activity of burrowing animals, the penetration of roots, frost and flood, or even moderate earth pressure, have caused the great majority to collapse, and many even to disintegrate, long before an excavator arrives to complete their destruction. It is often a matter requiring great care

[1] Out of more than four hundred urns from Caistor-by-Norwich, only five contained recognizable remains of brooches.

[2] At Little Wilbraham parts of three brooches and a considerable number of other objects found in urns were illustrated by R. C. Neville (*Saxon Obsequies* (1852)), but with no attribution to particular urns: at Girton eleven brooches occurred with urns but none of them can be individually assigned. It is worth noting that while objects likely to have been on the body, such as brooches, beads, or belt-fittings, were normally cremated with it, bone combs, though usually broken, are generally unburnt, and the same applies to other items in what are known as 'manicure sets', such as metal knives, razors, shears, and tweezers. Unfortunately such objects are less easy to date typologically than are brooches.

and skill to recover Anglo-Saxon pots from the ground in a state that will permit reconstruction,[1] and, in addition to the hazards already mentioned, their fragments are frequently so distorted by differential soil pressure that correct restoration may be virtually impossible. It is not surprising that many excavated cemeteries on record as containing large numbers of urns are now represented only by a handful of survivors, and in some instances by none at all.[2] If this has happened even in places which have been deliberately excavated, it goes without saying that the destruction of pots in cemeteries accidentally discovered during quarrying or civil engineering operations has been almost universal. Cases are indeed on record where urns found in reasonable preservation have been deliberately broken up by workmen hopeful of finding treasure in them, or have been set up in a row and used as cockshies during the dinner-break.[3]

In the face of all this unhappy history it may well be asked whether the subject is worth studying at all: whether the chance survivors of this orgy of destruction and neglect, most of them lacking all the information which a proper excavation report and the preservation of associated finds could give them, can tell the inquirer anything that is worth knowing of the beginnings of English history. It was no doubt the discouragement inspired by such considerations that drove an earlier generation of scholars to turn rather to the jewellery and other metal work, the glass and the weapons, in their search for enlightenment about the pagan Anglo-Saxons. And yet the surviving mass of the pottery is by no means negligible. We have a body of material comprising perhaps 4,000 individual pieces in a sufficient state of preservation for form and decoration to be recognized and assessed. In addition a vast number of fragments, most of them individually uninformative, can be used on occasion to provide additional evidence for the presence of a specialized group in an area where it is otherwise unrecorded, or the activities of an individual potter in a district outside his usual beat. Much can indeed be learnt from the distribution of the material, and this is the last subject to be covered in this introductory survey.

---

[1] At South Elkington, for example, where the subsoil was a stiff glacial clay and the urns had been spread with flints, most had been crushed to pieces and when first exposed had the consistency of wet blotting paper. They could only be removed after being allowed to dry out *in situ* and then, after careful bandaging, being cut out as a solid block of clay (*Arch. Journ.* cviii (1952), 27). There would have been nothing left of the pots from such a site had it been dug in pre-scientific times.

[2] e.g. the cemeteries of Wold Newton and South Willingham on the Lincolnshire Wolds (*Arch. Journ.* xci (1934), 139).

[3] As occurred with the earlier discoveries in the cemetery of Newark-on-Trent. Both at Kingston-on-Soar and at King's Newton about 200 urns were wantonly destroyed. G. Baldwin Brown, *The Arts in Early England* iv (1915), 770.

It is not wholly a matter of chance that some parts of eastern England are very much richer than others in the quantities of early Anglo-Saxon pottery that have been preserved (see Map 1). The burial customs of the invaders varied very greatly in accordance with a number of factors, of which the continental origin of the different groups, and the conditions determining the settlement of different parts of the country, are the most significant. In the coastal counties from east Yorkshire on the north to the Norfolk/Suffolk border on the south, forming the whole eastern part of the traditional area of Anglian settlement, the earliest settlers on the whole practised cremation, and many of the communities so established continued to cremate their dead during the greater part of the pagan period. This is therefore the region of the great cremation cemeteries, of which the examples mentioned earlier, Sancton in east Yorkshire, South Elkington and Loveden Hill in Lincolnshire, Caistor-by-Norwich and Illington in Norfolk, and Lackford in Suffolk, are the most informative, because large sections of all of them have been dug in modern conditions.

Cremation seems also to have prevailed normally further to the south and west across the eastern Midlands, especially in the neighbourhood of the main river systems which formed the natural channels of communication drawing seaborne settlers into the interior. Thus a large cremation cemetery was located in the nineteenth century at Newark-on-Trent, and has recently been re-examined: others were accessible from tributaries of the Trent such as that at Thurmaston (just north of Leicester), or from the Fenland rivers such as Kettering (Northants.), several (Girton, St. John's, Little Wilbraham) near Cambridge, or Kempston on the Ouse close to Bedford. In most of these inland areas, however, the cemeteries are more mixed in character, with a considerable proportion of inhumation burials in addition to those by cremation, so that the surviving pots include accessory vessels as well as cremation urns, and the total quantity of pottery is much less in relation to the number of burials than is the case in the great cremation cemeteries of the eastern seaboard. The same is true of the cremation elements in the burial grounds over the watershed in the valley of the Warwickshire Avon.

The explanation for these mixed cemeteries is rarely self-evident. Some may have been started, like those further east, to serve the needs of purely cremating communities, who, however, came to change their burial practice with the passage of time: others may have been mixed from the beginning: in others again there may be evidence for the subsequent intrusion of people practising one rite into country originally occupied by those favouring another. It is

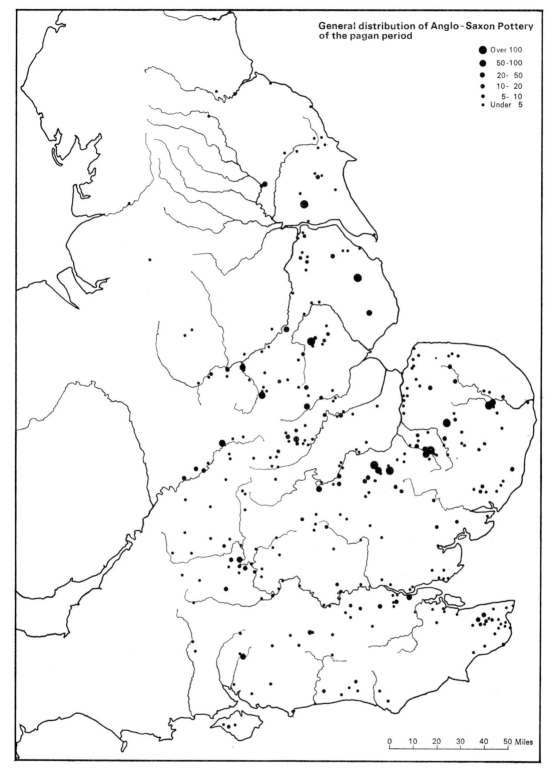

General distribution of Anglo-Saxon Pottery
of the pagan period

● Over 100
● 50-100
● 20- 50
● 10- 20
● 5- 10
· Under 5

0   10   20   30   40   50 Miles

Map 1

obvious that the clues to a good deal of history may await discovery in these mixed cemeteries, and that a detailed study of the pottery, whose evidence has hardly ever been examined with these possibilities in mind, gives by far the best hope of finding them.

Over all the south-east of Britain, including the Thames valley, the position seems different again. In most of this region cremation, though of more wide-spread occurrence than is often realized, is generally less prevalent in the cemeteries than inhumation. Some cemeteries, especially those on the south bank of the Thames, both downstream in Kent and Surrey and further west in Berkshire, have fairly substantial cremation elements, but everywhere they are in a minority, sometimes a very small minority, compared with the much more prevalent practice of inhumation.[1] Here again the dating of the cremation pottery and the accessory vessels found with inhumations seems to be an essential preliminary to any successful attempt to disentangle stages in the archaeological history of this region in the age of Anglo-Saxon settlement. And the contribution which archaeology should make to this story is all the more needed, because this is the one part of England for which, both in the Anglo-Saxon and the British literary sources, there are some significant pointers to the course of political events.

It will be clear from this summary that while the quantity of early Anglo-Saxon pottery known is substantial, its distribution over the eastern half of England is patchy, and this patchiness is due, not only to the accidents of survival and destruction, but to genuine differences in the culture of the settlers in different parts. Three-quarters of all we have come from no more than ten sites, the great cremation cemeteries of Norfolk, Suffolk, Lincolnshire, Cambridge, and the East Riding of Yorkshire. Five of these sites account between them for some 1,400 vessels, over a third of the whole number known. Yet every county east of a line from Derby to Southampton can make some significant contribution to the total, and it may give an indication of the overall spread of the material to set out the approximate number for each county in a rough order of magnitude. None of these figures are of course more than *minima*, and all could be upset by fresh discoveries: they are intended only to give the most general indication how the pottery is distributed.

---

[1] At Abingdon, where the highest ratio of cremations to inhumations in any Thames valley cemetery is recorded, the excavated portion of the site (estimated as between a half and two-thirds of the whole) produced 82 cremations against 119 inhumations, but it cannot be assumed that this high proportion would have applied had it been possible to examine the whole area. (*Abingdon* 9 and 11.)

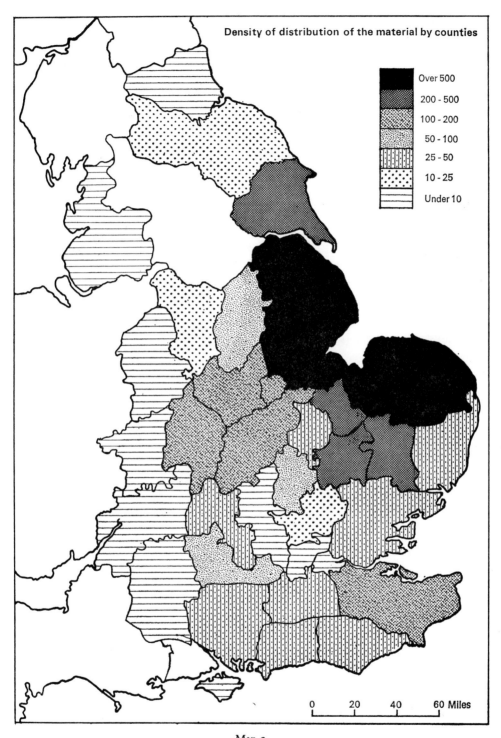

Map 2

(see note on p. 20)

Over 500   Norfolk, Lincs.
200–500   Cambridge, W. Suffolk, Yorks. (E. Riding and around York).
100–200   Northants., Leics. and Rutland, War., Kent.
50–100   Notts.,[1] Berks., Beds.
25–50   Hunts., Oxon., Sussex, Surrey, Essex, E. Suffolk, Hants.
10–25   Yorks. (N. Riding), Derbs., Herts.
Under 10   Bucks., Middx., Glos., Wilts., Worcs., Staffs., Durham, Lancs., Isle of Wight.

If these densities are plotted on a map (Map 2) it will be seen clearly enough that the distribution makes an intelligible pattern related to the earliest settlement areas of eastern England. The regions of primary cremation in East Anglia, Lincolnshire, and east Yorkshire, encompassing as they do the Humber estuary and the Wash as avenues of entry into Mercia and Middle Anglia, are most strongly emphasized. But the south side of the Thames valley and the south-east corner of England, as far west as Southampton Water, also produce an interesting pattern, especially in contrast with the comparatively empty areas north and north-west of London. Later on it will be necessary to examine these patterns more closely in the light of a typological classification of the pots themselves. To attempt such a classification must therefore be our next concern.

---

[1] Since these figures were compiled and incorporated in Map 2 the recent discoveries at Newark have raised the total for Notts. to at least 200.

II

THE TYPOLOGY OF FORM AND THE ELEMENTS OF DECORATION

THIS is much easier said than done. For this country indeed it has never been done as a whole before, though attempts have been made to nibble at the fringes of the subject and to pursue certain of the more obvious lines of inquiry rather deeper.[1] Some of the reasons which make the task one of special difficulty have already been mentioned. The pottery is all hand-made, and much of it from first to last was the product of domestic industry, informally operating in small communities, many of which may have lived for considerable periods in more or less self-sufficient conditions and to a large extent in isolation from one another. There was thus every opportunity for the development of local and even personal idiosyncrasies. These communities moreover had come into existence as a result of a process of migration which included for all the participants a sea-voyage, or at least a channel crossing:[2] a period, that is, of maximum personal and social disturbance enduring certainly for some months and often perhaps for some years, between leaving home and establishing a firm settlement in an unfamiliar and potentially hostile countryside. It is still a matter for argument whether the bulk of the

[1] See e.g. my articles on 'Three styles of decoration on Anglo-Saxon Pottery', *Ant. Journ.* xvii (1937), 424; 'Some English parallels to the Anglo-Saxon Pottery of Holland and Belgium in the Migration Period', *L'Antiquité classique* xvii (1948), 453; 'Two Saxon Urns from . . . Beds., and the Saxon Penetration of the Eastern Midlands', *Ant. Journ.* xxxiv (1954), 201.

[2] Technical reasons have been given by C. Green (*Sutton Hoo* (1963), 103) for believing that direct crossings of the North Sea were impracticable for the Anglo-Saxons of the fifth century. But these rest on the assumption that they had no masted sailing galleys at this time. Many of the invaders certainly reached Britain by coasting as far south as Texel or Flushing and so crossing to a landfall in Kent or Essex, but Green's argument makes it difficult to understand why the Romans set signal-stations on the Yorkshire coast, for these were clearly designed to give early warning of direct landfalls. A glance at the maps in this volume will suggest that the Angles at least were capable of reaching East Anglia, the Wash, and the Humber direct from their continental home, which lay north of the Saxon lands in Europe, just as their settlements in Britain did. Everything points to the use of masted sailing ships by the northern barbarians at this time, even though no remains of a vessel of this kind have yet been identified. A picture of one is engraved on a bronze strap-end from a north French cemetery of the seventh century: see *Revue Archeologique* (1939), 181–7.

newcomers arrived in well-organized and coherent social groups, large enough to transmit or impose traditions of common ancestry and a common culture, or whether the work of conquest and settlement was carried through mainly by bands of adventurers of mixed and diverse antecedents, temporarily united under warlords whose origins were as dubious as their own. The archaeological evidence suggests that, while both methods were employed, there was in any case no single pattern of social, let alone tribal, background, and that the main movements of population may have been spread over a considerable period of time. Later continental influences may thus have affected in quite different ways the development in different parts of the country.

In these circumstances it would be idle to expect that the pot-making traditions inherited, adopted, or improvised by the newcomers would exhibit a clear-cut series of well-defined ceramic types, or would develop as time passed in any uniform or easily intelligible sequence of evolving forms and ornament. It has furthermore to be remembered that along the greater part of the North Sea coast between Jutland and the Rhine mouths (the lands from which on any showing the great mass of the invaders came), there was already before the movement began a very considerable degree of tribal confusion. Whatever may have been the conditions in Jutland (the ultimate source of the Jutes), or in eastern Schleswig and Fünen (the parts from which the Angles came), the traditional lands of the Saxons in the valleys of the lower Elbe and Weser were by the later part of the fourth century the scene of a general mix-up of peoples resulting principally from the westward pressure of folk from east Holstein and the southward movement of others from the Danish peninsula. From this confused situation there seems to have emerged what the Germans aptly term a *Mischgruppe*, a mixed culture displaying elements derived from various sources.[1] The culture of this *Mischgruppe* is best represented at the great cemetery of Perlberg near Stade on the south bank of the lower Elbe, and, as J. M. Kemble noted with extraordinary insight more than a century ago, it is the pottery of the Perlberg cemetery that bears the strongest resemblance to much of what is found in this country.[2] We are dealing therefore to a substantial extent with the products of folk who were themselves a quite recent amalgam of different tribal elements in their continental homes, and could indeed, some of them, as well be termed Anglo-Saxon before the migration as after it. In considering the various elements of which the English ceramic

---

[1] The argument of this paragraph rests largely on the work summarized in Genrich (1954) and Tischler (1956).　　　　　　　　　　　[2] *Horae Ferales* (1863), Pl. xxx.

tradition is composed, it is thus necessary to remember the extent to which they were already mixed before the transfer to this country.

It is therefore not surprising that their pottery took many different forms and that many different styles of decoration were employed in its ornamentation. Not much will be said at this stage about the origins of these forms and styles, their geographical antecedents or their changing fashions, though it will be necessary to refer incidentally to all these things. The significance of these variations can best be understood after a general survey of the material has been made. At this stage we are dealing primarily with questions of typology and classification.

There are two main elements to be considered here, the study of forms, and the study of decoration. Both are of course indispensable to an understanding of the pottery, and to a large extent they inevitably interlock. This is because certain decorative schemes are specially appropriate to certain forms of pot, either because they are imposed by the limitations of shape, or because certain shapes alone give scope for their development. But this is not always so. There are many forms of pottery which it is possible and appropriate to decorate in all sorts of different ways, and the extraordinary inventiveness of Anglo-Saxon potters in ringing the changes on the limited range of decorative elements at their disposal is one of the most fascinating aspects of the whole subject. There is no other group of primitive hand-made pottery in Europe which displays anything approaching the imagination, variety, and spontaneity of the ornamental designs devised by Anglo-Saxon potters during the first two centuries of the settlement in Britain.

Foreign scholars have laid far more stress on form than on decoration in their classification of the continental counterparts of this pottery. The schemes worked out by Plettke, and developed or modified by his successors in Germany, rest largely on an analysis of shapes.[1] Comparatively little stress has been laid on the changing fashion in ornament. This was natural in handling the products of an industry with a long and more or less continuous tradition behind it, stretching back to the earlier phases of the Iron Age, and even in some of its aspects to Bronze Age times. In Denmark and north Germany, while tribal movements may have been frequent and important, there was no sharp cultural break comparable to that imposed on Britain by the Roman Conquest. The earlier Iron Age cultures of pre-Roman times developed on the whole continuously into the post-Roman cultures of the *Völkerwanderungszeit*. It is

[1] See the works of A. Plettke, A. Genrich, E. Grohne, F. Tischler, etc., already mentioned.

therefore natural and useful to trace these developments ceramically by pin-pointing the principal changes that took place in the forms of pots commonly used in different parts at different times, and to build these changes up into an integrated series of successive regional and chronological types. Such a method has its obvious advantages, and when linked to and checked at every stage by the corresponding evolution of contemporary brooches, buckles, and other significant artefacts found in association with the pottery, it provides a strong, if sometimes over-rigid, foundation for relative and even absolute chronology.

It is of course always necessary to guard against the temptations of excessive rigidity in applying such methods. It would be absurd, for example, to suppose that any culture could make do with only one type of pot at any one time, or that successive changes in type were necessarily simultaneous in different areas, or that personal preferences, or even errors of workmanship, never led to pots being produced of shapes that defy current fashion, and recall forms either earlier or later than their actual date.

But while such factors as these may create no more than a marginal risk of error in handling the products of a long-established and stable tradition, they could prove fatal to any attempt at classifying, by form alone, the pottery produced in such exceptional conditions as prevailed in Britain in the fifth and sixth centuries. Here many of the potters were no longer the expert ex-ponents of customary skills commonly accepted among a whole people: they could often be a chance assortment of uprooted amateurs doing their best to improvise for immediate needs on the basis of half-remembered forms, and misunderstood techniques of manufacture. In such conditions they would be most likely to recall and to imitate the simpler schemes of decoration familiar in their former homes, and to apply them to vessels of any shape that might emerge from their unskilled efforts. They would certainly be unlikely to maintain a typological exactitude of form above all else. As time passed, and the traditional skills were relearnt or new skills invented, it is likely that both forms and ornamental schemes would develop in their own way, the former on conservative lines and paying less attention to precision of contour than on the Continent, the latter increasing in originality and complexity, as confidence and competence returned, and diverging ever further from continental fashions.

This at any rate is the broad impression left on the student by comparing the continental and British series as a whole. And it follows that in any attempt to classify our pottery in this country at least as much attention must be paid to types of decoration as to the forms of the pots which carry them. It is in fact possible to establish a rough typology of schemes of decoration for our English pottery, and it will be found that this typology is broadly applicable over the whole range of the material, regardless of the precise shapes taken by the vessels concerned. This is not of course to deny that some forms of pots are normally early and some late, but it is in general true that obviously late forms are not found to carry obviously early schemes of decoration and vice versa. There is in fact a reasonably satisfactory coherence between the two criteria, so long as neither is applied too strictly. It will be found that, especially in the earlier periods, a considerable range of forms tends to carry the same general type of decoration, and these forms can therefore be presumed to be roughly contemporary with one another.

There is however one extensive series of pots which in the nature of the case cannot be classified by their decoration, because they are entirely plain and without ornament of any kind. This group can be conveniently used to illustrate, without the distraction imposed by decorative schemes, the very wide range of forms which our Anglo-Saxon pottery may take. I therefore propose to begin with these plain pots, which can be roughly classified into various basic types. In making this classification it must be understood that by no means all plain pots can be assigned categorically to one or other of these types. Indeed it would be safe to say that clear-cut examples of most of them are the exception rather than the rule, and that the great majority of plain vessels hover uneasily on the boundary between two or more of these groups: some may even lie outside all of them. This is of course but one illustration of the point just made, that to attempt a comprehensive classification by pure form of this English material would be not only unrewarding but also virtually impossible. There is in fact an infinite series of shapes, intermediate in every particular between every one type and every other. Any attempt to force a great number of these pots into one formal straitjacket will lead only to frustration.

When all allowance is made for these qualifications the following groups can be distinguished. First there are Biconical urns (Fig. 1), distinguished by a more or less pronounced carination at or not far away from the mid-point of the profile. Biconicals are treated as a fifth-century development on the Continent,[1] and the English examples come mostly from areas (east Yorkshire, Lincolnshire,

---

[1] An example from the Perlberg was found with a mid fifth-century equal-armed brooch. See also examples in Genrich (1954), Tafeln 1D: 2A: 5C: 15E, all found with brooches of late fourth- or early fifth-century types.

Norfolk, and the upper Thames valley) which will be constantly before us as providing abundant signs of early settlement. Second are the Hollow-necked urns (Fig. 2), a variety of the biconical type which displays a markedly concave neck and sometimes an exaggeratedly sharp carination or shoulder often set higher on the profile than with normal biconicals, so that many could as well be classified as shouldered types. This is a specifically early type on the Continent, with definitely northern associations,[1] and in this country is most strongly in evidence at Caistor-by-Norwich and Markshall (Norfolk), though examples occur also in Lincolnshire and east Yorkshire.

Deriving from these types is, third, the large and rather amorphous group of Sub-biconical pots (Fig. 3), characterized by a more rounded contour than the true biconicals, though retaining the tendency to have the maximum diameter at a point about half-way up the profile, and thus to lack a real shoulder. This very common form had undoubtedly a long life, the later examples typologically being those with a more sagging contour, and those of barrel shape.

Then there are, fourth, Shouldered pots (Fig. 4), distinguished from the sub-biconical group by having the centre of gravity set much higher on the body, though there is a continuous range of gradations between the two. To emphasize the distinction between them several markedly hump-shouldered urns are included on Fig. 4, a variety which seems to be datable by associated brooches, both on the Continent and in England, to the years around and following A.D. 500.[2] These extreme examples occur in this country mainly in the areas of early settlement near the east coast and on the upper Thames, though shouldered jars as a whole have a very much wider distribution, and a longer life.

Fifth should be mentioned Bowls of all kinds (Fig. 5), defining a bowl as a vessel whose rim diameter is at least equal to its height. It will be seen that these bowls include biconical, hollow-necked, and shouldered forms clearly related to the categories already discussed. As a group they fall early in the series, especially those similar in contour to the hollow-necked biconicals, and other forms occurring in fourth- and fifth-century contexts on the Continent. Plain bowls occur also in Kent and South Hampshire, in addition to the areas of early settlement already noted, although this may not have any special significance.

[1] e.g. Genrich (1954), Tafel 15C with fifth-century brooch. The type originates in Norway (see Bøe (1931), esp. Figs. 153–76), where in various forms it is exceedingly common.

[2] *Lackford*, Fig. 14. 50, 71, with a cruciform brooch and other objects indicating this date. A late fifth-century example from Borgstedt is illustrated by Genrich (1954), Tafel 7D.

Allied to all these types but especially to the biconicals, sub-biconicals, and bowls is a group of Small Accessory vessels (Fig. 6), normally found with inhumation burials, or used for child cremations, or sometimes in purely domestic contexts. Some of these are undoubtedly as early as the larger vessels of similar shape, notably most of those with hollow necks, which closely parallel a type very common in Norway. But so convenient a form for household use probably had a long life, and they occur occasionally in contexts suggesting a late date, like the one from Breedon-on-the-Hill (Leics.), which was the site of a seventh-century monastery.

Perhaps the most interesting of all the groups of plain pottery are the Globular vessels, of which there are two main types, those which have a short upright rim (Fig. 7), and those with a more everted or flaring rim (Fig. 8). There is little otherwise to distinguish them, though there is a tendency for the first type to exhibit a taller round-shouldered contour, while the latter are apt to be more perfectly spherical and are nearly always round-bottomed. The interest of both forms is that they are found among the characteristic pottery of the continental Angles in eastern Schleswig in the fifth and early sixth centuries, a fact which lends particular significance to their occurrence and distribution in this country.[1] It may be noted that they occur not only in the east coast areas of traditional Anglian settlement, but also (especially the sphericals with everted rim) on several sites in Kent and in the upper Thames valley. Wherever they are found, these distinctive vessels are a sure indication of direct derivation from the continental Angles.

One further group of plain pots may be isolated at this point, Vessels with a low bulbous or bag-shaped body merging into a tall, conical or cylindrical neck (Fig. 9). This is among the latest types to occur in the cemeteries, and it is characteristic of a special category in which burials by inhumation are set out in rows in the manner of the *Reihengräber* of the Merovingian Franks. It has recently been argued[2] that they may represent the first generation of Christian converts in the middle or late seventh century when cremation had been given up, and most of the older burial grounds with their pagan associations had been abandoned, but the practice of putting grave-goods with the bodies still

---

[1] As was first pointed out by H. Jankuhn, *Antiquity* xxvi (1952), 14–24, and especially Plate II. See also the examples in Genrich (1954), Tafeln 3C: 6E: 26A, all with fifth-century metal objects. An English example, Worthy Park C30, had been disturbed by an early sixth-century inhumation.

[2] By Miranda Hyslop in reporting on two cemeteries at Leighton Buzzard. *Arch. Journ.* cxx (1963), 161–200. Similar views were put forward by T. C. Lethbridge, *A Cemetery at Shudy Camps* (1936), 27–29 and Pl. 1.

persisted, at least in well-to-do families. If this is so, it is interesting to find a notable group of such late pottery in the great pagan cemetery of Loveden Hill in south Lincolnshire, and there is in general more of it available in normal pagan associations than is always realized. The transition to Christianity was of course a long and patchy process, especially in the Midlands and East Anglia, and it is perhaps safer to regard this kind of pottery as typical of the period of transition than to give it a specifically Christian significance.

Before leaving the undecorated pottery it may be as well to say something further about the plain domestic wares made for household use, which occur in quantity as broken sherds on occupation sites, and also on occasion as complete pots in the cemeteries, where they were used as accessory vessels or as cremation urns for poorer burials or for the ashes of children. Most of this household pottery is extremely crude and formless (Fig. 10), and the shapes are so lacking in specific character that any attempt to divide them into a meaningful series of types is likely to prove unrewarding. Perhaps the most distinctive group is that of Wide-mouthed Cook-pots (Fig. 11), with little or no indication of a neck, and plain upright or slightly everted rims sometimes faintly beaded. These range from comparatively tall forms through squarish types to hemispherical bowls with round bottoms. They often show a smoked or sooted outer surface or other indications of use for cooking. The cemetery evidence provides little close dating for these types, since, being mainly used for the poorer burials, they are rarely accompanied by grave-goods.[1] They were probably made throughout the pagan period and into Christian times until domestic needs were better supplied by the more serviceable products of the growing commercial industries such as the so-called Ipswich wares of the seventh century.

Among this domestic pottery attention should be drawn to a group of vessels that are provided with lugs (Fig. 12), either solid or horizontally pierced, with the object of facilitating suspension. These lugs, which are normally set on the shoulder, or near the point of maximum girth, were intended to support a cord or thong, lodged beneath them in the case of the solid variety, or threaded through them where they are pierced. The purpose is therefore strictly functional and not decorative, and it is obvious that vessels so equipped were designed primarily as household utensils, and came to be employed only secondarily as grave furniture, where the lugs would serve no practical end.

[1] One from Eriswell, Suffolk (Gr. 22), was found with a Group IV cruciform brooch: *C.A.S.* lix (1966), 9, Fig. 6(b)1; 12, Fig. 8(a)2.

It is a remarkable fact that functional lugs of this kind, on whatever form of pot they may be found, are nearly always three in number. This is no doubt partly due to the fact that three points on a pot are the minimum number required for safety in suspension. But there also appears to be a long ceramic tradition behind the practice. The Anglo-Saxon series evidently derives ultimately from the so-called *Dreiknubbentöpfe*, the three-knobbed pots, a recognized type in the Proto-Saxon Fuhlsbüttel culture of Holstein in the first and second centuries A.D.[1] The persistence of this tradition over several centuries, and its transfer to this country for use on vessels of various shapes, bearing no resemblance whatever to the Holstein prototypes, forms an interesting illustration of the occasional archaistic features that present themselves to the student of primitive ceramics. It will be seen from Fig. 12 that the three lugs, whether solid or pierced, occur on cook-pots of many forms, of which wide-mouthed rounded bowls, smaller pots with splayed sides, and beaker-like vessels are the commonest. Many of these are provided with footrings or footstands to improve their stability. Occasionally, as with the vessel from Kempston in the British Museum, the lugs are so reduced in size, or so shaped, as to be useless for their functional purpose: in these cases they have become merely vestigial and are retained as a form of ornament only.

Lugs, whether functional or not, must be distinguished in origin and purpose from the ornamental bosses which come to be a recognized decorative device on Anglo-Saxon pottery in the fifth century. These bosses, unlike the lugs which are normally either applied to the outside of the pot or roughly pinched up from the surface of it, are generally hollow. They are formed by being pushed out from the inside, where they leave a corresponding cavity. They may be of every shape or form, circular, vertical, horizontal, diagonal, or curvilinear. They are never pierced as an aid to suspension, and only very rarely are they as few as three in number, any quantity from four to twelve being common. Occasionally as many as twenty-two or twenty-four occur, if the decorative design of which they form a part so requires.

As an ornamental feature these bosses are normally used as part of schemes which include linear and often stamped decoration also, and some of the commonest basic designs involving bosses will be examined in the next chapter. But, before finally leaving the plain pottery, it may be noted that bosses may appear alone as the only decoration on almost every form which plain pottery can take. On Fig. 13 are examples of bowls, shouldered jars, and large biconical

[1] *Fuhlsbüttel*, 17–20.

urns on which bosses occur as the sole decoration. Usually in such cases they are placed on the shoulder or on the point of maximum girth to add emphasis to these formal features, but occasionally long vertical bosses may be used by themselves on the lower part of the vessel. These sometimes produce an effect of continuous ribbing or fluting, and in such cases there is probably a deliberate imitation of Roman silver or glass ware. These are most frequently found in the south-east, where they match similar examples in Holland and Belgium. There is, for example, a little vessel from Drury Lane, London, which seems to show the last end of the fluted tradition, probably in the seventh century.[1]

But bosses and other excrescences, such as raised collars, are only one element in the decorative repertoire used by Anglo-Saxon potters. They had, broadly speaking, two other principal resources at their disposal, linear ornament and stamps. By using one, two, or all three of these methods in combination they were able to produce a vast range of decorative effects, and the analysis of these designs and their significance will occupy the next two chapters. At this point something further should be said about linear and stamped ornament in themselves.

Linear ornament is of course the simplest and most elementary method employed by all primitive peoples for decorating pottery, and there is no need to spend time in discussing the background to its use by Anglo-Saxon potters. Here it should only be noted that the phrase covers a very wide range of decorative techniques. Lines may be wide or narrow, deep or shallow, close-set to produce ribbed or corrugated surfaces, or widely spaced to demarcate areas either left plain or decorated in other ways. Lines may be produced by every sort of tool, broad-ended for the wide shallow effects, sharp-pointed for the deep or narrow: notched lines may be made by a roulette: slashed lines by a twisted cord or thong, and groups of parallel lines by the points of a small comb. Combinations of lines of different kinds may occur; for example, what I term the 'line-and-groove' technique, in which a broad groove is bordered on each side by one or more finer lines, producing an emphatic, almost plastic, effect. This device is significant for dating because it is very commonly employed on the continental pottery of the fourth and fifth centuries and seems to have gone out of use everywhere by about A.D. 500.[2] So too the habit of decorating plain surfaces by close-set broadly tooled lines, producing a cor-

---

[1] Fluting as a decorative device on Anglo-Saxon pottery is discussed by me, in connection with the Drury Lane vessel, in *Ant. Journ.* xvii (1937), 432–6.

[2] See e.g. its use on vessels of Plettke's Type A7a from Quelkhorn and Westerwanna (Plettke, Tafel 32, 1–6).

rugated or furrowed surface, is characteristic of the Anglian and other northern peoples on the Continent in the fourth and early fifth centuries, and its occurrence in this country, as we shall see later,[1] is a sure indication of northern influence and an early date.

If one may venture a chronological generalization about linear ornament on our English pottery, it is that broad tooling and deeply furrowed lines are more likely to occur on fifth- than on sixth-century pots, and that finer and more lightly tooled lines, while they may be used at any time, are characteristic of the later, rather than the earlier, pottery of the pagan period. The use of finger-tipping, slashed collars (whether raised or flat), and line-and-dot designs, are also likely to be early rather than late; finger-tipping, and the use of small dots, in particular, seem to go out of fashion as the popularity of stamped ornament increases in the early part of the sixth century.

This use of stamped ornament is at once the most characteristic and the most perplexing feature of Anglo-Saxon ceramics. Its origin and its significance are alike somewhat obscure. Stamped wares occur of course among the commercial fabrics of the Roman Empire, and in Britain indeed even earlier, in various groups of Early Iron Age pottery. The popularity of this form of decoration greatly increased in the fourth century, both in the frontier provinces of the Rhineland, and in Roman Britain, where it became characteristic of certain rural industries such as that which sprang up in the New Forest. It begins to appear at much the same time, though generally used in a more restrained fashion, among the barbarian tribes beyond the Imperial frontiers in Frisia, north Germany, and the Rhineland, though not until much later in the Jutish peninsula and the rest of Scandinavia.

This distribution suggests that stamped ornament on pottery was one of the many borrowings by the free Germans from the industrial art of the late Empire, at a time when the frontiers were ceasing to maintain what significance they had ever possessed as cultural barriers. But, if this is so, the barbarians quickly adopted the technique as their own, and they always used it, at any rate in the Saxon lands, with a difference. On most of the late Roman stamped wares, which are of course wheel-made, the stamps are used to produce one or more lines of horizontal ornament, and very often the impressions are crowded together, sometimes one stamp half on top of the next.[2] This tradition was taken over in the wheel-made Frankish pottery of the Rhineland, and is frequently found on the biconical bowls and other rather monotonous products

---

[1] See pp. 52–3. [2] As e.g. with those in *Richborough* i (1926), Pls. XXIX, 133, and XXX, 4 and 11.

of that unimaginative industry.[1] So too the range of stamps employed both on the Roman and Frankish wares is somewhat limited, being mainly confined to cross-in-circle and rosette types, criss-cross patterns mostly in squares and rectangles, and segmented rectangles of the 'Union Jack' variety. It is related to, and sometimes used in combination with, the patterned or notched rouletting that is also characteristic of Frankish pottery.[2]

In both these respects the free Germans between the lower Elbe and the Rhine mouths made a much more uninhibited use of this technique. Horizontal zones of stamps are of course commonly employed on their hand-made pots, as they are on the wheel-made vessels of the Rhineland. But more care is taken with the individual placing of the stamps, which are hardly ever crowded one upon another, and they are also used very freely to add emphasis or diversification to all the many varieties of linear and bossed designs in which the potters took such evident delight. At the same time the range of stamps employed is very much greater, and far more significance seems to be attached to the employment of particular stamps, and combinations of stamps, and to the symbolism which some of them apparently display. This is a subject which will be discussed later, but it is worth stating at the outset, because of the much more prominent part which stamped ornament came to play in the English pottery of the sixth century than it had ever done on the Continent.

This freedom and spontaneity in the early use of stamps on pottery in the traditional Saxon regions on the Continent, and its development still further in England, especially, as we shall see, in those parts of the southern Midlands where Saxon influences were strongest, have led to the suggestion that there is something more than an accidental association between the popularity of stamped ornament and the spread of specifically Saxon culture. It could be argued not only that this is a case where an originally barbarian technique was borrowed into the artistic repertoire of Roman provincial industry, but that, later on, after the breakdown of the Roman economy in Britain, it was developed here in its own right as an element in the Saxon cultural dominance of certain parts of the country. This view might derive some support from the obvious contrast between the Anglian culture of Schleswig and Fünen, where stamped decoration on pottery is virtually unknown, and the Saxon areas from the Elbe westwards where it was undoubtedly becoming popular, whatever its

[1] A valuable recent study of this industry is W. Hübener's article, Topographisch-statistische Untersuchungen zur merowingerzeitlichen Keramik in Süddeutschland, in the *Alemannisches Jahr*buch 1964/5, but he does not deal specifically with the stamped wares.

[2] As e.g. on a vessel from Gr. 93 at Beerlegem (*Arch. Belg.* 91 (1966), 43, Fig. 14. 6).

origins, just when the migrations to Britain were starting up. It would be natural to draw the obvious conclusion that, of the peoples mainly concerned in these migrations, the Saxons rather than the Angles brought the taste for stamped ornament with them.

Continental scholars are, however, understandably reluctant to attach a specifically Saxon label to stamped ornament. This is partly because of the prevalent view that it was in origin not a barbarian technique at all, but one borrowed by the free Germans from the stock-in-trade of late Roman industrial art. It has been suggested on this ground that the increasing popularity of the technique in Britain in the century after the migrations may have been due to a hangover from Roman provincial taste in Britain itself. Whatever may be the origin of the fashion, a direct transfer of this kind seems to be very unlikely. It would imply a cultural relationship between the native population and the invaders in the early stages of the conquest that is not supported in the other evidence. Nor is there any reason to suppose that by the sixth century, when the fashion for stamped ornament really gets going, the surviving Romano-British population were in a position to exert any influence whatever on the ceramic fashions of their conquerors.[1] Had they been able to do so, the first thing they would have passed on would surely have been the use of the potter's wheel.[2] But by that time the whole technical background of Roman industry had been long forgotten. The situation in Britain, even in Kent, is really quite different from that in the Rhineland, where the Franks seem to have taken over the technical apparatus and skill necessary to maintain a commercial industry producing wheel-made pottery more or less complete from their Roman predecessors. In Britain the potter's wheel was never adopted by the great mass of the newcomers in the pagan period. Their increasing use of stamped ornament on their hand-made wares grew directly out of the traditions they brought with them. It owed little or nothing to native taste. The few pots whose decoration might be interpreted as owing something to Roman fashion are either very early, before the Romano-British economy had completely broken down, or else they are hand-made echoes of contemporary Frankish models. In neither case are they relevant to the main question under discussion.

[1] I find myself quite unable to accept the contrary view put forward by T. C. Lethbridge on this matter in *Dark Age Britain* (1956), 112–22.

[2] Mr. Hayo Vierck has suggested to me that the failure of the Anglo-Saxons to adopt the use of the potter's wheel was due to the fact that the ceramic forms which appealed to their taste could not readily be made in this way. This may be true of the more elaborate bossed pottery, but it could never have applied to the much wider range of their unbossed types.

D

Another reason for caution in associating stamped ornament with the Saxons arises from the reluctance of German scholars to identify a single cultural complex to which the term Saxon can properly be given. The state of tribal confusion which seems to have prevailed in the traditional Saxon homelands at the time when the movement to Britain began has already been mentioned. German archaeologists have been much preoccupied in sorting out the various elements in this hotch-potch. There has been much·discussion on the parts played in it not only by Saxons but by such historic peoples as the Chauci or the neighbouring Frisians to the west, or even the Lombards or Suebi originally seated further inland up the Elbe valley.[1] Much work has been devoted to disentangling a *Nordseegruppe*, or a *Westgruppe*, or a *Mischgruppe*, among the overcrowded population of these coastal areas. And in formulating these internal distinctions there has been a tendency to avoid using the term 'Saxon' even for characteristics like the use of stamped pottery which they seem to have in common. However important it may be to isolate these various groups—and the distinctions between them are of great interest for English as well as for German studies—it is perhaps natural for us in this country rather to seek the features which can be attributed to a common Saxon culture, than to discriminate so meticulously between its various elements that the common culture itself seems to disappear.

This brief discussion of the three main decorative elements—lines, bosses, stamps—employed on Anglo-Saxon pottery may be summarized by saying that, whereas all three may be found throughout the period of settlement, there is a change of character and emphasis in the use of each as time passes. In the early fifth century designs are characterized, at first, by the vigour and sometimes by the simplicity of their linear patterns, often carried out with furrowed lines or the line-and-groove technique, and emphasized by finger-tipping or dots: there is a comparatively restrained use of bossed ornament and stamps, though raised and slashed collars are in vogue from the start. Later in the century bossed ornament becomes more exuberant: these are the days of its culminating fashion in the curvilinear extravagancies of the bizarre *Buckelurnen*, about which more will be said later. In the sixth century the earlier years are marked by a growing restraint in the use of bosses, now largely restricted to shoulder-bosses of various forms, and by the increasing popularity of stamps,

---

[1] The bibliography attached to Tischler (1956) lists most of the relevant literature before that date: see especially the entries under W. D. Asmus, A. Genrich, H. Jankuhn, G. Körner, F. Tischler, and K. Waller. A recent summary by A. Genrich, 'Zur Geschichte der Altsachsen auf dem Kontinent' is in *Die Kunde* 16 (1965), 107–29. See also the Supplementary Bibliography, ibid. 130–6.

which, used in combination with bosses and lines, gradually become the most important part of the decorative repertoire. After the middle of the sixth century bosses go generally out of fashion, and stamped linear designs, often of considerable elaboration, tend to predominate. Later still there is a tendency for stamped patterns to lose their guiding lines and so to break down into a random medley of meaningless ornamentation with little or no attempt at a design. From this it is an easy step to that abandonment of all the traditional forms of decoration which brings the period with which we are concerned to a close in the course of the seventh century.

III

THE TYPOLOGY OF DECORATION

1. HORIZONTAL, BICONICAL, AND CURVILINEAR SCHEMES

FROM this general account of the rise and fall of ceramic fashions, for which, perhaps too rashly, a broad chronological framework has been suggested, let us turn to the typological evolution of the main schemes of decoration as they can be traced out by applying the principles here laid down. It will be found that most of the commoner schemes, including even the most elaborate, go back to a very few simple and basic ideas, developed either singly or in various combinations.

The simplest of all ways of decorating a pot, whatever its form, is to put one or more horizontal lines around its neck. This was done not infrequently by Anglo-Saxon potters, but the very simplicity of the device deprives the group of pots so treated of any single significance as a group. Some of them certainly belong to the first Anglian or Anglo-Frisian settlers in East Anglia and the eastern Midlands. Such are most of those shown on Fig. 14, several of which are of early forms, such as the biconical pieces from Peterborough and the Roman *civitas* of Leicester, or the sharply shouldered bowl from Pensthorpe.[1] It will be noted that the round-bottomed globular urn from Girton, itself an early Anglian shape, is decorated in the line-and-groove technique characteristic of fifth-century craftsmanship. There are, however, also some certainly late pieces with simple horizontal linear decoration, not here illustrated, such as a bag-shaped pot from Fonaby (Lincs.) or the slapdash example from Laceby in the same county. This is of the tall beaker-shaped type of the seventh

---

[1] A very close parallel to the Peterborough vessel was found at Liebenau (Brandgrab II/28) with one of the earliest types of equal-armed brooch, datable about 400. The Leicester urn is similar to one from Liebenau (Brandgrab II/58) with somewhat later associations. *Nachrichten aus Nieder-sachsens Urgeschichte* xxxiii (1964), 24–51. Abb. 1. 6 and Tafel. 1. 8. The grounds for placing bowls like that from Pensthorpe among the earliest groups of Anglo-Saxon pottery in Britain are discussed by me in connection with this piece in *Norf. Arch.* xxvii. 201.

century (Fig. 9) and was found with a large late square-headed brooch of Leeds Type B1.[1]

Variants of this simple design, in which the group of horizontal necklines includes, or encloses, a flat slashed or feathered collar, also occur both early and late. An early one from Lackford is shown on Fig. 14, where the feathered zone seems simply a contemporary alternative to the more usual raised slashed collar. On the other hand, the barrel-shaped pot with flaring rim from an inhumation at Horndean (Hants) has late sixth-century associations and must represent the final phase of the same tradition.[2] In a few instances urns with simple horizontal linear decoration also carry shoulder-bosses.[3]

Horizontal designs of this kind offer a ready field for stamped ornament, and an early form like the Illington piece on Fig. 14, which is decorated with four bands of horizontal lines separated by tempting blank spaces, seems almost to invite the attention of a craftsman with a bunch of stamps. Pots with horizontal zones of lines and stamps ranging in number from one to six constitute one of the largest groups of decorated pottery (Fig. 15). They occur in all the areas in which this pottery is found, though with less frequency in Kent and the south generally than in East or Middle Anglia. It is noteworthy that while the simpler examples are mostly found in the eastern areas of early settlement, the Cambridgeshire cemeteries are prominent among those producing pots with two or three stamped zones, and the most elaborate sort with four or more zones occur also further inland in Northamptonshire and Bedfordshire. The emphasis in this distribution, typified by the examples on Fig. 15 from Girton (Cambs.), Kempston (Beds.), and Holdenby (Northants.), thus points to a fact that will constantly recur at later stages in this analysis, namely the great popularity of elaborately stamped wares of all kinds in Middle Anglia.

The series also illustrates the dangers inherent in a purely typological dating. While it would be natural to assume a general chronological progression from the simpler to the more elaborate types, it so happens that two rather similar examples of the simplest form which this stamped horizontal decoration can take—a group of lines above a single line of stamps—can be shown to date from after the middle of the sixth century. One of these (Lackford 50, 78) contained a cruciform brooch of Group III/IV (about 550), while on the other (Loveden

[1] Illustrated and discussed by me in *Arch. Journ.* cviii (1952), 89 and Fig. 10. 1. The brooch is no. 53 in E. T. Leeds, *Corpus of Early Anglo-Saxon Great Squareheaded Brooches* (1949).

[2] Illustrated and discussed by me in *Proc. Hants. F.C.* xix (1956), 146 and Fig. 17. 1.

[3] One of these, Loveden Hill 60/212, contained the fused foot of an early sixth-century cruciform brooch.

Hill A3/243) one of the stamps used was simply the swollen nose-piece of an almost exactly similar brooch. It is, however, interesting to note that the Lackford urn was found to underlie another (49, 429), evidently buried later, which also had this type of decoration, but more elaborate, showing three zones of small stamps separated by rouletted lines. Lethbridge has suggested that this upper burial may be as late as the seventh century, when the use of rouletted lines was popular, but in any case it could hardly be earlier than the last quarter of the sixth.[1] On the other hand, there can be little doubt that the elaborate urn on Fig. 15 from Shropham (Norfolk), with its sharply biconical form and three horizontal zones of large stamps separated by raised collars embellished with slashes and dots, is a very much earlier piece, probably antedating A.D. 500.

It will be noted in the case of the Shropham urn, and some others that exhibit the horizontal scheme of decoration in its more elaborate forms, that this scheme is especially appropriate to the decoration of biconical pots. The horizontal feature produced by a more or less sharp carination in these vessels forms a natural basis on which horizontal zones of ornament can rest, and from which they can be built upwards or downwards to cover as much of the pot as it is desired to decorate.

Before considering other schemes appropriate to the decoration of biconical pots there are two points of general application that should be made about the horizontal type of ornament. The first is that it may occur in combination with bosses. When this happens the bosses are normally set below the zone of horizontal ornament and generally in no particular organic relationship to it. There are two main groups here, although, as always in the classification of Anglo-Saxon pottery, they merge imperceptibly into one another. The first consists of shouldered pots where the presence of bosses emphasizing the shoulder is the focal point of the scheme. These shoulder-boss pots frequently have one or more horizontal zones of ornament on the neck. Occasionally the bosses intrude into these horizontal zones, so that the latter are broken up into panels separated by bosses, and each containing stamped ornament arranged horizontally. More will be said of this type later, when panel-style decoration is discussed. The second group includes biconical and sub-biconical types where the bosses are mostly set lower, and are quite subsidiary to the main horizontal scheme. The type is well illustrated by the Saxby urn on Fig. 15, where the

---

[1] See *Lackford* 18 and Fig. 16, for illustration and discussion of this chronologically important association.

bosses are both inconspicuous in profile and insignificant in number (there are only three), and seem quite irrelevant to the main horizontal stamped design, to which they give the impression of having been added as an afterthought. These cases are best treated as examples of a mixed style, and they are probably quite late in date.

The other point of general interest about horizontal schemes of decoration is that they represent the closest approximation among this hand-made pottery to designs appropriate to the decoration of wheel-made vessels. In the late Roman wares of the fourth century, as in the Frankish ceramics of the sixth and seventh, horizontal bands of stamped or rouletted ornament are normal. This is in part a technical matter, for it is obvious that the simplest method of decorating wheel-made vessels is by causing the ornament to follow closely what may be termed the horizontal 'grain' of the pot-wall produced by the horizontal motion of the wheel. Biconical pots decorated in this way became the standard stock-in-trade of the Rhineland industry in the centuries following the Anglo-Saxon movement into Britain, and it is most unusual, except among the Alamanni in south Germany,[1] for this wheel-made pottery to have bossed ornament other than raised or ridged collars.[2] We should therefore be on the look-out among our hand-made wares for vessels which may betray familiarity with these late Roman or Frankish fashions by a similar combination of biconical form, horizontal zones of stamped ornament, and an absence of bosses. A number of such pots can be found, especially at Sancton (Yorks.), where there is a notable group, and among the accessory vessels from inhumation graves in the south-east and the Thames valley.[3] Their significance will be discussed further in a later chapter.

The other main type of decoration appropriate to biconical vessels springs more readily from Germanic traditions of hand-made pottery (Fig. 16). In this the whole, or the greater part, of the top half of the pot is treated as a single decorative zone, demarcated above, and generally below also, by horizontal lines, though the latter are sometimes omitted where the zone rests directly on

[1] See the distribution map of this type of decoration in south Germany by W. Hübener in *Alemannisches Jahrbuch* 1964/5, 27, Karte 21.

[2] A few exceptional pieces, like that from Pondrome in the Namur Museum, have vertical bosses extending from a raised collar to the carination, as do the Alamannic types illustrated by Hübener from Ulm (op. cit. Taf. 6. 33–34).

[3] Some are shown on Fig. 41. A sign indicating Frankish influence is the occasional presence on such pots of rouletting, or of stamped or comb-point decoration arranged in small chevrons to imitate rouletting, such as occurs in the work of the Sancton potter, some of whose products are shown on Fig. 42. They are modelled on Frankish *biconi* of the type of that from Merlemont Gr. 27 (Y. Wautelet, *La Nécropole franque de Merlemont* (1967), Fig. 37. 5) which is dated about 550.

the carination of the pot. The whole of this zone is broken up by groups of
vertical or diagonal lines, often arranged as chevrons, and these spaces may contain further linear patterns, sometimes accompanied by finger-tipping, dots, or
stamps. The effect is thus of a broad diversified band of ornament bounded
above and below by horizontal lines. Sometimes, instead of a single broad band
of this kind, two narrower ones are found, usually with a similar internal
arrangement in each case.[1] In a few instances similar treatment is also given to
the lower half of a pot.

This type of ornament has a long history in the continental Iron Age. It is
commonly found, for example, in the pottery of the Oberjersdal culture of
southern Jutland,[2] and in the Fuhlsbüttel culture of Holstein,[3] both of which
played a part in the first two centuries of our era in the growth of the later
Saxon complex of the *Völkerwanderungszeit*. It is well represented in the pottery
of east Holstein in the fourth century,[4] one of the main constituents in the
Mischgruppe cemeteries like the Perlberg-bei-Stade that have the closest affinities
with England. There is therefore every reason to expect some of the earliest
Anglo-Saxon pottery in this country to carry decoration of this type, and the
continental parallels, which will be discussed later, suggest that such a vessel as
Caistor-by-Norwich P 15 was made in the fourth century,[5] while most of the
sharply biconical examples, with or without hollow necks, shown on Fig. 16,
are of the fifth. They form an important group in settling the early history of
the invasions.

But this type of decoration had a long life. It continued in vogue long after
the biconical form to which it was originally appropriate had been generally
replaced by sub-biconical and even more sagging and baggy shapes, as some of
the examples on Figs. 17–19 and Pl. 4 show. It became, on the one hand, a popular
framework for elaborate displays, first of line-and-dot decoration, as in the
Abingdon and Howletts pots on figure, 18, and then of stamped ornament, as on
those from Girton and Kettering on the same figure, which are typologically
later. It could be treated in a loose and decadent fashion, as on the two pieces
from Caistor on Fig. 17, or it could be reduced to a narrow strip embedded in
decorative schemes of different origin, where it may become almost indistinguishable from a flat slashed collar. It is still found in the late sixth or early

[1] As on urn 1649 from Caistor-by-Norwich on Fig. 16.
[2] See *Oberjersdal*, especially Tafel A, and 2, 3, 4, 7, 8, 14, 15, and 16.
[3] See *Fuhlsbüttel*, especially Abb. 3, 7, 15, 22, 23, 24, 25, and 27.
[4] Genrich (1954), Abb. 1, nos. 26, 27, 29.
[5] See p. 71, 1626 on Fig. 16, and Pl. I.

seventh century, as on the pot from Sutton Hoo (Mound 3),[1] or on seventh-century vessels with tall necks, sometimes executed in rouletted lines or in the comb-point technique that became popular at that time.[2] Its echo can be seen in the arrangement of the stamps on some late pots that have stamped decoration only, without any guiding lines, such as that from Little Wilbraham (Fig. 19). In most of these cases there is little or nothing left in the shape of the pots to suggest its earlier history as a form of decoration especially appropriate to biconical types.

One of the linear motives that appears frequently in association with this biconical decoration, and is especially characteristic of the earlier stages in its development, is the arched or eyebrow motive, for which the Germans use the convenient phrase *stehende Bogen*, standing curves, as opposed to *hängende Bogen*, hanging curves, or what we should call festoons or swags. These *stehende Bogen* may occur on biconical pottery either as a means of breaking up the main horizontal zone, alternative to the use of vertical or chevron lines, or they may appear independently below the main zone, or even, more rarely, above it. The examples on Fig. 20 illustrate all these varieties, and also the occasional use of the motif on biconical pots with bosses on the carination. It will be seen that all these come from the primary cremation cemeteries of Yorkshire, Lincolnshire, and Norfolk, and all, with the possible exception of that from Elkington, are obviously early in form, fabric, and decoration: the lines are broad, firm grooves, and the pattern is embellished, if at all, with finger-tipping or dots. Not many urns of this kind in Britain show the use of stamps.

The *stehende Bogen* motif is in fact of great importance in the fourth- and fifth-century pottery of the Elbe–Weser region.[3] It is the basic element in the development in that area of the fondness for curvilinear patterns, which culminates in the second half of the fifth century in the extravagantly decorated

[1] R. L. S. Bruce-Mitford in *Proc. Suff. Inst. of Arch.* xxx (1964), Fig. 3, p. 18.

[2] As in those from Leighton Buzzard, *Arch. Journ.* cxx (1963), 174 Fig. 8g and 178 Fig. 11a.

[3] Several sources for it can be suggested in late antique art. It is a familiar motif on late fourth-century bronze work, e.g. E. T. Leeds, *Early Anglo-Saxon Art and Archaeology* (1936), Figs. 4 and 5, especially the pieces from Miannay and Buire-sur-l'Ancre. The trailed ornament on late fourth-century glasses sometimes takes this form. An example from Furfooz came from a grave dated by J. Nenquin about 350 (*La Nécropole de Furfooz* (1953), 46 and Pl. III. 10) but regarded by C. Isings as perhaps somewhat later (*Roman Glass from Dated Finds* (1957), 135). There is another example, also in the Namur Museum, from Samson: for one found in an English (Anglo-Saxon) context see *Lackford*, Fig. 23. The motif also occurs on fourth-century Germanic pottery in association with symbols of magical or religious significance, such as rosettes, swastikas, serpents, etc.: e.g. *Westerwanna* i, Tafel 146, no. 1167.

Buckelurnen, about which more will be said shortly. But the significant point about these developments in Germany is that designs mainly consisting of linear *stehende Bogen*, often accompanied by finger-tipping, frequently arranged in rosette patterns, are the most characteristic decoration of the round-bellied pottery with narrow cylindrical or concave necks and well-moulded rims, that became so popular in the Elbe–Weser region in the late fourth and early fifth centuries. This style of decoration used on this type of pottery—called by Plettke A7(*a*),[1] and by Tischler the *Cuxhaven/Galgenberg Typ*[2]—and on forms related to it, is found over and over again on such sites as Westerwanna,[3] Mahndorf,[4] the Galgenberg near Cuxhaven,[5] Altenwalde,[6] Quelkhorn,[7] etc. It occurs generally in contexts which antedate the elaborate *Buckelurnen* that are contemporary with the main movement to Britain in the mid fifth century.

In all this group, however, *stehende Bogen* form the main element of the design. Their appearance as a subsidiary feature in such biconical schemes of decoration as are illustrated on Fig. 20 is thus indicative of a secondary though still early phase. It illustrates very well the conditions which produced the culture of the *Mischgruppe* in the Stade area, in which, as we have seen, fashions from south Jutland and Holstein, where decoration of biconical type was traditional, met and mingled with those already in vogue in the lower Elbe and Weser valleys. A number of cemeteries in this area, Altenwalde,[8] Westerwanna,[9] and Wehden[10] amongst them, have produced a few instances of this mixed style, as it appears more commonly in England in the forms shown on Fig. 20, and there are also one or two contemporary examples of a parallel development in Norway.[11] All this suggests that the mixture of the two styles was only in its early stages at the time of the main movement to Britain, where its development

[1] Plettke 46 and Tafel 32, especially nos. 3 and 6 from Westerwanna, and nos. 4 and 7 from Quelkhorn.

[2] Tischler (1956) 48, and Abb. 8, especially no. 2 from Wehden.

[3] *Westerwanna* i, especially Tafel 8, no. 45, with early fifth-century equal-armed brooch: Tafel 19, no. 148, with late fourth-century brooch: Tafel 157, no. 1239, with tubular bronze fitting of 'Dorchester' type: and many others without datable associations.

[4] *Mahndorf*, especially Abb. 19*b*, fourth century: Abb. 37A, with early fifth-century equal-armed brooch: and Abb. 60D, said, p. 162, to be about 350.

[5] *Galgenberg*, Tafeln 21. 7: 22. 3: 24. 6: 26. 3: 29. 1: none closely datable.

[6] *Altenwalde*, Tafeln 1. 6: 2. 17, with two decorated bronze rings: 3. 19 and 20: 4. 27, with Roman glass bowl, apparently fourth-century: 8. 60: 9. 66.

[7] *Hemmoor-Warstade*, Tafel 19, Grab 46: *Quelkhorn*, Tafel 30. 86: *Gudendorf*, Tafel 35. 43: *Duhnen-Wehrberg* ii, Tafel 47. 45: none closely datable.

[8] *Altenwalde*, Tafel 3. 19.

[9] *Westerwanna* i, Tafel 10. 69.

[10] *Wehden*, Tafeln 28. 275, and 29. 43, both placed by Waller among urns which he dates typologically 450–500: and Tafel 38. 77, which he places after 500.

[11] e.g. Oslo Museum *c* 6965–75 from Vestfold, said to be about 400: *c* 4054 from Vestagder, associated with a fifth-century cruciform brooch.

was stimulated, as perhaps also in Norway, by the general confusion of the times. The presence in the German cemeteries of a few stamped examples,[1] which are probably later, could indeed be explained as instances of that cultural back-wash from Britain after 500 of which there are further possible signs among the brooches and other metal work.

But there are one or two examples in Britain of the *Cuxhaven/Galgenberg Typ* in its pure fourth-century form, decorated solely with *stehende Bogen* designs and the characteristic finger-tip rosettes that go with them. These are of great interest as direct manifestations of the earlier phase. One is Caistor-by-Norwich R12,[2] which is typologically almost too good to be true, a perfect blueprint of the Cuxhaven/Galgenberg type, with its rounded form, upright neck, *stehende Bogen*, and neat finger-tip rosettes, all executed in the most stylish and professional manner. The other, unfortunately less complete, but similar in general character, comes from Brundall,[3] a few miles to the east down the River Yare between Norwich and Great Yarmouth. It is hard to believe that either can have reached this part of Norfolk much after A.D. 400, and their significance, as to both date and place, will be discussed in a later chapter.[4]

Apart from these purely continental examples, there is also a whole group of English urns (see Fig. 21) whose decoration consists, either entirely or pre-dominantly, of linear *stehende Bogen*, embellished on occasion with a restrained use of finger-tipping, or line-and-dot patterns. In some of these cases[5] the groups of dots or finger-tipping in the spaces between the *stehende Bogen* are clearly bungled memories of the rosettes in this position on the continental prototypes of this style. Most urns of this kind would be treated by continental scholars as antedating the elaborate *Buckelurnen*, and so would be placed at latest in the first half of the fifth century. One, Markshall IX, not here illustrated, contained the full-round knob of a Group I cruciform brooch, which is con-sistent with that early dating.[6] But not all need be so early. The urn from Castle

[1] e.g. *Wehden*, Tafel 13. 30, which looks late, though placed, surely wrongly, among urns dated by Waller typologically 350–400, and *Galgenberg*, Tafel 29. 2, which also looks late.

[2] *Ant. Journ.* xvii (1937), 429, Fig. 1(b). This urn did not come from Cmdr. Mann's excavations but was dug out of a rabbit-hole in perfect con-dition by a warrener, and, when I first saw it, some thirty years ago, was standing on the mantelpiece in the dining room at Caistor Hall: it is now with the rest of the Caistor material in the Norwich Castle Museum. A very close continental parallel

to its form and decoration is the fine fourth-century piece from Midlaren, now at Assen, illustrated in *Wijster* 164, Fig. 81.

[3] Illustrated and discussed by me in *Norf. Arch.* xxvii. 189 and 191, Fig. 1. 1.

[4] See p. 72.

[5] e.g. Elkington 109 (*Arch. Journ.* cviii (1952), 40, Fig. 8), for which again close German parallels could be given: e.g. *Altenwalde*, Tafel 1. 6: *Wehden*, Tafel 19. 250 (in the 400–450 group): Tafel 32. 25 (perhaps after 500).

[6] So did the Thurmaston urn on Fig. 21.

Acre on Fig. 21 was accompanied by a burnt cruciform brooch of Group II, which could make it as late as the early years of the sixth century. It is in fact here necessary to reckon with the possibility that the decoration on some of these urns, such as that from Fonaby on Fig. 21, must be read as derived from, rather than leading towards, the late fifth-century *Buckelurnen*.[1]

Nevertheless the distribution of those which show the *stehende Bogen* style at its best and simplest, and have the strongest claims to be treated as early, suggests that the group as a whole must be placed among the products of what will be called in a later chapter the 'transition phase' of the settlement, focused rather on the half-century following 400 than on that following 450. Vessels of this early group, some twenty-four in number, marked with a solid black circle on Map 3, come from four or five sites in Lincolnshire (nine examples), four in Norfolk (seven examples), two in Suffolk (two examples), two in east Yorkshire (two examples), one each in Cambridge, Middlesex, and Berkshire (five between them). The concentration in the familiar areas of primary cremation on the east coast between Suffolk and Yorkshire, and in the Thames valley, makes a pattern entirely consistent with the suggestion of a really early date. It is interesting also to record that more complex and sophisticated designs of this kind, with the *stehende Bogen* used in combination with bosses or other linear patterns (but not with stamps), and marked with an open circle on Map 3, have, as one would expect, a somewhat wider distribution in the eastern Midlands. They occur not only on the east coast and the Thames valley but also in a few examples from Leicestershire and Northamptonshire. There is even one which is believed to have come from Scotland, though this is probably later.[2] One or two of them, like the urn from Thurmaston (Leics.) or the one with bosses from Sancton (both on Fig. 21), seem already to be feeling their way in greater elaboration towards the *Buckelurnen*. The same is true of Markshall IX, which, as already mentioned, contained a Group I cruciform brooch. The deeply furrowed arcading on this pot has almost the plastic effect of bossed ornament, and, unlike any others of the group, it has, in common with many *Buckelurnen*, a well-moulded foot.

[1] The same may well be true of some comparable pieces from Germany. Waller places a number of the Wehden urns (e.g. 624, 263, 657, 723, 705, 582, 644, 667, 538, 38, 207, etc., see Tafeln 31–41) with this kind of decoration among those which he dates on typological grounds after 500. Though so late a date would seem questionable for many of these, several (e.g. 38, 207, 705) have the decadent and slapdash appearance characteristic of such late English examples as the Fonaby piece on Fig. 21. The latest surely datable German example known to me is that from Liebenau Gr. 1 with associated weapons of 450–525. *Studien aus Alt Europa* II (1965), 258 Abb. 1. 1.

[2] In the National Museum of Antiquities, Edinburgh, supposed to have been found in Buchan.

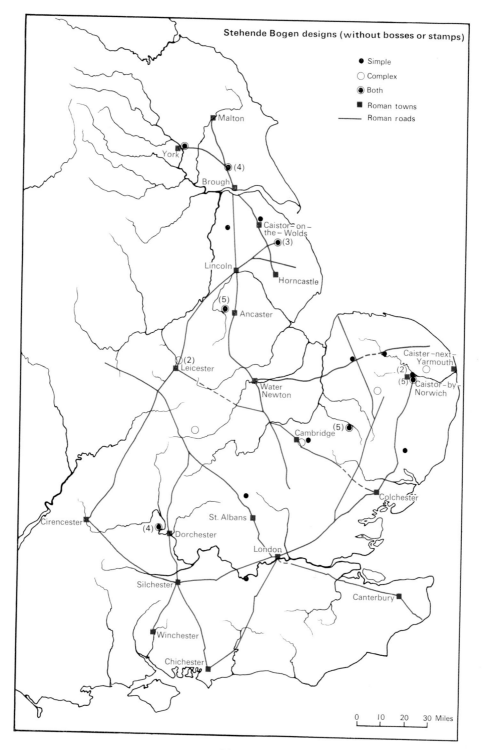

Stehende Bogen designs (without bosses or stamps)

- ● Simple
- ○ Complex
- ◉ Both
- ■ Roman towns
- — Roman roads

Malton

York

(4)

Brough

Caistor – on –
the – Wolds

(3)

Lincoln

Horncastle

(5)

Ancaster

(2)
Leicester

Water
Newton

Caister – next –
Yarmouth

(2)

(5) Caistor – by –
Norwich

(5)

Cambridge

Colchester

Cirencester

St. Albans

(4)
Dorchester

London

Silchester

Canterbury

Winchester

Chichester

0   10   20   30 Miles

MAP 3

It is when designs of this kind become, so to say, three-dimensional, and are executed no longer in pure line but partly in protuberant bosses of various sizes and shapes, that the true *Buckelurne* is born. Such vessels are securely dated on the Continent in the fifth century and predominantly in the second half of it.[1] They belong to a cultural complex that must be called Saxon and includes various other characteristic artefacts of which the fully developed types of equal-armed brooches are the most easily recognizable. While primarily at home in the so-called *Westgruppe* between Elbe and Weser (Westerwanna, Galgenberg, Mahndorf, Quelkhorn, Altenwalde, etc.), they occur also further west in Frisia, as at Beetgum, no doubt as a symptom of that westward movement of the Saxon peoples which led to their settlement in Britain.

I have distinguished five groups among the Saxon *Buckelurnen* of Britain:

    I. Those with feet, decorated with linear or line-and-groove designs, with or without finger-tipping and/or dots: but without stamps (Fig. 22).

    II. Those with similar decoration to those of Group I but without feet (Fig. 23 and Pl. 3).

    III. Those with feet, and with restrained use of stamps (Figs. 22 and 24 and Pl. 3).

    IV. Those without feet, and with restrained use of stamps (Fig. 24 and Pl. 3).

    V. Those with or without feet, and with free or exuberant use of stamps (Fig. 24 and Pl. 3).

The first two groups are alike in showing the style in its typologically earliest and purest form. The ornament, apart from the bosses, is here all executed in line, or line-and-groove, and embellished with finger-tipping and dots, including raised and slashed or dotted collars, but no stamps. These two groups are separated simply by the presence in the first and the absence in the second of a moulded footstand or footring, generally of no great height, but occasionally approaching pedestal form. The second two groups are similarly distinguished from one another by the presence or absence of a foot, and both are distinguished from the first two groups by the use of stamped ornament, though only in a sparing and restrained manner which does not dominate the design. In the fifth group stamps are freely used and frequently in such an exuberant

---

[1] Tischler (1954) 68. Among those with datable associations may be noted *Westerwanna* i, Tafeln 70. 525, with late fifth-century cruciform brooch: 78. 586, with late fourth-century brooch: 157. 1236, with late Roman zoomorphic buckle of Hawkes Type III A: *Galgenberg*, Tafel 34. 6, with late Roman bronze pincers.

manner that the plastic ornament of knobs and bosses ceases to be dominant and is sometimes almost overwhelmed.

These five groups of English *Buckelurnen* comprise between them about a hundred and thirty-five examples, of which rather over half are in the first two (unstamped) groups, about a fifth in Groups III and IV (with restrained stamping), and rather over a quarter in the fifth group comprising elaborately stamped urns.[1] In the first four groups there are nearly twice as many urns without feet as with feet: there are scarcely any vessels with feet in the fifth. It will be seen from these figures that some three-quarters of the English *Buckelurnen* either have no stamped ornament or show it only sparingly, and that, while about a quarter of the total have feet, two-thirds of these are unstamped. If one bears in mind the fact that, while stamped ornament may occur at any time, it attained its greatest popularity in the middle and late sixth century, it seems a reasonable conclusion from these figures that the great majority of English *Buckelurnen*, nearly all those in the first two groups, which are probably contemporary, and most of those in Groups III and IV, were made between 450 and 500. Unfortunately very few *Buckelurnen* can be dated by associated finds, but such evidence as exists (see Appendix) is consistent with this conclusion.

The distribution of the five groups is also interesting (Map 4). Group I is represented by at least nine examples from four sites in Norfolk and Suffolk, at least eight from seven sites in Cambridge, Bedfordshire, Northamptonshire, and Huntingdon, three from one site in Leicestershire, and singletons from Lincolnshire, east Yorkshire, and possibly Berkshire. The folk using these early urns with feet seem thus to be strongly focused in East Anglia, and to have spread thence, mainly south-westwards and to a lesser degree northwards, round the inner margin of the Fens into Middle Anglia.[2] Group II is again strongly represented in Norfolk and Suffolk with nineteen examples from seven sites, but east Yorkshire and Lincolnshire are now much more firmly in the picture with eighteen urns from four sites between them. There is also more emphasis on the Thames valley and its tributaries, with four examples from three sites in Middlesex and Berkshire, and outliers in Hertfordshire and Oxfordshire. But, apart from these, the weight is at least as much on the Humbrensian area as it is on East and Middle Anglia. Group III, urns with feet and restrained use of stamps, again shows best in Norfolk, spreading thence, through Northamp-

---

[1] The details on which the figures in this paragraph rest are given in the Appendix.

[2] As was first pointed out by me in *Ant. Journ.* xxxiv (1954), 201–8.

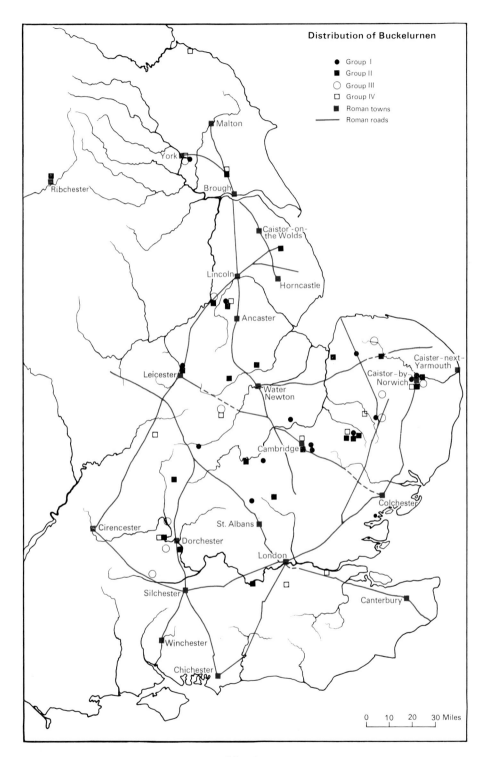

Distribution of Buckelurnen

● Group I
■ Group II
○ Group III
□ Group IV
■ Roman towns
— Roman roads

Malton

York

Ribchester

Brough

Caistor-on-
the Wolds

Lincoln

Horncastle

Ancaster

Leicester

Caister-next-
Yarmouth

Caistor-by-
Norwich

Water
Newton

Cambridge

Colchester

Cirencester

St. Albans

Dorchester

London

Silchester

Canterbury

Winchester

Chichester

0   10   20   30 Miles

MAP 4A

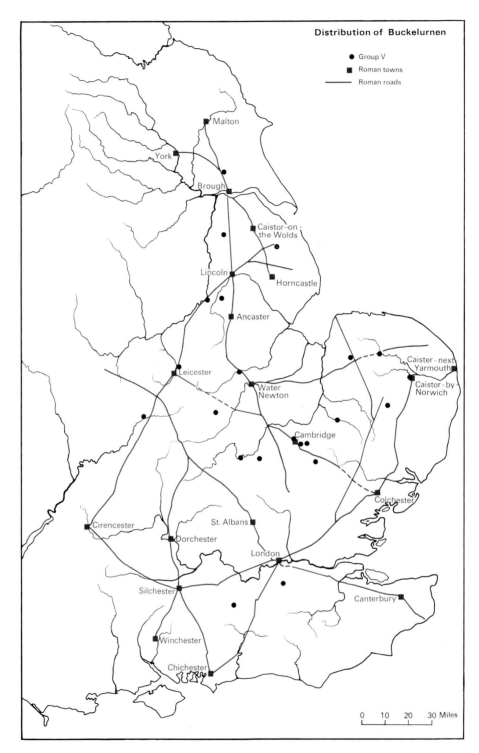

Distribution of Buckelurnen

● Group V
■ Roman towns
— Roman roads

Malton

York

Brough

Caistor-on-the Wolds

Lincoln

Horncastle

Ancaster

Caister-next-Yarmouth

Caistor-by-Norwich

Leicester

Water Newton

Cambridge

Colchester

Cirencester

St. Albans

Dorchester

London

Silchester

Canterbury

Winchester

Chichester

0 10 20 30 Miles

MAP 4B

tonshire, on to the upper Thames in Berkshire and Oxfordshire: north of the Trent there is only one in Yorkshire, and Lincolnshire has produced none at all. Group IV, on the other hand, gives much the same pattern as Group II; they show up best in Suffolk and Yorkshire, but there are now extensions westward into Warwickshire, and south into Kent and Surrey, as well as one other on the upper Thames in Berkshire. The late Group V, with its elaborate use of stamps, has a more restricted distribution. While especially popular in Cambridge, Suffolk, and Lincolnshire, where all forms of heavily stamped pottery were so much in evidence in the sixth century, it does not appear at all in the upper Thames valley or the regions east of it. A possible explanation for this unexpected restriction will be considered later.[1]

I have not attempted in discussing the *Buckelurnen* to suggest a typological analysis of the various designs which they display. There is very great variety in this matter, and all types are grouped together in the classification attempted above. While a number of elements can be distinguished (of which *stehende Bogen* bosses, split oval bosses, diagonal, vertical, horizontal, and circular bosses, with raised and slashed collars, are the commonest), they are found associated with one another in every possible combination and decorated in every sort of way to produce a bewildering number of different designs. Some general distinctions can perhaps be made between patterns based primarily on *stehende Bogen*, those based primarily on one or more tiers of bosses of various forms arranged horizontally, and those in which diagonal schemes are used to produce whirling effects. An analysis on these lines could be attempted and might prove significant. But even in postulating broad categories of this kind one soon encounters difficulties with hybrid and marginal examples, and these are sufficiently numerous and complex to make the task of resolving them more appropriate to a specialist study than to a general survey such as this.

Parallel with Group V, the heavily stamped *Buckelurnen* of the sixth century, there is also a related group of stamped urns with linear *stehende Bogen* as the main feature of the design. These arise no doubt directly from the intrusion of stamped ornament on to the earlier category which carries *stehende Bogen* designs in line only. There are not many of these stamped *stehende Bogen* urns, and for some reason they seem to be especially popular at Caistor-by-Norwich, which has produced six of the examples noticed by me: two of the others are also Norfolk urns from Illington and North Elmham, and the remainder are from Yorkshire, Lincolnshire, Oxfordshire, and Cambridge.

[1] See pp. 114–16.

Before leaving the *Buckelurnen*, this is the place to mention one or two special types which are perhaps more closely related to them than to the general run of shoulder-boss urns which will be discussed in the next chapter. The most interesting of these is the small group of so-called winged or horned urns that carry zoomorphic bosses. They are of rounded or shouldered form, mounted on a well-moulded foot, and have long vertical bosses, emphasized by feathering and stamps, which rise up to the shoulder from the constriction above the foot. In the characteristic form shown by those from Alfriston and London, the top of each boss is drawn up into a projecting head provided on each side with a stamped eye to indicate its zoomorphic character. The rest of the boss, with its linear feathering, is thus seen as the body of a legless serpent or *wyrm* climbing up the surface of the pot. In some examples, such as that from High Down (Sussex) or that from Northfleet (Kent), the heads of the zoomorphic bosses are more flattened, or the stamped eyes omitted, so that the likeness to an animal is less obvious.[1] These urns are especially at home in the south-east, Sussex, Kent, and London, with derivatives in Essex. The only close continental parallel known to me is from Norway, an urn in the Stavanger Museum from Varhaug, Hå, Rogaland,[2] which has no foot but six serpentine bosses rising from the base with horizontally barred bodies to end on the shoulder in prominent heads with stamped eyes. This urn is believed to date from about 400, and the English examples are likely to be of the fifth century, though none of them comes from a datable context. In view of the Jutish traditions of the south-east it is interesting to note this ceramic link with southern Norway.

Related to the south-eastern group, though different in form, are three other urns with zoomorphic bosses which may be mentioned at this point. One is a highly eccentric pot from St. John's, Cambridge,[3] where shoulder-bosses of otherwise normal type run up into long necks terminating in animal heads facing inwards. The second is an urn from Thurmaston (Leics.) by a potter who also worked at Lackford[4] (Suffolk) on which feathered bosses with stamped

---

[1] The examples from Alfriston, London, and High Down are illustrated by G. Baldwin Brown, *The Arts in Early England* iv (1915), Pl. cxxxvii, 1, 3, 4: for a sketch of the Alfriston piece, which better illustrates its zoomorphic character, first pointed out by Miss V. I. Evison, see her *Fifth Century Invasions south of the Thames* (1965), Fig. 16. 1: there is a drawing of the Northfleet example in R. F. Jessup, *Archaeology of Kent* (1930), 231, Fig. 32.

[2] Bøe 146, Fig. 225. I am indebted to Mr. Hayo Vierck for a drawing of this pot, which makes clearer its close relationship to the English group of urns with zoomorphic bosses.

[3] *Ant. Journ.* xvii (1937), Pl. xcii (*b*), bottom left.

[4] The Thurmaston urn shares four identical stamps with Lackford 50.33 (*Lackford*, Fig. 30), likewise an elaborate bossed urn, but without zoomorphic indications.

eyes are set diagonally on the shoulder of the pot (Fig. 45). The third is Sancton 204A which has solid lug-like bosses in the form of inverted animal heads set on the maximum diameter. There can be little doubt that in this whole group the zoomorphic bosses are not merely decorative but are intended as a protective or prophylactic device, designed to preserve the urn and its contents against desecration or disturbance.[1]

Another small group should be mentioned at this point. These are tall narrow vases, quite unlike the normal forms of Anglo-Saxon pottery, decorated with strong vertical fluting or line-and-groove ornament on the body, and usually mounted on pedestal feet. The type seems to be confined to Kent, and the known examples, five or six in number, may all have come from a single workshop.[2] The tall form, and especially the fluted decoration, might seem to mark them as fairly direct imitations of late Roman glass or silver ware, but the presence of at least two in Denmark, where such imitations are less likely, may suggest that this is just another link between Jutland and Kent.[3]

There is another small group, of which examples are shown on Fig. 25, which may also show some Roman influence. These are shoulder-bossed or long-bossed urns whose principal feature is that, like the Groups I and III *Buckelurnen*, they are mounted on well-moulded feet, sometimes approaching the pedestal form. A few of these, such as those from Frilford, Caistor, Girton, and Thurmaston, are decorated only with bosses and associated lines: they may perhaps owe something to memories of the late Roman folded beakers or thumb-pots. Others, like those from Woodston and Driffield, include a zone of stamped ornament: others again, like the very similar pieces from Thurmaston, Leicestershire, and from the churchyard at Waldringfield, Suffolk, are of more pronounced biconical profile and more strongly Germanic character.

[1] Another example, more stylized than the others, is from Sandy, Beds. (Bedford Museum 116), which has two stamps to indicate eyes at the head of otherwise normal bosses. One of the Castle Acre urns at Norwich has two of its five bosses capped by a two-eyed wyrm. The Sancton urn has been restored with the heads facing upwards, as in the other examples. But this may be incorrect as their form is quite different. They have no bodies and their shape appears to indicate intended use as handles or lugs, for which an inverted position would make them impracticable.

[2] For the Canterbury piece see *Ant. Journ.* xvii (1937), Pl. xciv (*b*): those from Westbere are in *Ant. Journ.* xxvi (1946), Pl. v. 18 and 20: one from

Eastry is illustrated *Proc. Soc. Ant.* xxii (1909), 367, Fig. 4: one from Ozingell, *Coll. Ant.* iii, Pl. IV. 4: and one from an unknown Kentish site, formerly in the Mayer collection at Liverpool, by E. T. Leeds, *Early Anglo-Saxon Art and Archaeology* (1936), Pl. XIII (*a*) centre: but this is probably identical with that from Ozingell.

[3] One is from Grave 1 at Røgnehoj, Gudme, in Fünen (H. Norling-Christensen, *Haraldstedgravpladsen* (1957), Fig. 19. 2); the other, which has no foot, is from Velling, Jutland (Ringkøbing Museum 1526). There was also one from the Hoogebeintum Terp in Dutch Friesland, there dated around 400.

It will be seen, however, that all these bossed urns with feet, though similar to the *Buckelurnen* in the extravagance of their form and sometimes in the elaboration of their ornament, are typologically shoulder-boss pots. As such they are related closely to classes which will be considered in the next chapter. It is therefore now necessary to go back to the beginning and consider further lines of development stemming from the basic principles outlined at the outset of this discussion. These are the lines of development that lead to the great variety of designs to which the main groups of shoulder-boss urns and their related types belong.

IV

THE TYPOLOGY OF DECORATION

2. RECTANGULAR AND TRIANGULAR SCHEMES

IN the preceding chapter designs were analysed which spring from three fundamentally different ways of decorating a pot: first, the purely horizontal schemes; second, what I have termed the biconical schemes; and third, the curvilinear schemes which arise from such simple motifs as *stehende Bogen* and develop into the over-all patterns of the elaborate *Buckelurnen*.

The remaining main groups of designs are based on what may be called the rectangular and triangular principles. In these schemes, which are particularly appropriate to shouldered pots, though they are found of course on vessels of every shape, the basic idea is to present a contrast between horizontal decoration on the neck and vertical or chevron decoration on the shoulder and below. In its simplest statement this takes shape as a group of horizontal lines on the neck, surmounting vertical lines on the shoulder, arranged either continuously or in groups with spaces left blank between them. From this simple idea it is easy to build up more complex patterns which, however, all have a basic rectangularity of form, horizontal above and vertical below, quite unlike the more uninhibited curvilinear designs arising from motives like *stehende Bogen*. Thus when the fashion for plastic ornament and bosses sets in, it will here take the form of raised collars or horizontal strips on the neck, and of vertical bosses on the shoulder, emphasizing the contrast between the two parts of the design.

It so happens that, while, as we have seen, curvilinear designs achieved a special popularity in the Saxon lands between the Elbe and the Weser during the fourth and fifth centuries, these rectangular patterns were far more in favour further north in Schleswig, Fünen, and southern Jutland at that time.[1] They were, of course, particularly appropriate for decorating the shouldered bowls,

[1] At least half of the thirty standard types of continental Anglian pottery illustrated by Genrich (1954), 29, Abb. 2, show straightforward patterns of rectangular type or simple variations on this theme: four others show triangular schemes of the same general character: there are no true curvilinear designs.

and shouldered urns with tall vertical or conical necks, which were so commonly made in those parts, just as the curvilinear designs were well suited to the more rounded contours favoured by many of the Westerwanna or Galgenberg potters.

These distinctions must not of course be pressed too hard. Many types, both of form and decoration, were shared between these closely related and contiguous folk, and these natural links were reinforced by the continuous southward pressure of the Angles and other northern peoples towards the Elbe. This led, as we have seen,[1] to the hybrid culture of the *Mischgruppe* which itself spread westwards into Friesland, so that what have been termed Anglo-Frisian types include elements of both sorts and some hybrids between them.[2] It is, nevertheless, impossible to ignore the difference in feeling between the Anglian pottery of Schleswig and Fünen, and the fashions characteristic of Westerwanna or the Galgenberg. It is indeed the first thing that must strike anyone who passes from the museums of Bremen, Hannover, or Hamburg to those of Schleswig, Odense, or Copenhagen.

There is a further contrast which should be mentioned. In the north—and this goes for Norway and Jutland as well as the more restricted Anglian home-land in Schleswig—there is a fondness for massed parallel lines, whether horizontal or vertical, a practice which, when carried out in broad, shallow tooling, produces the effect of a rippled surface, which I have called 'corrugation' and the Germans term *Kannellierung*.[3] This technique of course strongly em-phasizes the rectangular effect of designs based on horizontal necklines and vertical shoulderlines, and may itself be used as a background to further plastic ornament of horizontal and vertical strips and bosses.[4] This kind of 'two decker' ornament is characteristic of the whole northern *Kulturkreis* and is an un-

[1] See pp. 22, 34.

[2] See my article 'Some English Parallels to the Anglo-Saxon Pottery of Holland and Belgium in the Migration Period' in *L'Antiquité classique* xvii (1948), 453–72, where Figs. 1–4 show vessels with rectangular and triangular schemes, and Fig. 5, nos. 1–7, some of the less common curvilinear designs. Fig. 5, nos. 8–10, illustrate the way in which these traditions became mixed, for here *stehende Bogen* designs are in process of breaking down into groups of diagonal and vertical lines, in much the same way as fifth-century animal ornament broke down towards the end of the century into the *disjecta membra* characteristic of

Salin's Style I. The same process can be seen occur-ring on the Ingham pot on Fig. 26 or on the Sancton *Buckelurne* on Fig. 23: a good example of the final stage in the breakdown of *stehende Bogen* bosses is the very degenerate *Buckelurne* from Worthy Park C 23.

[3] The technique is well shown in the examples from Schleswig, Fünen, and Norway illustrated in Mackeprang (1943), Tafeln 18–21: or in those from Denmark in H. Norling-Christensen, *Harald-stedgravpladsen* (1957), Figs. 13, 15, 33–6.

[4] As on the urns from Hammoor (164) or Borgstedt (189) illustrated in Genrich (1954), Tafeln 50. 5; 51. 1.

mistakable sign of direct northern influence wherever it may be encountered on pottery, in England or on the Continent, outside those parts.

Corrugated pots occur in some numbers in two of the great English cremation cemeteries, Caistor-by-Norwich in Norfolk[1] and Sancton in the East Riding of Yorkshire. They are found sporadically elsewhere,[2] but on these two sites they form a substantial element in the total. Their precise dating and their historical significance will be further considered later: at this point it need only be said that they belong at latest to the fifth century, and many of them to an early date in it. In Denmark, for example, where the museums at Copenhagen and Odense are full of corrugated urns that would be equally at home in Norfolk or east Yorkshire, they are regarded as essentially a late fourth-century type, and some very English-looking examples from various sites in Schleswig, Fünen, and Norway are dated by brooches in use there around 400.[3]

This corrugated pottery is of course only one element among the wares carrying simple linear decoration of the rectangular type. Such schemes are frequently carried out in sharp line or more softly tooled effects, in line-and-groove, or even in faint scratches. However it is produced, rectangular decoration occurs over almost every part of England in which Anglo-Saxon pottery is found. It may take the form of massed lines, groups of lines with blank spaces between, basketry patterns with alternate groups of horizontal and vertical lines, or it may be diversified on occasion with diagonals, or with feathering or fish-bone motives.[4]

All these simple linear arrangements, whether corrugated or otherwise, can occur equally on pots carrying shoulder-bosses, and such bosses are then treated as an integral part of the design. Generally they are themselves left plain, but outlined with vertical lines, and the panels between them then invite individual treatment. But the bosses themselves may be emphasized by linear ornament, such as feathering or slashing, or they may carry a vertical line of finger-tipping or stamps. The intention in all these cases is to provide a contrast with the treatment of the intervening panels. The bosses, when not circular, are normally oval with the long axis vertical, though sometimes they may be much longer, extending all or most of the way from the shoulder to the base.

---

[1] See, e.g. four of those from Caistor in *Med. Arch.* iii (1959), Pl. II A–D: and A11, X2 on Pl. 1 below.

[2] Two from Ancaster and Loveden Hill (Lincs.) are on Fig. 26.

[3] Genrich (1954), Tafeln 4A, Borgstedt; 12D, Hamburg/Alt-Rahlstedt; H. Norling-Christensen, *Haraldstedgravpladsen* (1957), Fig. 15, Signekaerskov; Fig. 24, Alenbaekhuse; and the Norwegian examples from Fuskeland and Foss there quoted (p. 80).

[4] See the examples of these variations on Fig. 26.

Whatever form they take, and whatever their number, they underline the rectangularity of the design by breaking up the surface into panels which themselves require vertical or horizontal treatment. Shoulder-bosses thus seem naturally at home on pottery bearing decoration of the rectangular type, for they serve to emphasize the essential nature of designs of this kind in a way that is not the case when they are introduced on pots displaying other types of decoration.

The treatment of the panels on this panel-style pottery opens up a wide range of possibilities for typological development.[1] They range from a complete blank in the case of those basically horizontal designs which occasionally have bosses set below the main scheme, to various combinations of horizontal and vertical zones. Sometimes the panels are used to continue the horizontal treatment of the neck with one or more lower zones of lines and stamps. More often vertical zones of stamps are intruded, at first singly, among the vertical lines of the shoulder, and gradually, as the fashion for stamped ornament spreads, these stamps may come to fill the whole of the panel, forcing back the vertical lines against the sides of the bosses. The next stage is when the stamped panels come to dominate the design, and the bosses are reduced in size and either ignored in the layout, or are even themselves overrun with stamps. From this it is a short step to the disappearance of the bosses, so that the stamped panels either hang free from the lowest neckline, or coalesce into a continuous zone of random stamping, which comes in the final stage, to lose its guiding lines altogether.

In all these phases except the last, the basic rectangularity of the scheme is retained. But there is a very common alternative treatment of the shoulder on pots of this general class, which leads by a closely parallel development to a series of designs which produce a different effect. Much of the corrugated pottery at Sancton, in contrast with most of that at Caistor, has linear decoration on the shoulder in the form of chevrons or swags, *hängende Bogen*, rather than massed vertical lines. These motives, which are very popular on the Continent in the fourth and fifth centuries,[2] can be used to produce, whether in the corrugated

---

[1] As shown on Fig. 27 and Pl. 5.

[2] Chevron lines on the shoulder occur in all areas, and examples need not be quoted: swags, *hängende Bogen*, are especially characteristic of the pottery of east Holstein type in the fourth century and earlier: see the dated examples in Genrich (1954), Tafeln 2C, Bordesholm (275–350); 10B,

Gleschendorf (c. 350); 15D, E, Hammoor (c. 450); 17K, 18D, 20A, 21A, all Krummensee/Pötterberg (c. 300); 21B Lassahn (before 300). A late example from Liebenau Gr. 57 d. was found with objects dating about 500. *Nachrichten aus Niedersachsens Urgeschichte* 33 (1964), 41. Abb. 8. 5.

or simple linear techniques, patterns based on triangular rather than rectangular designs.[1] They are equally susceptible to the intrusion of stamped ornament, indeed even more so, for the zig-zag lines of the chevrons can be emphasized in various ways by being outlined with stamps, as with the two Loveden Hill urns on Fig. 28, and the same is true of the triangular panels which they enclose, as has happened on the Peterborough, Brixworth, and Leicestershire pieces on the same figure. When, as commonly occurs, shoulder-bosses are introduced into these schemes, muddles can well develop, as, for example, in the case of one of the Girton potters, who normally favoured a typologically fairly early variety of the stamped chevron style, but, on introducing bosses, got out of step with the main pattern so that the panels are asymetrically arranged.[2]

But more thoughtful artists than this potter realized that, while shoulder-bosses may not be so intrinsically natural to these schemes as they are to the more strictly rectangular kind, they can be combined with them in a very effective way. This is done by introducing the bosses at the upper points of the chevrons, so that the panels between them come to be filled with one or more pendent triangles or swags, which appear to be hanging from the bosses themselves. The arrangement is well shown on the vessel from Caistor-by-Norwich, by the larger one from St. John's, and the smaller from Baginton, all on Fig. 29. The pendent triangles and even the intervening bosses can then be treated as the framework or vehicle for every sort of arrangement of stamps, culminating with the exuberant displays that became so popular among potters in the course of the sixth century.

This bossed panel-style, in which the panels are occupied with pendent triangles or *hängende Bogen* filled with stamps, goes hand in hand with the rectangular stamped panel-style already discussed, and both alike are characteristic of the Middle Anglian and south Mercian cemeteries in the central decades of the sixth century.[3] Cambridge, Northamptonshire, Leicestershire, and south Lincolnshire are the homes of the style, and it spills over into the valley of the Warwickshire Avon, where the cemetery at Baginton (see, for example, the smaller urn from this site on Fig. 29) exhibits the pendent triangle version of it at its most effective. The evolution of this variety follows an exactly similar

---

[1] *Hängende Bogen*, like *stehende Bogen* (see p. 52, fn. 2), easily lose their curvilinear form by breaking down into straight-sided chevron or zigzag lines.

[2] See the three examples of this potter's work in *Antiquity* xi (1937), 397, Fig. 9, top row. It will not escape notice that confusion can often arise between these triangular designs and the chevron patterns of the biconical style. This has occured in the work of this Girton potter: the two Loveden Hill urns on Fig. 28 are also hybrids of this kind.

[3] See Pl. 6.

course to that taken by the rectangular style. As time goes on, the bosses come
to play a dwindling part in designs dominated by an abundant use of stamps,[1]
and in due course disappear, leaving the stamped pendent triangles by themselves as the main element in the decoration. In this form the style has an even
greater popularity, and an even wider appeal. It spreads from Middle Anglia
into the upper Thames valley,[2] where the normal bossed variety had been
uncommon. It becomes, as we shall see, the principal style affected by the
so-called Illington/Lackford pottery on the borders of west Norfolk and
Suffolk, the most prolific and successful workshop, and the nearest approach to
a commercial ceramic industry, that was achieved in this period.[3] Eventually,
however, as with the rectangular designs, the fashion for formal arrangement
in pendent triangles and *hängende Bogen* lost its power to please, the guiding
lines disappear,[4] and the designs break down, probably in the early part of the
seventh century, into a meaningless jumble of random stamping.

These developments, though primarily of course to be thought of as a
typological rather than a chronological sequence, can in fact be roughly checked
against the passage of time, both by some associated finds of brooches, and by
the occasional stratigraphical relationships of particular urns. There are not at
all as many of these check-points as one would like to see, and they are not
sufficiently decisive to establish a certainty of dating for every vessel bearing
this kind of decoration, but they are broadly consistent with the course of
development outlined above. Thus a pot from Holywell Row, Suffolk, with
slashed bosses separating panels partly filled with vertical lines, and a single
horizontal zone of jabs above—a design typologically early in the series—
came from a grave dated by Lethbridge on other grounds about 500.[5] Caistor-
by-Norwich M47 represents the next stage, a wide-mouthed vessel with plain

[1] The Caistor urn on Fig. 29 well illustrates this stage of development.

[2] e.g. examples from Abingdon, East Shefford, Frilford, Long Wittenham, and Reading in Berks.: and from Kingsey and Cassington, Oxon. The whole distribution is shown on Map 9.

[3] See pp. 132–6 and Fig. 48, 2060 and 2625. Some other products of this workshop are illustrated in *Lackford*, Fig. 18: see also *Antiquity* xi (1937), 392, Pl. I, Fig. 3. Their distribution is shown on Map 10.

[4] As on the Girton urn on Fig. 29. This final stage occurs also on the Continent: see e.g. an eighth-century example from Sahlenburg-Silberberg Gr. 3 in F. Stein, *Adelsgräber des 8. Jahr-*

hunderts (1967), Tafel 61. 16.

[5] Cambridge 2. 7142C. It was associated with a late Group I cruciform brooch. A simpler continental example of this stage came from Liebenau Gr. 1 dated by associated weapons 450–525. *Studien aus Alt Europa* II (1965), 258, Abb. 1. 2. A comparable Norwegian piece from Linnestad i Ramnes (Vestfold) is datable 500–50 by associated gold bracteates and glass: *Oslo Universitetets Oldsaksamlings Arbok* (1961), 7–29 and Fig. 9. Another from Staßfurt Gr. 1 (Mecklenburg) is dated 450–500 by B. Schmidt on the strength of associated brooches (*Jahrbuch für Bodendenkmalpflege in Mecklenburg* (1964), 248 and Abb. 125).

bosses separating half-empty panels, and a single horizontal zone of stamps above: it contained parts of two cruciform brooches of the first half of the sixth century. There is good evidence for dating the stamped panel-style without bosses to the second half of the sixth century. Lackford 50. 126 and 50. 234 were both found with florid square-headed brooches of that date:[1] Illington 102 contained a Group III cruciform brooch: a Group IV cruciform brooch came from the same grave at Woodston, near Peterborough, as an inhumation accessory vessel in this style: and the larger Baginton urn on Fig. 29 was associated with a saucer brooch decorated with elevenfold running spirals, by no means the earliest variety of this type. At Lackford the relationship in time between bossed and unbossed panel-style pots is neatly illustrated by a case in which an unbossed pot with stamped pendent triangles overlay, and was evidently buried later than, a large shoulder-boss urn with five zones of horizontal stamping on the neck, and a vertical line of stamps on each side of the bosses, leaving the rest of the panels empty.[2]

It also seems clear that these developments took place over a sufficient length of time and in sufficiently settled conditions to permit the evolution of local variations in different parts of the country. In the upper Thames valley, for example, the earlier phases of the bossed panel-style are scarcely represented in the form so popular in Middle Anglia, being apparently replaced by a local variety in which the ornament is concentrated between long bosses on the lower half of the pot.[3] But later on the unbossed panel-style with stamped pendent triangles was here very popular, and there are even two examples with feet, an unusual feature at this late date.[4] In Yorkshire, on the other hand, large and prominently stamped *hängende Bogen* seem to have become fashionable, and these were sometimes arranged in an elaborate overlapping fashion, as by the Sancton potter, one of whose products, along with simpler examples from other Yorkshire sites, is on Fig. 30. A further suggestion of late date for the style is given by the Loveden Hill urn on Fig. 30, for here very large stamped *hängende Bogen* decorate a vessel of the sagging bag-shaped contour with tall neck that is characteristic of the seventh century. It also occurs in the work of the Sancton potter who imitated Frankish *biconi* of the late sixth century.[5]

Panel-style decoration did indeed persist occasionally, and in a decadent form, on pottery of the Middle Saxon period in this country, particularly in East

[1] *Lackford*, Fig. 17.
[2] *Lackford*, 21 and Fig. 31, 49. 2478 and 49. 247A.
[3] e.g. examples from Abingdon, East Shefford, Frilford, Long Wittenham, and Wallingford, Berks.: and from Brighthampton, Oxon. (Figs. 38 and 39).
[4] From East Shefford and Reading, Berks.
[5] Fig. 42, 2293.

Anglia.[1] It forms one of the more interesting links in the little-studied transition between the ceramic fashions of pagan and Christian times. Although to pursue the matter further would lead beyond the chronological limits of this book, the point is worth making because of its bearing on the relationship between English and continental pottery in the latter part of our period. It is a remarkable fact that the evolution of panel-style stamped decoration, as it is so powerfully in evidence in sixth-century England, should have so few parallels in the nearer parts of the Continent from which the bulk of our Anglo-Saxon settlers came, and with which they must have maintained some degree of cultural contact.[2] It seems to have been an almost purely English development, and the few pieces from continental sites in north Germany and the Low Countries which hint at similar fashions are too isolated and out of place to represent an indigenous evolution. Some of them may perhaps be best explained as elements of that cultural backwash from England to the mainland of Europe of which other signs have been noted at this time.

The problem is of course to some extent bound up with the general reduction of population which must have taken place in these coastal areas of the Continent in consequence of the migrations to England. Few, if any, of the great cemeteries between the Elbe and the Weser seem to have continued in active use after about 500, and many came to an end well before that time. The sixth century, and even indeed the later part of the fifth, are something of an archaeological blank in Schleswig and Fünen, a fact which has very naturally been linked with Bede's positive assertion that Angulus, the homeland of the Angles, was deserted after the migration to Britain.[3] But it is probable that too much emphasis has been laid in the past on the completeness of this cultural break. Recent work on settlement sites has corrected the notion of a total evacuation that earlier scholars had based too firmly on Bede's statement and the apparent evidence of the great cremation cemeteries. It is probable that a number of these cemeteries continued in use, if more spasmodically, for

---

[1] e.g. the vessels from Ipswich, Suffolk: and from St. Osyth and Shoebury, Essex, illustrated in *Med Arch*. iii (1959), 22, Fig. 5.

[2] There are more at Wehden than in most other cemeteries: e.g. Tafeln 33. 27: 34, middle top row (unnumbered but ? 150); 39. 737; all these in the group dated typologically by Waller after 500: among the earlier groups Tafeln 18. 703 and 26. 44 are approaching the style. Elsewhere I have noticed only *Gudendorf*, Tafeln 33. 8 and 34. 22:

Galgenberg, Tafeln 34. 1 (an exceptional unbossed piece with twelve different stamps) and 35. 1. There appear to be none at Westerwanna: but one with no bosses from Nesse (5486) was formerly in the museum at Wesermünde: the material from this cemetery has a very English look.

[3] *Hist. Eccles*. i. 15. The Angles came from '. . . illa patria, quae Angulus dicitur, et ab eo tempore usque hodie manere desertus inter provincias Iutarum et Saxonum perhibetur . . .'.

longer than has been supposed, for they contain a quantity of objects, and not least of pottery, that in England would readily be dated in the sixth century, and can indeed only be forced back into the fifth by imposing a needless strain on the principles of typology.[1]

However that may be, the comparative rarity of the elaborately stamped wares characteristic of sixth-century English ceramics remains a puzzling feature of the Anglo-Saxon homelands on the Continent. This is all the more so, because some other parts of the Germanic world, whose connections with Britain might be supposed far less close, do show a similar fondness for the use of stamped pottery in the century between 550 and 650. This is especially true of some parts of Scandinavia on the one side and of central and southern Germany on the other. The stamped pottery of Norway comes mainly from the eastern side of the country, and, since associated finds rarely occur, can be dated only on typological grounds. While it mostly displays horizontal or biconical schemes of decoration, there is at least one globular piece from Brunlanes which has, below two horizontal stamped zones, large pendent triangles filled with stamps in exactly the English manner.[2] In Sweden most of the stamped pottery of this period comes from Gotland, but there are a few examples from Bohuslan, presumably related in some way to the similar material from eastern Norway. Nearly all of it shows wide zones of horizontal stamping, but there is at least one piece from Gotland with a more elaborate design including small stamped pendent triangles.[3]

The position in central and southern Germany is more puzzling, for there, both in Mittelfranken and also among the Alamanni in Württemberg, there appears to have developed a taste for stamped pottery, some of it showing panel designs with bosses, at a date after the middle of the sixth century, when bossed designs of this sort were going out of fashion altogether in northern Europe.[4] Moreover the style apparently continued well into the seventh

---

[1] Wehden and Nesse are among the most obvious cases, but the material from such a site as Rahnstorf in the Helms Museum at Harburg gives a similar impression to anyone familiar with English sixth-century cemeteries.

[2] See the pieces from Brunlanes, Eidsvoll, and Skjeberg illustrated by Bøe, Figs. 337–42. I am grateful to Dr. Wencke Slomann for further information on the stamped pottery of Norway.

[3] For information on the dating of this stamped pottery in Sweden I am indebted to Dr. W. Holmquist. A number of metal objects of English origin

found their way to Sweden, Gotland, and Finland in the sixth century: see H. Vierck in *Suomen Museo* (1967), 54–63. This stamped pottery may be a further indication of cultural contacts at this time.

[4] W. Veeck, *Die Alamannen in Württemberg* (1931), i. 24–5 and Tafeln B10 and C1 and 3; ii, Tafel 13; B. Schmidt, *Die späte Völkerwanderungszeit in Mitteldeutschland* (1961), 88–106 and Tafeln 7–18; H. Dannheimer, *Die germanischen Funde . . . in Mittelfranken* (1962), Tafeln 25B; 26B; 29; 30B, C; 35G; 37A; 42D, E; 43B; 44; 67C, and the stamps shown on Tafel 81.

century,[1] and may have exerted some influence further north in the lower Rhineland, where a few examples of bossed pottery, for which a seventh-century date has been claimed, occur in Frankish cemeteries in Holland.[2] This is not the place to go into the complications both for typology and for dating which here arise: indeed they have not yet been fully worked out. But it is necessary to refer to them briefly because of the resemblance which such pots sometimes bear to English forms current about a hundred years earlier.

Before leaving this brief typological analysis of the forms and decoration employed on pagan Anglo-Saxon pottery, which has occupied the last three chapters, it should be stressed once again that there is a great deal of hybridization to be found between the various schemes whose individual evolution has here been traced. It has already been noticed how shoulder-bosses are introduced on forms not really suited to them, and how, for example, *stehende Bogen* are commonly found in apparently irrelevant combination with biconical schemes. It is not at all unusual to observe a broad band of biconical ornament appearing on the neck of a bossed panel-style urn, and forming so conspicuous an element in the decoration that it is impossible to dismiss it as just an over-grown flat collar.[3] These combinations may be exceedingly perplexing to the tidy-minded classifier intent on fitting all the decorated pottery into the water-tight compartments of a fool-proof system. But they are, after all, only to be expected in the confused conditions which brought folk of many different cultural antecedents to take part in the common enterprise of the English

---

[1] The view held by Veeck that the bossed pottery of the Alamanni belongs to the period before they passed under Frankish control in 536 has been challenged by R. Roeren (*Germania* xxxii (1954), 183–8) on the strength of four closed finds from Steinheim, Nusplingen, Herbrechtingen, and Schretzheim, which contained objects of the seventh century. On the other hand, J. Werner, *Munzdatierte Austrasische Grabfunde* (1935), Tafeln 2A and 6A, illustrates two shoulder-boss pots with unstamped panels from Remagen and Worms-Bollwerk dated by associated finds 520–50 and 550–600 respectively. It seems clear that the bossed panel-style pottery of south-west Germany started early in the sixth century as it did in England, but survived much longer. The most remarkable case is the bossed pot with stamped pendent triangles from Schretzheim, Grave 580, illustrated by Roeren, which is decorated with animals in Salin's Style II. A sequence more in accord with the English

dating has recently been published from Sontheim, Kr. Heidenheim (C. Neuffer-Müller, *Ein Reihengräberfriedhof in Sontheim an der Brenz* (1966)). It includes both stamped hand-made *biconi* and hand-made vessels decorated with stamped pendent triangles without lines, all dated to the sixth century. The latter group would here be placed shortly before 600. Roeren is criticized (p. 12) for taking the bossed *Rippengefässe*, of which there were two small examples at Sontheim, too far into the seventh century.

[2] e.g. *Wageningen* 273–4, Fig. 94, 4 and 5: and similar pieces there quoted from Rhenen, Rijnsburg, and Monster.

[3] As e.g. in the products of the Girton potter, five of whose urns are discussed and illustrated in *Antiquity* xi (1937), 392 and Pl. III, Fig. 6: or the St. John's urn on Fig. 19, which has stamped pendent triangles in this unusual position.

conquest. They should lead one to regard the different main styles of ornamentation here disentangled, not as individually self-sufficient or mutually
exclusive schemes, but rather as elements with different roots in a mixed cultural heritage, ready to be used as tradition or the whimsy of individual taste
might suggest, in a bewildering variety of different mixtures. It is in fact the
perennial freshness of these combinations, and the imaginative fertility to which
they bear witness, that gives this fascinating and frustrating subject both its
challenge and its charm.

V

THE SETTLEMENT OF ENGLAND

1. THE PHASE OF OVERLAP AND
CONTROLLED SETTLEMENT

FROM the typological studies which have occupied the last three chapters we must now turn to consider how these various kinds of pottery, their geographical distribution, and the various ways and proportions in which they are combined and related to one another on Anglo-Saxon sites of settlement or burial, can help us to understand the course and character of the invasions. The discussion of these questions in one form or another will occupy the rest of this book, and it will involve the examination of many issues which any student of these difficult centuries finds confronting him, as he tries to obtain an understanding of what took place. There are questions of political history; what was the course of events? When, and in what circumstances, did the various phases in the settlement occur? There are questions of origin: who were the newcomers, and where did they come from? And there are questions of a social and economic nature: how did these invading folk establish themselves, and what were their relations both with the existing population, and with one another? On all these matters their pottery may be expected to tell us something of interest to add to the information that can be drawn from evidence of other kinds.

It is of course impossible to deal with any of these groups of questions wholly in isolation from the others: questions of date cannot be profitably discussed independently of questions of origin: political history inevitably raises social and economic issues: and the nature of the settlement is not only a matter of method but also a matter of time and place. Nevertheless an attempt will be made to deal broadly with these aspects in succession, beginning with the political history and questions of origin, and leaving social and economic matters to the end.

First, then, let us inquire what the pottery can tell us about the political transition from Roman Britain to Saxon England, and about the timing of the successive phases through which that transformation was effected. To answer that inquiry it is first necessary to be clear what those successive phases are likely to have been. To provide such a framework it may be convenient to divide the period from the fourth to the seventh century into five sections, each roughly, but not of course precisely, covering some fifty years. In each of these sections it would of course be desirable to see the changing circumstances of British history, as the literary record and the archaeological evidence broadly reveal them, against the known course of events in Europe in these momentous years. To do so adequately in these pages would go far beyond the scope of this book: but it must throughout be remembered that, however separated this country may have become from continental affairs at this time, the archaeological material here under review cannot be treated in isolation, and indeed only becomes intelligible in the reflected light of continental parallels. Some knowledge of the European background, both political and cultural, is thus essential to an understanding of this whole sequence of events; and in endeavouring to ascertain what information the pottery can provide on each of these successive phases of the transition from Roman Britain to Christian England, the changing situation in the lands beyond the Channel and the North Sea must constantly be kept in mind.

The five phases, in each of which the salient features of the ceramic evidence must be indicated, may be briefly distinguished as follows:

I. *The phase of overlap and controlled settlement*, say, 360–410.

Here it is necessary to consider what signs there may be either for the influence of barbarian taste on the ceramic fashions prevalent in the last days of Roman Britain, or for the presence of barbarian groups with their own ceramic traditions within the continuing framework of Romano-British life.

II. *The phase of transition*, say, 410–50.

There is reason to believe that for some time after the direct administrative links with the Imperial government were broken, local Romano-British regimes were able to maintain themselves against barbarian pressure with or without the help of federate settlers. There may be ceramic evidence for the extent and expansion of barbarian settlement, whether friendly or hostile, in sub-Roman Britain.

III. *The phase of invasion and destruction*, say, 450–500.

The literary record, both British and Anglo-Saxon, points to this half-century as the time of massive and uncontrolled land-seizure by Anglo-Saxon and other barbarian peoples, and for the accompanying destruction of Romano-British civilization. The contemporary pottery should throw some light on the nature and range of these movements, and on the background of the principal groups of settlers in different parts.

IV. *The phase of reaction and British recovery*, say, 500–50.

There is literary evidence, principally but not exclusively from Gildas, that the initial force of the invasions was spent by about 500, and that further advance was halted for at least a generation owing to successful resistance by the Britons at that time. There could be ceramic evidence for local differences in the density or continuity of Anglo-Saxon settlement in this phase, or even for some backwash of invaders from Britain to the Continent.

V. *The phase of consolidation*, after, say, 550.

This is the phase in which many of the Anglo-Saxon kingdoms first took their historic form, and began to expand. Does the pottery throw any light on these developments?

None of these phases is of course to be thought of as rigidly demarcated from those before or after it, and the dates suggested for each are intended only to supply the most generalized chronology, which may not be universally applicable to all parts of the country. Such variations will become apparent as the ceramic evidence for each of these phases is examined in greater detail. More space will be devoted to the earlier than to the later phases because of their greater basic importance, and because the material relating to them has not been assembled before.

In considering the earliest of these phases the first point to grasp is that throughout the fourth century, if not indeed from the late third, there had been the mounting pressure of barbarian menace against the exposed frontiers of Roman Britain. The reality of that menace, and the changes that it enforced on the civilian life of the provincials, can be demonstrated archaeologically in several ways. It is most strikingly evident in the building, or rebuilding, of what came to be known as the fortresses of the Saxon Shore,[1] whose massive and sometimes spectacular remains still stand on many of the principal harbours and anchorages on the east and south coasts between the Wash and the Isle of Wight. It can be seen in the construction later in the century of coastal signal-stations in Yorkshire and elsewhere to give early warning of approaching fleets. Perhaps most significant of all, it is apparent in the modernization of the fortifications of many, if not most, of the civilian towns of eastern Britain from Isurium Brigantum (Aldborough, near Boroughbridge) in the north to London and Chichester in the south.

This policy of urban refortification, carried through in the third quarter of the fourth century,[2] was especially significant because of the change that it implied in the role which the towns would now play. They had mostly been given ramparts and walls during the second and third centuries for reasons which are still not wholly clear, but may well have been mainly administrative. The late fourth-century refortification meant that they were now being thought of as focal points in a system of military defence, and not just as centres of administration and civilization in a peaceful countryside. The security of that countryside could no longer be safely left to the distant garrisons of Hadrian's Wall, the Pennines, and Wales: it was something quite literally at their own gates. Whether a town was fortified or not, and whether its walls could be brought up to date by the addition of the new fashionable bastions for *ballista* platforms, and the extension of the ditch system, was now a matter of urgent military consequence, and no longer one merely of administrative convenience or of civic pride.

This need to treat towns as fortresses, and to provide along the east and south coasts a broad military zone under the command of an officer who could be described as '*Comes litoris Saxonici*',[3] can mean only one thing—a very real danger of barbarian penetration, not merely in the form of transient raiders

---

[1] The most recent study is D. A. White, *Litus Saxonicum* (1961), a Wisconsin doctoral thesis, which, in the manner of its kind, is more useful as a descriptive and historical summary of present knowledge than remarkable for the reliability of its judgement or the soundness of its positive contribution to the outstanding questions, historical and archaeological, that the subject presents.

[2] The significance of this phase in the urban history of Roman Britain was first emphasized by P. Corder in *Arch. Journ.* cxii (1956), 20–42. His suggestion that it might be associated with the visit of Constans in 343 is now superseded, and the latest suggestion proposes the restoration of the *civitates* by Count Theodosius after the *barbarica conspiratio* of 367 as a more likely moment: B. R. Hartley in *The Civitas Capitals of Roman Britain* (1966), 52–3.

[3] *Not. Dig. Occ.* xxviii. The most stimulating commentary on the British sections of the *Notitia Dignitatum* is still that of C. E. Stevens in *Arch. Journ.* xcvii (1941), 125–54. For a more recent summary, see S. S. Frere, *Britannia* (1967), 228–38.

in search of loot, but of substantial war-bands intent on permanent settlement. And though it can be argued that the reorganization of town defences may have been intended primarily to cope with an overland danger from the Picts of the north, the Saxon Shore system, as the name it came to bear distinctly implies, was designed to meet a sea-borne menace originating beyond the North Sea and the Channel. Roman authority had thus devised new military measures to meet a risk of massive barbarian infiltration, and for perhaps half a century from around 350 to around 400 these measures may have broadly met the strain they were intended to carry, though on occasions the defences are known to have been temporarily overwhelmed. But we do not know what lasting effect in the form of intrusive settlers these temporary disasters may have left behind.

Nor do we know the extent to which the deliberate settlement of barbarian *laeti* by Roman authority itself may have formed part of the military measures designed to protect the Romano-British countryside. Both the new fortresses and the newly fortified towns required garrisons, and the employment of friendly barbarians, sometimes under regular officers, but often under their own tribal chieftains, was the normal method of meeting such para-military requirements. That it had been followed on occasion in Britain even as early as the second century is shown by the literary references to the settlement of Marcomanni by Marcus Aurelius,[1] of Burgundians under Igillus in the late third,[2] and of Alamanni under Fraomar in the later fourth.[3] The acclamation of Constantine as Emperor at York in 306 was apparently the work of one Erocus, king of the Alamanni, most likely the leader of locally settled *laeti*.[4] What light, if any, can a study of the pottery throw on the extent to which, in this phase of overlap, the provincial society of Roman Britain was already being penetrated by the taste of Germanic *laeti* or of less official intruders forcing their way onto and through the Saxon Shore?

More than ten years ago I called attention to several different categories of late Roman wheel-made pottery that were decorated in ways which suggested the influence of Germanic taste.[5] The distribution of these wares lay in the eastern

[1] Dio lxxi. 16.
[2] Zosimus i. 68.
[3] Ammianus Marcellinus xxix. 4. It has recently been suggested (S. S. Frere, *Britannia* (1967), 220) that Fraomar was transferred to Britain to take command of Alamanni who were already part of the garrison. But Ammianus gives overpopulation as a reason for the move (they were *multitudine viribusque ea tempestate florenti*) which surely implies the siphoning off of excess numbers to Britain to form Fraomar's new command.
[4] Victor, *Ep. de Caesaribus* xli. 3.
[5] *Dark Age Britain*, ed. D. B. Harden (1956), 16–39.

coastal regions of the country, and especially in and around the Saxon Shore forts themselves, the eastern ports, like Caister-by-Yarmouth, Colchester, London, or Richborough, and the main walled towns of the immediate hinterland, which must have served as the principal supply-bases for the defence system. This strongly suggested the presence in these areas of folk who liked their crockery to be decorated in this barbaric fashion. The wares concerned were mostly dated to the fourth century and in a number of cases to the last quarter of it.

As I made clear at the time, my article was not intended to be more than a *ballon d'essai*, and it served its purpose in provoking discussion and in stimulating excavators and museum curators to look out for and report the occurrence of other material of the kind. In consequence many further finds of these so-called Romano-Saxon wares have come to notice, and their general distribution has become clearer. The principal additions to the map which accompanied my article are to be found in Yorkshire, where it has been noted at Aldborough (Isurium Brigantum) and on a number of sites in and around York itself; at Ancaster and elsewhere in Lincolnshire; at Great Casterton and several places in the neighbourhood of the Castor potteries; at the Saxon Shore fort at Brancaster on the north Norfolk coast and elsewhere in East Anglia; and at Leicester. All this strengthens the original case for a distribution significantly related to the defences of the east coast, to its principal ports, and to the walled towns of the immediate hinterland, whose new military importance after the middle of the fourth century has been already stressed. It will be noticed that it also bears a striking resemblance to the distribution of the earliest Anglo-Saxon cemeteries.

There remains therefore a strong presumption that the popularity of these types of pottery in eastern Britain at this time is related in some way to the social and military changes created by the Saxon Shore defences and the deployment of the forces, whether friendly or hostile, which their new situation implied.

The nature of the relationship is, however, not altogether clear, and it is necessary to look a little closer into the probable antecedents of the principal types of decoration involved. There are two main classes of these wares, apart from a number of minor groups. There are first those in which stamps and bosses are combined in various patterns, the stamps being normally set on bosses formed by pressing the clay out from inside the vessel against a stamp held on the outside of it.[1] This technique is now known to have a wide chronological

---

[1] Group I of my provisional classification of these wares: *Dark Age Britain*, 32–4, and Fig. 7.

range in Roman Britain. It occurs not only, as I noted, at the Antonine potteries at South Carlton in Lincolnshire,[1] but also in the late third and early fourth centuries at other east Midland workshops, such as those at Sibson and Stibbington in Huntingdonshire, from the latter of which has come one of the actual pottery dies used for making the stamped impressions.[2] These workshops, which no doubt supplied many of the Lincolnshire, Yorkshire, and Nene valley sites, where these wares have more recently been found, were operating too early to have started up the fashion in response to a demand initiated by barbarian *laeti* in the fourth century, though, as we have seen, there is literary evidence for some Germanic settlement in Britain much earlier than this. It has been claimed that they rather represent the development of a native tradition of stamped pottery, the so-called Parisian wares, that goes back on both sides of the Humber estuary to early Roman and indeed pre-Roman times.[3] This may be held to make any initial borrowing of barbarian fashions by Romano-British craftsmen unlikely, but it remains true that the technique became increasingly popular in the mid and late fourth century, and was used not only to produce rosette designs of the kind so familiar in Germanic contexts, but also on vessels whose form directly echoes Germanic types.[4] It must therefore be taken as illustrating the two-way traffic in decorative ideas so characteristic of the times. These wares certainly deserve more intensive study, for they may well provide a clue to the extended use of stamped decoration on the pottery of the Saxon homelands on the Continent in later centuries.

If so-called Romano-Saxon wares of this class may throw light on the adoption of a fondness for stamped decoration in barbarian circles at this time, it is possible that the other main class of these wares may be related to their growing interest in bossed ornament as such. This is the class of unstamped vessels decorated with a combination of circular bosses and finger-tip depressions, frequently but not invariably arranged in triangular groups.[5] Just as the curvilinear combinations of bosses and stamps on some later examples of the previous group seem to anticipate features of the *Buckelurnen*, so these unstamped bossed vessels of Roman date appear related to the origin

[1] *Ant. Journ.* xxiv (1944), 141 and Fig. 6, 7.
[2] I am grateful to Mr. Brian Hartley for information on these sites, and for the chance to examine some of the relevant material.
[3] I am indebted to Mr. Jeffrey May for information on this point.
[4] See *Med. Arch.* iii (1959), Pl. I, where the close relationship in form and decoration between the Romano-Saxon vessel from the Roman villa at Great Casterton, Rutland, and an Anglo-Saxon urn from North Elmham, Norfolk, is too strong to be merely a coincidence.
[5] Groups B and C of my provisional classification: *Dark Age Britain*, 22–6, Pl. IV, and Figs. 3 and 4.

of the bossed panel-style of later times. But here too the style seems to echo Roman as well as Germanic models. The suggestion which I made that some features of these groups could be derived from late Roman metal or glass wares is one which requires to be emphasized more strongly. Roman embossed silver was very popular in barbarian circles, and it was natural, both within and without the frontiers, to imitate its attractive appearance in pottery. It was moreover a very common fashion in the fourth century for Roman glass vessels to be decorated with applied blobs or roundels arranged as pendent triangles, or in straight lines, or scattered at random over the surface. The technique is not necessarily of barbarian origin, nor is it confined to the western parts of the Empire: it occurs, for example, in fourth-century levels in the Fayum and on other Egyptian sites,[1] where direct Germanic influence may be thought improbable: it appears indeed to be a universal fashion in the glassware of that time. The larger applied roundels could be readily copied as bosses on pottery,[2] and so could the smaller blobs as dimples in reverse. There is of course a difference in technique between the applied blobs of the Roman glasses and the recessed dimples found on this class of pottery, but the decorative effect is often very similar, especially since both commonly use the pendent triangle motive in grouping the spots, whether raised or sunken, which compose the designs. It would seem likely therefore that, both in Roman Britain and also in free Germany, where similar motives are found on some earlier pottery from sites in Thuringia and the Low Countries,[3] the inspiration reached barbarians and provincials alike from the silver and glass industries whose products were equally popular on both sides of the frontier. It remains true of course both that there is an obvious link with the development of panel-style designs in the barbarian repertoire, and also that, whatever their derivation, these patterns were used in the last days of Roman Britain to decorate wheel-made vessels, whose shape is clearly inspired by Germanic forms.[4]

[1] D. B. Harden, *Roman Glass from Karanis* (1936), Pl. XV, 331: XVI, 440, 457: and pp. 100, 103, 197–8 for similar pieces from other parts of the Empire. See also C. Isings, *Roman Glass from Dated Finds* (1957), forms 96 and 107 (*b*), pp. 131, 133 where many fourth-century examples are quoted. It is perhaps worth noting that some auxiliary cohorts of German origin were stationed in Egypt at this time.

[2] On Romano-Saxon pottery of Groups B and C the circular bosses are normally surrounded by a slight sunk groove, suggesting that, though themselves pushed out from the pot-wall, they are copied from a medium in which the effect was produced by applied blobs. Germanic parallels for this feature occur in the first- and second-century pottery of Jutland. A. Genrich in *Archiv für Landes- und Volkskunde von Niedersachsen* (1943), 101 and Abb. 23.

[3] *Med. Arch.* iii (1959), 10, Fig. 2. *Wijster*, 278, Fig. 166, and *Probleme der Küstenforschung im südlichen Nordseegebiet* VI (1957), Tafeln 8. 9: 14. 4: 16. 2, 12: 17. 5a: and 23. 2.

[4] e.g. *Dark Age Britain*, 24, Fig. 3, 1 and 4.

Apart from these two major classes of Romano-Saxon pottery, there are smaller groups which show more obviously the adoption by Romano-British potters of tricks familiar to the continental Germans. There is a clear parallelism between the linear chevron and diagonal designs of my Groups F and G, and the use of such designs on north German pottery, especially when, as in Group F, linear chevrons are combined with finger-tipping or dots to produce patterns which, as we shall see, are characteristic of Germanic practice both in this country and on the Continent in the early part of the fifth century.[1]

It is therefore reasonable to continue the use of the term 'Romano-Saxon' for much of this pottery. Even if many of the motives employed spring from sources used equally by Roman and barbarian craftsmen it was their evident popularity in barbarian society that gives significance to the growing fashion for them at this time. Most of this material belongs to the last phase of the Roman economy in Britain. It is wheel-turned in the hard, efficient, durable fabrics, bright red or grey in colour, that are typical of Roman commercial industry; it was made alongside other Roman coarse wares in typically Roman kilns, some of which were in use for many years, and it was used almost exclusively on Roman occupation sites, whether towns, villas, or forts.[2] How long it continued to be made in the eastern parts of Britain, which happen of course to be also those which the cremation cemeteries show to have been first occupied by Anglo-Saxon settlers, is anybody's guess; perhaps its manufacture could have continued as long as such fortified centres of sub-Roman life as York or Colchester or Verulamium were able to offer some protection to the tattered relics of Roman economy, say, into the second quarter of the fifth century. But a fixed terminal date for this, as for other aspects of Romano-British life, is likely to defy discovery.

Here, then, is a group of ceramic products from the phase of overlap that is firmly set on the Romano-British side of the cultural divide, however strongly it may hint at the intrusive presence of Germanic folk. Are there any comparable Saxo-Roman hybrids to be set beside the Romano-Saxon; wares, that is, which, coming from an Anglo-Saxon milieu, none the less echo in a significant way the essentials of the Roman ceramic tradition? There are very few certain cases, but one from the Caistor-by-Norwich cemetery, urn Y 36,[3]

---

[1] *Dark Age Britain*, 30, Fig. 5, where Romano-Saxon and Anglo-Saxon examples of both are illustrated together. See also pp. 80–1 below.

[2] Examples of Groups B and C have recently been found associated with very early Saxon occupation in hut floors at Mucking, Essex. I am indebted for information on this interesting site to its excavator Mrs. M. U. Jones. An interim report on it is in *Ant. Journ.* xlviii (1968), 210–30.

[3] Pl. I.

deserves mention as a wholly exceptional product of this overlap phase seen, so to speak, from the Anglo-Saxon side. This is a large biconical bowl, used in the ordinary way as a cremation urn. It is very well made of a fine hard pale-grey paste, quite unlike normal Anglo-Saxon pottery, but indistinguishable from a commercial Roman fabric: it is very thin-walled and has certainly been formed with the aid of a turntable or a slow wheel. The decoration also markedly recalls Romano-British ceramic fashions, and that in two ways. The stamps in the single horizontal zone are set so close together that they sometimes touch or even overlap, as is often the case with late Roman stamped wares: and the wide criss-cross trellis of lines below the stamps is, of course, characteristic of Romano-British coarse wares, but very unusual, though not wholly unparalleled, on Anglo-Saxon pottery. This urn, so obviously hybrid in fabric and decoration, must surely have been made at a time when the techniques of Romano-British pot-making were still remembered at Venta Icenorum, and the early years of the fifth century would seem the last possible moment when such conditions could still have prevailed on this exposed part of the Saxon Shore. It is in fact one of the strongest arguments in favour of some period of physical overlap between the last days of the Roman urban economy and the first establishment of cremating barbarians in the immediate vicinity of the town.

The case for postulating such a physical overlap at Caistor is greatly strengthened by an examination of the earliest types of purely Anglo-Saxon pottery to be found in that cemetery. In this examination we are no longer considering hybrid products linking the ceramic traditions of the two cultures, but rather the earliest examples in this country of the barbarian tradition uninfluenced by Romano-British ways. At Caistor there are a number of purely Germanic urns of types which on the Continent are dated in the fourth or at latest in the early years of the fifth century. A remarkable instance is P 15, a large carinated bowl with an early form of biconical linear ornament and small hanging swags.[1] This is exceedingly well made, and, like Y 36, appears to have been formed on some kind of simple turntable. In shape and decoration it strikingly recalls two bowls with handles from Ringe, Fünen, one of which is dated as early as the third century by an associated brooch.[2] While this is undoubtedly too early for P 15, which has no handles, its decoration is certainly closer

---

[1] Fig. 16. 1626 and Pl. I.
[2] Mackeprang (1943), 42 and Tafel 12. Similar pieces occurred in second-century levels at

Feddersen Wierde: *Germania* xxxv (1957), 307, Abb. 9. 2.

typologically to the Ringe pieces than it is to another somewhat similar bowl from Hammoor[1] which was accompanied by an early fifth-century brooch. Bracketed between these two dates, it would seem reasonable to put P 15 no later than the second half of the fourth century.

Another group of Caistor pots, whose continental associations are in this early period, comprises the large strongly made urns with linear decoration, such as N 52, X 35, P 23, E 5, and P 53, shown on Fig. 31. Of these, E 5 and N 52, with their wide mouths and simple chevron decoration, recall Plettke's Type A3, dated by him before 300, while X 35 and P 23 seem closer to his rather taller Type A4, which with the more elaborately decorated Type A5 he places in the first half of the fourth century.[2] These dates may well be fifty years too high,[3] but even so these great urns would seem to belong to at least one generation before the complete collapse of Roman rule in Britain. E 14 and P 53, the latter with a zone of *stehende Bogen* jabs above the linear decoration, are also related to these fourth-century types, though they might here be somewhat later: all can be closely paralleled among the fourth-century pottery at Westerwanna.[4]

It has already been noted that Caistor R 12 and a similar piece from Brundall,[5] a little further down the Yare valley, are two examples of Plettke's Type A7(a)[6]—the *Cuxhaven/Galgenberg Typ* of Tischler—both in its purest form and hardly datable after 400. Another significant piece is K 7 (Fig. 31), a bowl related to Plettke's Type C. It closely resembles an urn from Dingen that would be placed by continental scholars not long after 400.[7] As Plettke notes,[8] the distribution of these large bowls of his Type C seems related to the fourth-century movement of the Suebi from Mecklenburg on to the lower Elbe. It is interesting in that context to recall place-names such as Swaffham, which occurs three

---

[1] Genrich (1954), Tafel 15 E.

[2] Plettke, 42–5 and Tafeln 28 and 29.

[3] Tischler (1956), 66–7, places A5 in the second half of the fourth century.

[4] Among the Westerwanna urns of types A3–6 the following seem most relevant to the dating of these Caistor pieces. *Westerwanna* i. 388, with two fourth-century brooches (A3): 454, a plain urn with a tutulus brooch (A3): 11 with fourth-century brooch (A4): 848, with fourth-century brooch (A4): 861, with an early form of equal-armed brooch (A4): 727, with rosette attachment of 'Dorchester' type (A5): 507, with three fourth-century brooches (A6): 1342, with fourth-century

brooch (A6). As Tischler has pointed out (op. cit., 66), there is probably less difference in time than Plettke supposed between his types A3–6.

[5] See p. 43. The fragmentary Brundall piece is illustrated in *Norf. Arch.* xxvii. 191, Fig. 1. i.

[6] Plettke, 46 and Tafel 32.

[7] The Dingen urn is Plettke, Tafel 40, 6. K7 contained well-made bronze tweezers of late Roman type. It is very similar in form and decoration to an urn from Bordesholm dated late fourth century by Genrich (1954), 21 and Tafel 3A, which also contained bronze tweezers. The type is characteristic of East Holstein 350–400.

[8] Plettke 48.

times in Norfolk, Suffolk, and Cambridge, and Swavesey (Cambridge), that bear witness to the presence of communities with the name of Suebi among the Teutonic settlers of East Anglia.[1]

There is finally the difficult question of the date of the Anglian corrugated pots, which have already been noticed as especially frequent in the Caistor cemetery. In Denmark these are regarded as a fourth-century group, and in Fünen the fashion is believed not to have lasted much after 400.[2] Further south in Schleswig, the centre of Angle influence, much of this corrugated pottery is placed early in the fifth century, though some of the more elaborate bossed pieces may be dated after 450 and treated as the Anglian equivalent of the Saxon *Buckelurnen*. At Caistor many of the examples are simple bowls or jars without bosses, characteristic of the earlier group.[3] There are also bossed bowls,[4] and shoulder-boss urns with tall conical necks.[5] But only one or two carry the two-decker decoration with overlying strips that often accompanies the more elaborate bossed effects.[6] Although this whole group is notoriously difficult to date owing to the scarcity of distinctive associated finds,[7] it seems reasonable in view of the close continental parallels to regard the Caistor corrugated pottery as starting around 400 and continuing throughout the fifth century.

The evidence that the Caistor cemetery came into use at or before this date is particularly impressive because it is so broadly based on urns of different kinds. But while it is perhaps the best case hitherto established for so early a date for the beginning of the Anglo-Saxon settlement, it is by no means alone in this respect. Most of the great cremation cemeteries of eastern England con-

---

[1] Swaton and Swaby (Lincs.) may contain the same tribe name, but the latter of course has in that case been scandinavianized.

[2] See the dated examples noted in Chapter IV, p. 53, fn. 3.

[3] Such as N 53, N 75, N 86, N 94, X 2. (Pl. I.)

[4] Such as E 9, M 54.

[5] Such as A 11 (Pl. I), K 5, M 41.

[6] B 2 is the best case. This vessel bears so striking a resemblance in its detail to two large urns from Hammoor (KS 12084, 24) and Sörup in Schleswig as to raise the presumption that they all come from one workshop. If this is so, and the suggestion here made is correct, that the more elaborately decorated corrugated pots with bosses fall late in the series, it would form a strong argument for the view that direct contact between Caistor and the continental

Angles was maintained until at least the end of the fifth century, probably accompanied by further immigration. Tischler holds that it continued even later: 'a fresh influx into England from the north can be seen in the sixth century', *Med. Arch.* iii (1959), 4. Some of the bossed corrugated pottery of Norway is datable around 500 according to Bøe 141, Figs. 215–16, and Mackeprang (1943), 55: this, though not directly related to the English series, represents a parallel development. W. Slomann (*Die Kunde* xii (1961), 2–15) places it 400–50.

[7] It is a remarkable fact that while the corrugated pottery of continental cemeteries is singularly lacking in associated objects, it is normal at Caistor for such urns to contain manicure sets (knife, shears, tweezers, etc.) of iron. Unfortunately these are not helpful in dating their containers.

tain some pottery that has its closest parallels among the continental wares of the half-century before 400, though there may be no other that has so many distinct varieties that seem to date from that time. Thus the profusion of early corrugated bowls at Sancton, and their occurrence in smaller numbers else-where, has already been mentioned: tall rounded vessels with high upstanding necks related to Plettke's Type A6 are on record not only from Sancton and Heworth (Yorks.), but from Elkington and Loveden Hill (Lincs.), Lackford (Suffolk), Girton (Cambs.), and from Leicestershire.[1] This type is associated with the settlement of Germanic *laeti* on the Roman frontiers on the Continent over the years around 400, and this, as we shall see, is of especial significance to the situation in this country.[2] They constitute at least presumptive evidence that many of the great cremation cemeteries were coming into use towards the end of the fourth century.

If this is so there is only one conclusion to be drawn. These cemeteries must have begun as the burial places of barbarian *laeti*, brought in with their wives and families during the last days of Roman rule and deliberately planted in eastern Britain to act as a reinforcement to, or a substitute for, more regular garrisons in the protection of the province against invasion. This was a normal Roman practice in disturbed frontier areas, and there is, as we have already seen,[3] literary evidence for its use in Britain on several occasions from the third century onwards. This phase is thus, at least in part, a phase of controlled settle-ment, the areas chosen being those which appeared to the Roman authorities as requiring or justifying such special protection.

With this idea in mind it is worth while to look at the distribution of the cremation cemeteries in eastern England and especially of those which have produced evidence of use before the collapse of Roman authority. A number of them are in obvious and direct relationship to Roman fortified towns, and to the principal lines of communication between them. As we have seen, both Caistor and Markshall lie within a mile of Venta Icenorum: Brundall is close to a Roman site on the direct route down the Yare valley from Venta to its fortified port at Caister-next-Yarmouth. In Yorkshire, York itself has produced a number of early cremation burials, and the notable cemetery at Heworth is only a mile or two to the east on the road to Malton.[4] Sancton lies significantly

---

[1] See Fig. 32.
[2] Tischler (1954), 66.
[3] p. 66.
[4] Malton, itself in all probability the supply base for the late fourth-century coastal signal stations, is

not a certain case. The provenance of the urns now at York that are supposed to have come from near-by Broughton is dubious. I owe this information to the kindness of Mr. G. F. Willmot.

under the inner escarpment of the Wolds on the Roman road south from Malton to the fortified town of Petuaria at Brough-on-Humber and close to its junction with the road from Brough to York. There is Anglo-Saxon pottery from Catterick, and evidence for at least one inhumation burial at the Brigantian cantonal capital at Aldborough (Isurium). One could hardly imagine a more obviously strategic disposition in relation to the centres of Roman power and the lines of communication between them.

It is indeed just possible, though the possibility should not be stressed, that in these Yorkshire arrangements there survives a trace, however heavily over-laid by later Anglian intrusions, of the settlement of those Alamannic *laeti* for whose presence in fourth-century Britain there is contemporary witness.[1] A sixth-century inhumation burial at Londesborough close to Sancton con-tained the remains of a rare type of fourth-century Alamannic brooch, evidently an heirloom in that context; an Alamannic spearhead comes from Driffield, which has also produced a wheel-made pot of Frankish character whose unusual stamped decoration is exactly paralleled on a handled jug from Ulm. Among the pottery from Sancton there is not only a remarkable group of vessels which seem to be hand-made copies of Frankish biconical pots of very similar types to those found among the Alamanni and their neighbours in Württemberg and Mittelfranken,[2] but at least two others of earlier forms which can be exactly paralleled in central or south-west Germany. The only complete Anglo-Saxon vessel from Catterick is also a hand-made imitation of a stamped Frankish biconical vessel of south German type. It is of interest to recall in this connection the early *francisca* from the cremation cemetery at Saltburn,[3] and the group of place-names in the West Riding containing the element 'Almond'. In the light of the literary and archaeological hints it may be well to look again at the old suggestion that some of these may contain the name Alamanni, especially as the early forms of the best-attested case, Almond-bury near Huddersfield, relate to a prehistoric fortress that could well have been reoccupied as the headquarters of *laeti* in late Roman times. Nor should it be objected that these names belong rather to the West Riding than east Yorkshire, for on any showing the place-names of the East Riding have been heavily overlaid by later Anglian and Scandinavian settlement, while

[1] This paragraph summarizes the case for Ala-mannic settlement in Yorkshire outlined by M. Swanton and myself in *Ant. Journ.* xlvii (1967), 43–50, and should be read with the references there cited.

[2] Including those made by the workshop some of whose products are shown on Fig. 42.

[3] Illustrated by F. and H. W. Elgee, *Archaeology of Yorkshire* (1933), 181, Fig. 32A.

west Yorkshire long retained its native independence to which such survivals as the British district names Elmet and Loidis (Leeds) bear witness.

Further south in Lincolnshire and the east Midlands something of the same pattern recurs. The early cremations at Kirton Lindsey are close to the Roman road running south, from the Humber crossing at Ferriby, down Lincoln Edge to Lincoln. Eastwards on the Lincolnshire Wolds, the Fonaby burials lie close to fortified Caistor, and even closer was an inhumation cemetery to the south on the way to Nettleton. There could well be a relationship between the cremation cemetery at West Keal and Roman Horncastle. The walls of both Caistor and Horncastle are of fourth-century type with projecting bastions.[1] The position at Lincoln itself is obscure, for neither of the two early urns once thought to come from the city has a good local pedigree, and there is no certain evidence for the major cremation cemetery that one would expect. It is, however, of interest that a small plain biconical accessory vessel was found in the Greetwell Roman villa two miles east of Lincoln (Fig. 6).[2] Further south down Lincoln Edge the area around Roman Causennae in the Ancaster gap is also full of interest. All the urns known from the cemetery at the south gate of Causennae itself are early, and the great urnfield at Loveden Hill, certainly originating at this time, is only a few miles to the west, while to the east down the Slea valley is Sleaford, the site of one of the largest mixed cemeteries in Britain, though not one that is known to have produced the earliest types of cremation urns.[3]

From Lincoln the Fosse Way runs south-west to Leicester, and at Newark, where it touches the Trent, there was an early cremation cemetery: at Thurmaston, just north of Leicester and in the same relation to it as Heworth bears to York, there was another, also on the Fosse. Leicester itself, Ratae Coritanorum, has produced at least one early cremation urn (Fig. 14) from a site just outside the Roman fortifications. East and south around the inner margin of the Fens, there is ceramic evidence for early settlement at a number of sites that could be related to the Roman pottery towns at Casterton and Water Newton, notably at Stamford, Peterborough, Woodston, and Nassington, but no major cremation cemetery has been recorded. Casterton itself has now produced both cremation and inhumation burials immediately outside its Roman walls. Further south the little walled town of Cambridge,

[1] *Arch. Journ.* ciii (1947), 21–3.
[2] See my note ibid., pp. 85–8.
[3] The pottery from Ancaster and Sleaford, as well as the small group from the earlier excavations at Loveden Hill (Hough-on-the-Hill), is published in my 'Anglo-Saxon Pottery of Lincolnshire', *Arch. Journ.* cviii (1952), 65–99.

described three centuries later by Bede as a *civitatula . . . desolata*,[1] is the focus of a remarkable concentration of early cemeteries. Those of St. John's cricket ground and Newnham are close at hand: Girton is a mile or two north-west up the Roman road to Godmanchester (in exactly the same relationship that Thurmaston bears to Roman Leicester or Heworth to Roman York), and Little Wilbraham is only a little further away to the east. It is difficult to treat the obvious uniformity of this pattern over nearly the whole of the cremation area as the unplanned product of coincidence. Only the concentration of early cremation cemeteries on the borders of west Suffolk and west Norfolk, that focuses upon Illington and Lackford, seems less obviously related to the administrative pattern of Roman Britain.

But outside the main cremation area this appearance of a deliberately planned relationship is not so clear. With the exception of Dorchester-on-Thames, whose special interest will be discussed shortly, the Roman towns of the south and south-east seem to have no really early Germanic settlements in their immediate proximity. Colchester, St. Albans, Silchester, London, Chichester, and Cirencester are without early cremation burials or substantial Saxon cemeteries of any kind close at hand. It is true that Canterbury has produced Saxon huts and occupation debris within its walls[2] and that the cemetery at Westbere is near by,[3] but in neither case is there reason to date the material much earlier than the middle of the fifth century. At Winchester the recently discovered mixed cemetery at Worthy Park two miles north up the Roman road to Silchester certainly looks like another instance of the same relationship as has already been noted between Thurmaston and Roman Leicester, Heworth and Roman York, and Girton and Roman Cambridge. But none of the burials from the carefully conducted excavations at Worthy Park need be much earlier than 500, and, if the beginnings of the cemetery lie in that period, its proximity to Winchester must have been due to different causes from those that were operating a century earlier in the last days of Roman Britain.

None the less there are parts of southern Britain that can show ceramic evidence for the presence of barbarians settled before the end of the Roman occupation. This comes for the most part not from the urns of cremation cemeteries but from accessory vessels used with inhumation burials. Most informative perhaps is the distribution of carinated bowls mounted on pedestal

---

[1] *Hist. Eccles.* iv. 19.
[2] The evidence is now most conveniently collected in *The Civitas Capitals of Roman Britain*, ed. J. S. Wacher (1966), 90–3 and Figs. 18–20.
[3] *Ant. Journ.* xxvi (1946), 11–21.

feet, a characteristic fourth-century type on the Continent.[1] Very few of these have so far been noted in this country and nearly all are from Thames valley sites, only one of which is a Roman town. The best known, and most complete, is that from Grave 205 at Mitcham in Surrey,[2] a cemetery which has produced other very early objects. Parts of several come from Linford and Mucking on the Essex shore of the Thames, a site whose magnificent visual command of the Thames estuary makes it ideal as a look-out point against any sea-borne threat to Roman London.[3] Another is from Ham on the Surrey bank of the river near Richmond, and the fourth, again only a fragment, is from inside the Roman defences of Dorchester-on-Thames. This distribution (Map 5(a)), re-inforced as it is by the parallel occurrence of contemporary imported metal-work at other Thames estuary and Thames valley sites,[4] conveys a strong hint of barbarian folk officially settled on the main route into the heart of Roman Britain by the very early years of the fifth century.

The occurrence of a sherd from one of these fourth-century pedestalled bowls inside Roman Dorchester is of especial significance. It was found during the 1963 excavations in the south-west quarter of the town, where traces of rough structures overlying earlier buildings and streets represented the final phase of the Roman or sub-Roman occupation.[5] Such ramshackle living quarters and such pottery seem exactly to fit the barbarian *laeti* whose presence at Dorchester is already demonstrated by the well-known burials found both north and south of the town. The personal equipment found with these interments places them unequivocally in this context, for it is characteristic of that used by barbarians recruited into Roman service at this time.[6] This equipment, studied by Joachim Werner on the Continent,[7] and more recently by Mrs. Hawkes in this country,[8]

---

[1] Its history is summarized by Tischler (1956), 56–9 and Abb. 13 and 14. The type is characteristic of north German cemeteries associated with the Chauci in the second and third centuries and passes over into the fourth-century stock-in-trade of the continental Saxons, ending as Tischler's *Dingener Typ* in the early fifth. Plettke, Tafel 27. 8 shows a vessel of this kind used as a lid to a fourth-century urn at Westerwanna. It also occurs in the Low Countries as Van Es's type 1D: *Wijster*, 298–300 and Figs. 104–6.

[2] Pl. 2. J. Morris, in *Surr. Arch. Coll.* lvi (1959), 114, points out that the apparent association with two applied saucer brooches is doubtful.

[3] One of these (*Trs. Ess. Arch. Soc.* iii, ser. I. 34 and Pl. V. 2) has been dated by Genrich to the

fourth century. See also *Ant. Journ.* xlviii (1968), 222–8 and Fig. 5.

[4] S. Hawkes has analysed this metal-work in *Med. Arch.* v (1961), 10–21. Her map, Fig. 4, shows a Thames valley distribution exactly in line with that of these carinated pedestal bowls. This can now be reinforced by the discovery of several pieces at the Mucking settlement.

[5] As described by S. S. Frere in *The Civitas Capitals of Roman Britain* (1966), 93–4.

[6] As first pointed out by Joan Kirk and E. T. Leeds in *Oxoniensia* xvii/xviii (1953), 63–76.

[7] *Bonner Jahrbücher* clviii (1958), 372.

[8] *Med. Arch.* v (1961), 1–70: a revised version in German is in 43–4 *Bericht der Römisch-germanischen Kommission* (1964), 156–231.

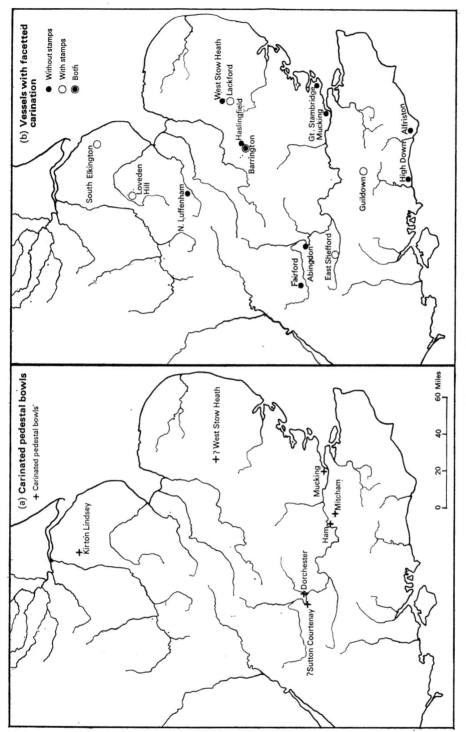

(a) Carinated pedestal bowls

+ Carinated pedestal bowls

Kirton Lindsey +

+ ? West Stow Heath

?Sutton Courtenay +
+ Dorchester

Ham +
+ Mucking
+ Mitcham

0   20   40   60 Miles

(b) Vessels with facetted carination

● Without stamps
○ With stamps
◉ Both

South Elkington ○

Loveden Hill ○

N. Luffenham ●

Fairford ●
Abingdon ●
East Shefford ○

West Stow Heath ●
Lackford ○

Haslingfield ●
Barrington ●

Gt. Stambridge ●
Mucking ◉

Guildown ○

High Down ●
Alfriston ●

Map 5 a and b

is sufficiently distinctive to be recognized wherever it is found, and to have led German scholars to give the name *Laetenhorizont* to a complex of archaeological fashions securely dated in the last third of the fourth century and the opening years of the fifth. As such it is invaluable as a dating instrument. So far as Britain is concerned, for example, it is most unlikely that fresh supplies of such equipment would reach the province after the official withdrawals of the army and the civilian administration in 408–10, though before that date it would almost certainly have been supplied to any barbarian irregulars, such as those at Dorchester, employed to reinforce the defences of Britain.

The characteristic features of this equipment, the belt fittings with their zoomorphic buckles, strap-ends, rosette attachment plates, tubular fittings, and so on—and the brooches that go with them—need not be described here. They are in fact very well and fully represented in the finds from the Dorchester burials,[1] and few other sets are so complete. But it is of the utmost importance, in our study of Anglo-Saxon ceramics, to note any pottery that occurs in association with these *Kriegergräber*, the graves of warriors equipped in this way, for such pottery will give precious information on the types in use in this phase of controlled Anglo-Saxon settlement.

The Dorchester burials themselves unfortunately contained no pottery, though we have seen one type, the carinated pedestal bowls, occurring at Dorchester in a context contemporary with them. But one or two comparable burials on the Continent have been associated with pottery, and the types can be checked against corresponding material in this country. At Blumenthal, near Bremen, a carinated pedestal bowl was in fact found in almost certain association with a burial containing belt-fittings of Dorchester type.[2] At Liebenau, Kr. Nienburg, Grave 57/1, which contained a zoomorphic buckle, Dorchester-type belt-fittings, and a shield-boss with silver studs, had also a pot some six inches high with a tall hollow neck and upstanding rim, ornamented with two finger-tipped collars above multiple chevron lines, with a single finger-tip in each triangular space. The pot is of a type well known in late fourth-century contexts in the cemeteries of the *Nordseekustengruppe* of west Schleswig and in the Elbe-Weser area. Quite apart from its association

---

[1] *Oxoniensia* xvii/xviii (1953), Fig. 27.

[2] *Mahndorf*, 137–8 and Abb. 47 d–g. The objects were a group found by chance and with them were three large urns of late fourth-century type. Since none of the belt-fittings were burnt, and both they and the pedestal bowl are of types commonly found with inhumations, it seems likely that they all come from a single burial in a cemetery which also contained contemporary cremation urns.

with this *Kriegergrab*, it is unusually well-attested in contexts datable to this time.[1]

Now pots of this general character and closely similar in decoration, with a combination of chevron lines and restrained finger-tipping, are not uncommon in our eastern cremation cemeteries. The closest parallels are shown on Fig. 33: they come from Cambridge, Kettering, and Elkington, but the Lackford and Castle Acre vessels are not far from the type. There were several with chevron designs, diversified in various ways with finger-tipping and dots, at Caistor-by-Norwich, and others of this kind come from Heworth (Yorks.), Loveden Hill and Ancaster (Lincs.), North Luffenham (Rutland), Thetford and Illington (Norfolk), Hoxne (Suffolk), Great Stambridge (Essex), and Oxford and Abingdon on the upper Thames. Their distribution is of great interest, and their presence at or near the Roman walled towns of York, Ancaster, Cambridge, and Venta Icenorum is surely significant, as well as in the upper Thames valley at Oxford and Abingdon in an area doubtless controlled by the *laeti* of Roman Dorchester. There need be little doubt that we are here on the track of controlled barbarian settlement in the last days of Roman Britain. How pottery of this kind, with its chevrons, finger-tipping, and line-and-dot designs, may have developed in the course of the fifth century, as a feature of subsequent phases of the settlement, will become apparent later. Here it is of particular interest to recall that chevron-and-dot designs of this type are characteristic of one of the classes, Group F, of the Romano-Saxon pottery.[2] There is a direct link here between the latest Romano-British and the earliest Anglo-Saxon decorative fashions in this country. The two are doubtless contemporary.

One other continental cemetery containing pottery associated with a *Krieger-grab* of the early fifth century is significant in this connection. This is at Helle, near Oldenburg, between Bremen and the Dutch frontier. Grave I in this small

[1] The following are parallels with datable associations: *Westerwanna* i. 174, with tutulus brooch: 1122 with late fourth-century brooch: Genrich (1954), Tafeln 25c from Stenderup, near Haderslev, with late fourth-century brooch: and 8F from Borgstedt, with bronze pincers of late Roman type. In the Cuxhaven Museum is a pot of this kind from Wingst (1297) that is actually decorated with impressions from the coiled spring of a brooch of the sort found with the Stenderup and Westerwanna 1122 vessels. I am indebted to the late Karl Waller, Director of the Cuxhaven Museum, for knowledge of this interesting piece.

Ornament that may be made by impressions of brooch-springs also occurs on the contemporary pedestal bowls, e.g. the example from Hooghalen: *Wijster*, 207 and Fig. 105. 3.

[2] *Dark Age Britain*, 30, Fig. 5, where Anglo-Saxon examples from Abingdon and Cambridge are set side by side with Romano-Saxon pieces from Caister-by-Yarmouth (Norfolk), Sawbridgeworth (Herts.), and Colchester (Essex). An instance of this chevron-and-dot decoration on a pot from Nordre Ferang, Vestfold, Norway, is dated by W. Slomann 400/450. *Die Kunde* xii (1961), 6 and Tafel 1 E.

burial ground contained Dorchester-type bronze belt-fittings, a shield-boss of conical form with a large knob not unlike the one at Liebenau, 57/1, a small glass cup of an early fifth-century type with vertical ribs, and a hand-made pot, a sharply biconical bowl decorated only with three horizontal lines above the carination.[1] Carinated bowls of this kind, known to German scholars as *Schalenurnen*, are closely related to the pedestal bowls already discussed in this context: the carinated contour of the upper part is very similar in the two forms, and the only difference lies in the replacement of the pedestal foot by a flat or simply rounded base. They occur repeatedly in contexts around 400 on the Continent.[2] English parallels to the Helle pot are not far to seek. It can in fact be closely matched in size, form, and ornament by urn 75 from Thurmaston,[3] and also by the bowl from Peterborough on Fig. 14. The undecorated biconical accessories from Frilford and Long Wittenham (Berks.) on Fig. 6 are similar in form. It is tempting also in this context to note the similarity of its decoration to that of the urn from Roman Leicester on Fig. 14. Though this is a larger and taller piece, and less sharply biconical in form, the setting of its decoration is identical, and its fabric is the hard, dark, polished ware characteristic of this early period.[4] Here then are three varieties of pottery, all associated with the *Laetenhorizont* in Germany, and all with parallels in this country. It would be difficult to find better evidence for some degree of Anglo-Saxon settlement in the years around 400.

The phase of overlap ends politically with the collapse of the central Roman administration, both civil and military, between 408 and 410. As Stevens has demonstrated, the British sections of the *Notitia Dignitatum* can be interpreted to show many of the regular army units on the way out of Britain, or in process of dissolution, at this time, and the literary evidence for the ejection of the civil administration by a spontaneous uprising in the *civitates*, the fortified cantonal capitals, and other urban centres of the province, is very strong.[5]

[1] *Bonner Jahrbücher* clviii (1958), 372, Abb. 11. 1–3 and Abb. 12.

[2] As e.g. in Liebenau Grab 11/28, with the earliest form of equal-armed brooch (discussed by A. Genrich in *Nachrichten aus Niedersachsens Urgeschichte* xxxiii (1964), 27, Abb. 1): Genrich (1954), Tafel 15E from Hammoor, with early fifth-century brooch. The type is common in the Low Countries: see the examples (van Es's types VIII A and B) illustrated in *Wijster* Fig. 160. 7, 11, 12 and discussed on pp. 315–17.

[3] Leicester Museum 580/1954/75.

[4] On the other hand a very similar vessel from Liebenau (Brandgrab 11. 58) was found with a round-headed brooch with five radiating knobs, of the early sixth century: *Nachrichten aus Niedersachsens Urgeschichte* xxxiii (1964), Tafel 1, 7a and 8. The brooch is discussed ibid. xxx (1961), 38–9.

[5] I follow the analysis of these confused years worked out by C. E. Stevens in *Arch. Journ.* xcvii (1941), 125–54, and Pavia *Athenaeum* xxxv (1957), 316–47: and summarized in my own article on 'Pelagius and the End of Roman Rule in Britain' in *J.R.S.* l (1960), 21–36.

But although these dramatic events, rightly emphasized in our history books as marking the political end of Roman Britain, were of the first importance for the future of this country, they were not of a kind which can be expected to leave direct archaeological traces. It is impossible even to guess what immediate effect, if any, they may have had on such barbarian communities as were already established in Britain. In the absence of any direct evidence it is idle to speculate on the attitude that would be taken towards these communities by those tyrants, the local emperors in the lowland *civitates* or the tribal chieftains in the Highland zone, who, if Procopius is correct,[1] continued to rule Britain after the direct links with the western Empire had been broken. What light the pottery can shed on this phase of transition will be considered in the next chapter.

[1] *Vandal.* i. 2.

VI

THE SETTLEMENT OF ENGLAND

2. THE PHASE OF TRANSITION

WE know very little about Britain in the generation that passed between 410 and the 440s, but two things seem certain. The first is that the Romanized part of the population was still sufficiently coherent to be passionately concerned in the religious controversies provoked by the teachings of Pelagius on social morality, and the relation between human free will and divine omnipotence.[1] The second is that its rulers were still troubled by Saxon raiding, and apparently unable to cope with it without external aid.[2] The religious disputes of the time will have left no archaeological record, but they are at least evidence for the continuance of some degree of urban life.[3] The menace of Saxon raiding and settlement may well have left archaeological traces.

In discussing the phase of controlled Anglo-Saxon settlement, we have seen reason to believe that the defence of many of the lowland *civitates* was already nominally in the hands of Germanic settlers, whose presence is vouched for by the earliest pottery in the cremation cemeteries that were coming into use in their immediate proximity. Such forces may have been assisted by local levies of provincials from the *civitates* themselves, and there would also appear to have been places, especially south of the Thames and in the west Midlands beyond the area of foreign settlement, where such native levies would be the sole source of defence, and the only basis of a tyrant's power.

In the generation that followed 410, therefore, we have to think of Britain as passing through a phase of transition, in which an uneasy balance of authority subsisted between native tyrants supported by forces composed partly of barbarian mercenaries and partly of provincial levies. The sources of instability

[1] See my article on 'Pelagius and the End of Roman Rule in Britain' in *J.R.S.* 1 (1960), 21–36.

[2] This is clear from the Alleluia victory affair recorded by Constantius, *Vita Germani*, in connection with the first visit of St. Germanus in 428/9.

[3] The archaeological evidence for the survival of Roman life in Verulamium until the middle of the fifth century is summarized by S. Frere in *The Civitas Capitals of Roman Britain* (1966), 97–8.

inherent in such a situation were aggravated on one hand by bitter theological disputes over Pelagianism, on another by the mounting pressure of Picts and Scots from the north and west, and of Saxons from the east and south, and on yet a third by the differences which, if our analysis has been correct, existed from the start between the cremating—and therefore pagan—settlers in the country north of the Thames and the quite different situation in the south. The religious divisions between Catholics and Pelagians among the rulers of the *civitates* were so deep and bitter that the former, no doubt led mainly by the urban clergy, could seek aid from the bishops of Gaul in their efforts to suppress the heretics. It was this which led to St. Germanus's two visits in 428/9 and in the 440s. The persistence of the barbarian menace is well illustrated not only by the Alleluia campaign recorded in connection with the first of Germanus's visits, but also by the notice of a near-contemporary, but not necessarily well-informed, Gaulish chronicler, who reported that by 442 Britain was wholly under Saxon sway.[1] To add to the confusion, the evidence of the pottery itself bears witness to a widening gap between the political situations north and south of the Thames valley.

The great cremation cemeteries of the east coast and the east Midlands show every sign of a continuously rising Germanic population in those areas in the first half of the fifth century. There is an uninterrupted progression of ceramic forms and a natural evolution in styles of decoration over all this region through this time. This is the period in which, for example, the more elaborate line-and-dot designs grow into popularity out of the earlier restrained use of finger-tipping:[2] it is the period when the more complex *stehende Bogen* designs develop from types such as Caistor-by-Norwich R12[3] (Map 3), and pave the way for the *Buckelurnen* of the years from about 450 onwards: it is the period in which the fondness for shoulder-bosses begins tentatively to show itself in pottery of the Anglian tradition, and when such bosses combined with linear and corru-gated designs to provide the roots from which panel-style decoration was to spring. There seems no obvious interruption in the steady evolution of these styles as they are revealed in the pottery of the great cremation cemeteries.

There is unfortunately no scrap of surviving literary tradition to indicate the course of political history in the parts of Britain where this pattern of settle-ment prevailed in the first half of the fifth century. One may guess that such

---

[1] *M.G.H. Auct. Ant.* ix. 660.

[2] e.g. Fig. 18, the Abingdon urn: Fig. 20, the Sancton (2003) and Shropham urns.

[3] e.g. Fig. 20, and the Thurmaston and Sancton urns on Fig. 21.

authority as the *civitates* had over the settlers planted around them gradually declined, and that the relations between them, never very friendly, deteriorated as the worsening economic situation and the political fragmentation of Britain made Romanized town life a less and less viable proposition. It is abundantly clear that, whatever the relations between the two communities may have been, they remained rigidly distinct and no attempt whatever was made to weld them into one. This follows not only from the obstinate adherence of the German settlers to their ancestral practice of cremation, which implies on the religious plane that they were never converted to Christianity, but from the still more remarkable fact that they never adopted the simplest technical improvements in their domestic economy, such as the use of the potter's wheel, which must have been a familiar object wherever Roman pottery was still made. The rarity of objects of barbarian manufacture or association that occur, even as chance finds, inside Roman towns suggests too that they lived their lives apart and that there was little or no social intercourse between them. There is no reason to suppose that the language barrier was ever effectively surmounted at this stage: certainly no effort was made by the barbarians to master the Latin that in the early years of the fifth century must still have been the normal usage of the Church, the market place, and such courts as still functioned in the towns.[1]

In view of this evidence for the absence of effective social contacts it is probable that the barbarians soon lost interest in the ostensible purpose of their presence in the neighbourhood of Roman towns. They probably encouraged other settlers from their homelands to join them and increased their hold on the countryside with or without formal agreement with their nominal employers. They may well have quarrelled with, and even eliminated here and there, what was left of Roman urban life in some of the smaller towns that they were supposed to protect. They seem in any case to have ceased to provide any effective defence against Saxon incursions of the type with which St. Germanus was confronted in the Alleluia victory campaign. The whole point of that story, in which the saint resorted to an ingenious ruse to inspire panic in the enemy, lies in the fact that the only forces at his disposal were native levies of such poor quality that he could not risk committing them to a direct engagement with the invaders.[2]

[1] K. Jackson, *Language and History in Early Britain* (1953), 261, and my review in *E.H.R.* lxx (1955), 630–3.

[2] Constantius, *Vita Germani*, 17–18. These levies were still pagan in both senses, and it is interesting that Germanus's first act on assuming command was to baptize his ramshackle army.

There is a definite contrast between this picture of the transition phase in the parts of England where cremation cemeteries are the main indication of barbarian settlement and the situation further south. Here, as we have seen, cremation cemeteries, or indeed any substantial cemeteries set in direct relationship to the larger Roman towns, seem unusual, and the few examples of fourth-century Germanic pottery, with the exception of the piece from Dorchester, come from sites of no special significance in Roman times.

It is not at all easy to see what this contrast implies for the situation in southern Britain. It could mean that for a generation or more after the first controlled settlement in eastern England, and even for some years after the break-down of Roman rule, the cities of the south were strong enough to control their own affairs without the dubious assistance of barbarian mercenaries: or it could mean that such barbarians as they employed came, like those at Dorchester, of folk sufficiently in sympathy with Roman ways to inhume their dead and to leave few traces, other than occasional bits of uniform equipment, to betray their presence to the modern archaeologist. In fact it is only such bits of buckles, belt-fittings, strap-ends, and the like, casually preserved in contexts both sub-Roman and early Anglo-Saxon, and a few accessory vessels mostly associated with inhumation burials, that give any real evidence for the presence of such soldier-settlers in this part of England during the first half of the fifth century.

There are several points of interest to be noted about this admittedly rather scanty and uninformative material. The first is that stylistically the metal work does appear to show a genuine sequence.[1] At the beginning comes the imported late Roman equipment of the kind found with the Dorchester burials; then types whose distribution is virtually limited to Britain, and so is almost certainly of British manufacture; and finally the earliest brooches and other metal work of admittedly Anglo-Saxon origin dating from about the middle of the fifth century onwards. This, for what it is worth, suggests some continuity through these years, producing a situation perhaps similar to that which we have pictured further north, in which controlled settlement on a small scale was turning irresistibly into uncontrolled settlement on a large scale, and more or less organized warrior bands were changing gradually into a settled agricultural peasantry.

Then, too, the pottery from inhumation burials, though also scanty in quantity and for the most part lacking in datable associations, does seem to include a few pieces that are typologically at home in this transition phase. Biconical accessory vessels, mostly small bowls with simple linear decoration

[1] As demonstrated by Mrs. Hawkes in *Med. Arch.* v (1961), 1–70.

above the carination, have been found at several places in the south-east, as at Little Oakley,[1] Feering,[2] and Mucking in Essex, the first carrying a simple *stehende Bogen* design characteristic of this time, and the second associated with a bronze penannular brooch decorated with the same chevron-and-dot ornament that occurs on the Abingdon accessory vessel,[3] and on Group F of the Romano-Saxon pottery.[4] Similar biconical bowls with continuous diagonal lines or nicks on the carination are familiar in Brandenburg[5] and East Holstein[6] in the early fifth century: further west, they occur in similar and rather later contexts at the Galgenberg, near Cuxhaven,[7] and one was found at Helle in a grave dated by Werner about a generation later than the *Kriegergrab* already discussed.[8] They are very common in the latest levels at Feddersen Wierde where the main occupation seems to have ended about 450.[9] An English example from Kempston is on Fig. 35, and related pieces of larger size used as cremation urns occur at Caistor-by-Norwich (Y29), Lackford (49. 579A), Haslingfield (Ashmolean 1874. 5), and elsewhere. A variety of this type of bowl, carrying continuous facetting on the carination, is characteristic of sites in East Holstein,[10] soon after 400, and also appears in the latest levels at Feddersen Wierde. In this country unstamped examples occur at North Luffenham (Rutland), Great Stambridge and Mucking (Essex), in Berkshire at Abingdon, further west in Gloucestershire at Fairford, in Sussex at Alfriston and High Down, in Suffolk at West Stow Heath, and in Cambridgeshire at Barrington (three examples) and Haslingfield.[11] Not all these are necessarily so early, and stamped examples like those from Guildown, in Surrey, and East Shefford in Berks., a type that occurs also in larger form both at Lackford and in Lincolnshire,[12] carry on the style into the years around 500. There is here, as with the corresponding metalwork, a continuous development for a century or more from the traditions

[1] Fig. 36.
[2] Fig. 35.
[3] Fig. 36.   [4] See p. 81.
[5] As, e.g., at Butzow (*Veröffentlichungen des Museums für Ur- und Frühgeschichte Potsdam* ii (1963), 68–88, especially Tafeln 8. 122, 124, and 9. 138).
[6] Genrich (1954), Abb. 1. 19 from Hammoor.
[7] *Galgenberg*, Tafeln 47. 4 and 6 (the former with a Group II cruciform brooch): 48. 1: 49. 13.
[8] Helle, Grab 7: *Bonner Jahrbücher* clviii (1958), 385, Abb. 11. 5, and see pp. 81–2 above.
[9] I am greatly indebted to Dr. P. Schmid of Wilhelmshaven for information about Feddersen Wierde.

[10] Genrich (1954), Abb. 1. 20 from Borgstedt. Tafel 14B from Hammoor, with brooch about 400. The form is included in Plettke's Type C, Plettke 48 and Tafel 40, especially 9 and 11 from Dingen and Oberndorf: 13 from Altenwalde, itself a form approaching the *Buckelurne* type with a foot, had the broken lower half of such a bowl used as a lid, suggesting a date for the latter before 450. See also Tischler (1956), 63 and A. Genrich in *Archiv für Landes- und Volkskunde von Niedersachsen* (1943), 83. The type also occurs in the Low Countries, e.g. the piece from Borger (*Wijster*, Fig. 160. 3).
[11] Fig. 37 and Map 5b.
[12] *Lackford*, Fig. 12. 49A 13: Elkington 108 (*Arch. Journ.* lviii (1952), Fig. 9): Loveden Hill NE 19.

introduced to Britain with the soldier-settlers at the end of the fourth or very early in the fifth century.

A further point of interest is the distribution of so much of this material along the south bank of the Thames below Oxford, at places many of which, though not in any sense towns, seem originally to have been occupied by small rural communities in Roman times, and became eventually the sites of substantial Anglo-Saxon cemeteries. Frilford, Abingdon, Long Wittenham, Wallingford, and several places in and around Reading, all fall into this group, which includes also Lower Shiplake and Aston-next-Remenham further down the river. Above Dorchester, Cassington and Brighthampton on the Oxfordshire bank of the river may well have a similar origin. If, in fact, most of these Anglo-Saxon communities began as groups of barbarian soldier-settlers planted out among the existing villages on the riverside gravels, and dependent perhaps in the first instance on the fortified bridgehead at Dorchester, we seem to be in the presence of something that looks uncommonly like a political frontier along the Berkshire bank of the upper Thames. The mass of very late Roman material, recovered unfortunately without stratigraphical associations, from the excavation of Silchester (Calleva Atrebatum), coupled with the apparent absence of early Anglo-Saxon settlement in its immediate neighbourhood,[1] can well mean that, for this period of transition at any rate, there was some sub-Roman power centred in that area that was in a position to hold hostile barbarians at arm's length, and perhaps to employ more friendly ones to defend its northern frontiers in the Thames valley.

Against whom was such a defence required? In the total absence of any political record for this place and period, the question cannot be answered. But it has been stressed already that this part of the Thames valley lies like a boundary between two regions in which, on the pottery evidence especially, Anglo-Saxon settlement seems to have taken two different forms. To the north and east lies the region of cemeteries in which cremation is dominant or at least substantially represented, cemeteries, for the most part, closely related to the pattern of the greater Roman centres: to the south and east lies a region where inhumation from the start is dominant, and where the Roman cities seem to shun the close presence of systematic barbarian settlement. Whatever the historic reasons for this contrast, it is easy to guess that political friction

[1] G. C. Boon in *Med. Arch.* iii (1959), 79–88, discusses the latest metal objects. Some of the pottery is shown in T. May, *The Pottery found at Silchester* (1916), Pls. LI–LVII, but his dating is not reliable. B. H. St. J. O'Neil in *Antiquity* xviii (1944), 113–22, has conveniently assembled the topographical evidence from the Silchester area.

could well have been generated in these formative if chaotic years along this obvious frontier line that geography has drawn between them.

It is worth looking for a moment at the Abingdon cemetery in this connection, for here, at the junction of the Thames with its Berkshire tributary the Ock, lies one site which, set on the frontier between them, seems to combine the features of both worlds. The cemetery is characteristically placed on the south bank of the Ock just across the stream from the small Roman settlement of rather indeterminate nature which occupied the site of the later abbey and the adjacent centre of the present town. The relationship seems typical of the cremation area, and the excavated part of the cemetery in fact contained 82 cremations against 121 inhumations, a much higher proportion than is normal in the larger cemeteries of the south, even at other Thames-side sites like Long Wittenham, its nearest rival in this respect.[1] Moreover, the cremation urns themselves include an unusually large proportion of really early types. A surprising number of them, for example, are decorated with the finger-tipping or line-and-dot designs, which are directly derived from those which have already been discussed in connection with German warrior-graves of the late fourth century. There is also considerable use of those *stehende Bogen* motives which we have seen as typical of ceramic decoration in the first half of the fifth century. Abingdon is indeed the most westerly site on the distribution map (Map 3) of this sort of pottery.[2] To this same phase, or very soon after, must also surely belong two early urns in the British Museum from near Oxford,[3] one of which has strongly grooved linear ornament, and the other an elaborate pattern of chevrons and dots. Quite apart from the bits of early metal-work for which the Abingdon cemetery is well known,[4] the evidence of the pottery makes it abundantly clear that settlements both of cremating and of inhuming Saxons were established in this part of the upper Thames valley quite early in the fifth century.

There are two instances a little further down stream, one from Long Witten-

[1] See *Abingdon*, 11. Long Wittenham had 46 cremations and 188 inhumations. The significance of the varying incidence of cremation and inhumation in the upper Thames valley is discussed by Joan Kirk in *Dark Age Britain* (1956), 123–31.

[2] e.g. C17, C38, C64, C67, C74, C76, and the inhumation accessories B24 and B111. Of these C64 is on Fig. 21 (2032), B24 on Fig. 36 (41), and B111 on Fig. 37 (2035). Unfortunately none have datable associations.

[3] BM. 68. 7–9, 77 (here shown on Fig. 26) and 68. 7–9, 78. The decoration of the latter, a natural development from the simpler chevron-and-dot designs of the *Laetenhorizont* type shown on Fig. 33 and Abingdon B24 (Fig. 36) is closely paralleled by Abingdon C17, Caistor-by-Norwich N32, N40, N44(a), Y19, and Elkington 63 (*Arch. Journ.* cviii (1952), 38, Fig. 7).

[4] e.g. the equal-armed brooch from C26, the *tutulus* brooch from B106, and the sword from B42.

ham and one from Reading, in which early fifth-century buckles have been found associated with pots. Although their discussion may raise wider issues, this would seem the best point to examine them. At Reading, Grave 13 contained, among other metal objects, the loop of a Type IA buckle with confronted dolphin heads, and a hand-made pot on a pedestal foot decorated with necklines, a single horizontal zone of alternate dots and stamps, and groups of chevron lines on the shoulder, with a similar combination of dots and stamps in the triangular spaces above and below them.[1] Mrs. Hawkes has described Type I buckles as representing 'the last recognizable phase of provincial Roman metal work in Britain',[2] and, as such, as she points out, they may well have been treated as 'precious and had a long life'. The pot (Pl. 2) is of great interest, for both its decoration and its form are clearly developed versions of those already noted as characteristic of *Kriegergrab* pottery. At Reading, the use of simple finger-tipping in the collar and among the chevrons on the shoulder has been replaced by a mixture of dots and stamps, while the form is developed direct from that of the carinated pedestal bowls. This combination is typologically the next stage following the use of line-and-dot designs of the kind so popular in the Abingdon cemetery.[3] Now Silchester is one of the late Roman towns from which several examples of Type I buckles have come, a place indeed where they may well have been made, and it is entirely consistent with the suggestion put forward here for the origin of the Thames-side Anglo-Saxon settlements that such a piece should be found associated, at Reading, with an Anglo-Saxon pot whose position in the typological series makes a date around 450 probable. Several examples of this sort of decoration from Wehden-bei-Lehe are dated typologically by Waller between 400 and 450.[4] A date about the middle of the fifth century would seem on all grounds acceptable for Reading Grave 13.

The other pot associated with a fifth-century buckle in this area is that from Long Wittenham Grave 57.[5] The buckle in this case is of Type IIIB, a type apparently manufactured in the Meuse valley, and closely paralleled by one from the earliest grave, Grave 11, at Haillot, near Namur, datable about 425.[6] The

---

[1] See Pl. 2, and *Med. Arch.* v (1961), 44, Fig. 14 b. A bronze ring from this burial is decorated with the chevron-and-dot pattern already noted as characteristic of this phase.   [2] *Ibid.*, 26.

[3] Dr. P. Schmid tells me that pottery with this type of decoration occurs in the latest phase at Feddersen Wierde, abandoned about 450.

[4] e.g. *Wehden*, Tafel 18, 537 and 680.

[5] First published in *Arch.* xxxviii (1861), 16 and Pls. XIX 10 and XX 2: here shown Fig. 38 and Pl. 2.

[6] J. Breuer and H. Roosens, *Haillot* (*Arch. Belg.* xxxiv (1957)), Fig. 12. 8.

continental associations of this type of buckle are with the early Frankish settlement of Belgium, carried out under Chlodio before his defeat by Aetius at Vicus Helenae in 446, after which his people were established around Tournai as *foederati*. The occurrence of this buckle at Long Wittenham, and another smaller one of the same kind at Sarre in Thanet, together with some other categories of objects from the parts of Gaul occupied by the Franks at this time, such as the sword from Grave B42 at Abingdon, has been recently used in support of a claim that most of England south of the Thames was settled by Franks in the years following the middle of the fifth century.[1]

This is not the place, nor the occasion, to examine this claim in detail, since it would take us too far afield from a study of the pottery.[2] But it does raise one point directly relevant to our present purpose, the scarcity of Frankish pottery from all the parts of Britain in which these objects occur. With the exception of one piece of developed Argonne ware from the Chessell Down cemetery in the Isle of Wight,[3] and one or two in Surrey and Kent,[4] there is no Frankish pottery on record from the cemeteries here under discussion. The contrast which this presents with the great quantities of wheel-made vessels which accompany the inhumation burials in the cemeteries of the Low Countries and northern Gaul makes it as certain as it can be that there was no massive movement of Frankish people into Britain south of the Thames during the fifth century. Frankish immigrants would never have tolerated such a lack of the strong, serviceable, wheel-made pottery to which they were accustomed in their continental homes.

The pot found with the buckle from Long Wittenham, Grave 57, has no direct Frankish associations. It belongs to a category of bossed hand-made wares that were particularly popular among the Thames valley Saxons. These vessels (Figs. 38 and 39) are mostly of conical or sloping form in the upper part, with the maximum girth set rather low on the body, below which are long,

[1] V. I. Evison, *The Fifth Century Invasions south of the Thames* (1965), who illustrates the pot and buckle Fig. 12 a–c.

[2] For a full discussion see my review in *E.H.R.* lxxxi (1966), 340–5.

[3] Illustrated by Miss Evison, op. cit., Fig. 9 f, and datable, if her assessment of its position in the typological series is acceptable, around 500. Another piece of Argonne ware has recently come from a hut floor at Mucking, Essex.

[4] e.g. an accessory from Sarre (Maidstone Museum) and another from Wickhambreux (Canterbury Museum, RM 4927). It is significant that the little pot from Lyminge, Grave 24 (*Arch. Cant.* lxix (1955), 31, Fig. 12. 1), though said to be wheel-turned, and found in a cemetery with strongly Frankish associations, is typologically closer to north German accessories, such as that from Kempston on Fig. 35, than it is to normal Frankish *biconi*. The wheel-turned plain *biconus* found near Mitcham 68 (*Surr. Arch. Coll.* lvi (1959), Pl. XVIII), now at Cambridge, seems to be a similar case.

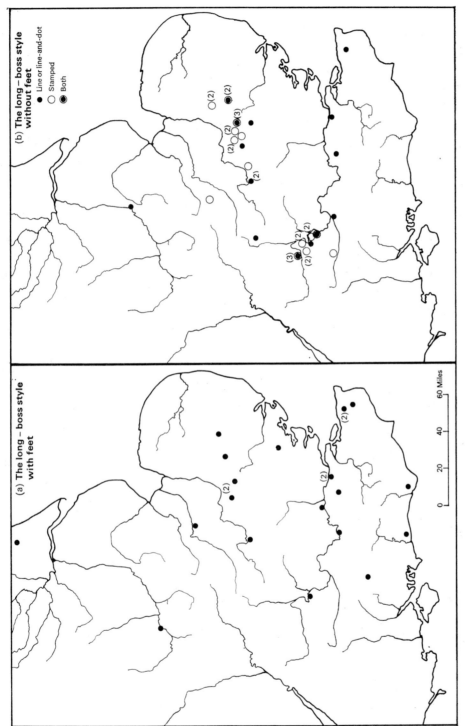

Map 6 a and b

vertical, hollow bosses reaching to the generally rounded base: the panels between the bosses are sometimes left empty, as in the Abingdon and Walling-ford examples, but are more often partly filled with vertical lines, or groups of vertical lines and stamps, as at Long Wittenham and Frilford. The form is in fact a variety of the bossed panel-style, not limited in its occurrence to the upper Thames valley, but especially common in the north Berkshire cemeteries, nearly all of which have produced one or more examples, either in a size large enough to take cremated bones, or on a small scale more suitable for use as inhumation accessories. A further group occurs in Middle-Anglia. Map 6(b) indicates the two main centres of their distribution in this country.

There is no reason to suppose that any of these pieces antedates the sixth century. Such a date is suggested by the short–long brooches found with the Wallingford example.[1] As a variety of the bossed panel-style one would expect its development to follow a course parallel to that style in the years after 500. It is true that the earliest and simplest forms may well have been inspired by the little late Roman glasses with vertical ribs on the lower part, such as are occasionally found, as at Helle, with *Kriegergrab* burials, and seem to have been made in the Meuse valley. But such convenient little vessels doubtless lasted long in use through the fifth century, and it is of interest that one found its way to north Jutland.[2] Continental parallels to the English series in pottery occur occasionally in the Low Countries, and, where datable, seem also to belong to the first half of the sixth century.[3] This fits the English sequence quite well, and makes it clear that the Long Wittenham buckle was about a century old when it came to rest with our pot. It is evident that such objects were widely appreciated and long treasured. As with many such imports it may be unwise to draw firm conclusions from the distribution of their ultimate resting-places as to the race of their owners or even the date or circumstances in which they entered Britain.

[1] Fig. 39.

[2] See J. Werner's distribution map of these glasses in *Bonner Jahrbücher* clviii (1958), 385–7 and Abb. 13.

[3] One in Grave 25 at St. Gilles-lez-Termonde occurred with two radiate-headed brooches of 525–50 (*Arch. Belg.* xli (1958), 91 and Fig. 18a). At Rhenen one from Grave 373 was accompanied by bird brooches of about 500, and another from Grave 380 by radiate-headed brooches of 500–25. I owe this information to the kindness of Mr. J. Ypey. Among the Alamanni of south-west Germany somewhat similar forms among the so-called *Rippengefäße* persisted into the seventh century, as, e.g., the pot from Steinheim, Kr. Heidenheim, discussed by Roeren, *Germania* xxxii (1954), 184 and Tafel 23. 4. But there is no reason to suppose that this dating is relevant to the English series (if it were, one would expect such vessels to occur in seventh-century burials in Kent). Some of the parallels quoted by Roeren are not strictly relevant, e.g. that from Herbrechtingen (J. Werner, *Münzdatierte austrasische Grabfunde* (1935), Tafel 11A), which lacks the characteristic bosses and is merely a hand-made copy of a Frankish *biconus*.

This discussion has taken us in time far beyond the transition phase of settlement in the Thames valley. To return to that phase we must consider one further local group of pottery which is relevant to the period before the main Anglo-Saxon invasions of the mid fifth century. This is the material which comes in particular from some of the earliest cemeteries of Kent, and indeed from some hut floors and occupation debris within the walls of Roman Canterbury (Durovernum Cantiacorum) itself.[1] It consists for the most part of round-shouldered jars and bowls with tall, hollow necks, flaring or everted rims, and rounded bases. They are decorated with simple linear patterns, sometimes verging on the curvilinear in character, and frequently executed in strongly grooved lines or the line-and-groove technique. There are also small, somewhat squat, biconical vessels, decorated in the same way, like that from Canterbury. While some plastic ornament, in the form of raised slashed collars, applied strips, and so on, appears, bosses as such do not occur.

Though there is little direct evidence for its date in Kent, pottery of this kind belongs typologically to the first half of the fifth century. It seems to be related on the one side to the earlier grooved and corrugated wares of Angle Schleswig, which we have seen to date both before and after 400, and on the other to those which are found with some frequency in the latest levels of north German settlements such as Feddersen Wierde or in the Frisian *terpen*,[2] datable in the first half of the fifth century. It is significant, in view of the literary traditions of Jutish settlement in Kent, that the closest parallels of all come from Jutland itself, where pottery of very similar forms and decoration has been recorded from at least twelve places, mostly in western coastal areas around Ribe and Esbjerg, then as now the natural point of departure for a voyage both to Frisia and to south-eastern Britain.[3]

This is the moment at which the study of Anglo-Saxon pottery brings us for the first time face to face with specific historical events. For in addition to Bede's statement that the first settlers of Kent were Jutes,[4] there is, in the

[1] See the examples on Fig. 40. For the Canterbury pottery see S. Frere in *The Civitas Capitals of Roman Britain* (1966), 91 and Fig. 18. 1, 7, 11, 19–22, 24–30.

[2] Among the Dutch *terpen*, Hoogebeintum, Ezinge, and Beetgum have produced material very similar to this Kentish type: e.g. Hoogebeintum 28. 326 in the Leeuwarden Museum. The same is true of such sites as Raard and Kimswerd (Leiden Museum): *Wageningen*, Fig. 94. 3, and Terp 101 bis 1927 (Leeuwarden).

[3] See Map 7 and the references there given. I am particularly indebted to Dr. O. Voss for information about such pottery from his excavations at Drengsted and other sites in Jutland. Among the closest parallels to this Jutish pottery in Kent are Drengsted 1963. 1: Fourfeld, near Esbjerg, C17206: Herredsbjerget, near Ribe, 826/58: and Rubjerg Knude, C26826.

[4] *Hist. Eccles.* i. 15. See my discussion of this passage in *Roman Britain and the English Settlements* (ed. 1937), 336–7.

familiar tale of Vortigern's arrangements with Hengist and Horsa, a tradition of federate settlement hereabouts[1] by folk whose leaders at least are associated

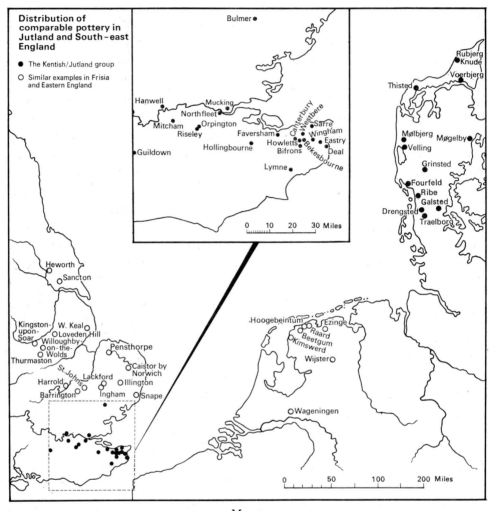

Map 7

in the literature with both Jutland and Frisia.[2] Some of the Kentish pottery, it is true, might be placed a little earlier than the second quarter of the century when Vortigern's need for protection against invasion from Roman Gaul

[1] Gildas, *De Excidio* 24; *Hist. Britt.* 31, 36–8.

[2] I see no reason to doubt the identification of the Kentish Hengist with the Jutish chieftain whose earlier adventures in Frisia are the subject of allusions in Beowulf and the Finnsburh fragment.

would make his arrangements with Hengist in the south-east strategically most sensible, but no fourth-century types are recorded, such as those noted at Caistor-by-Norwich, to suggest the presence of *laeti* in Kent before the breakdown of direct Roman rule. Moreover the absence of shoulder-boss pottery, which is also almost unrepresented in the latest levels at Feddersen Wierde, abandoned about 450, is consistent with the view that this Kentish group antedates the main invasions in the middle of the century. It is in fact very close in character and period to what we are told of Hengist's date and antecedents. If one had been asked to guess the style of pottery which a Jutish chieftain with Frisian contacts would have used towards the middle of the fifth century this is very much the answer that one would give. The distribution is also suggestive. Not only are there the pieces from the occupation debris of huts in Canterbury: others (on Fig. 40) come from Sarre in Thanet, where the first settlements of these folk are supposed to have been made, from Westbere close to Canterbury, from Faversham on the Roman Watling Street leading towards London, and from Hanwell in Middlesex, representing perhaps the first encroachment on British territory beyond the limits of Kent. Map 7 shows that it occurs sporadically elsewhere *in orientali parte insulae*, but its significant concentration is in Kent.

The federate phase in Kent was, however, of brief duration. If the literary traditions have any truth, it soon broke down in the quarrels between Vortigern and Hengist, which touched off the disastrous conflict in which what still remained of Roman civilization in Britain was destroyed. It can hardly have lasted a generation, probably much less. It is thus remarkable that any certain traces of so transient a phase should be discoverable. But it is difficult to see what other explanation of this material can be offered.

Before we pass on to consider what pottery evidence there may be for the phase of destruction which followed, one final comment may be made. If our interpretation of the ceramic record in this and the preceding chapter is correct, some considerable revision of the standard account of our earliest English history is required. In the story of Hengist and his Jutish or Frisian followers, we are dealing, not with the first occurrence in Britain of the familiar Roman practice of controlled barbarian settlement, but with the last. The pottery we have been studying shows in its dating and its distribution that the Kentish settlements come at the end of a series of such movements, not at their beginning. They have left some detailed impact on the literary traditions on both sides of the subsequent conflict, just because they were the last of their kind, and thus focused attention on the memorable climax to the long and disastrous process of official and non-official barbarian infiltration.

As such the Kentish story in the literary sources makes far better sense than if it has to be regarded as the first incident of its kind in the defence of Britain. For Kent, after all, is no place in which to base a force intended primarily for action against the Picts and Scots of the north, or even against Angles and Saxons making a landfall in the Wash or the Humber. Such a federate establishment in Kent is intelligible only in a context in which similar expedients, against threats to the northern frontier and the eastern coasts, had already been tried, and had either already failed or had proved all too successful in providing a bridgehead for uncontrolled barbarian penetration. It is intelligible moreover only in a context in which the main source of political danger to the independence of sub-Roman Britain had shifted to Roman Gaul, so that it became essential to close the invasion routes that led from Richborough and the other ports of the south-east to London and the Midlands. This is precisely the situation which Vortigern had finally to face, when, as the *Historia Brittonum* so aptly recalls, he could be described as living in fear not only of the northern barbarians and of the internal opposition led by Ambrosius, but also of Roman invasion.[1] Even before 451, when the defeat of Attila on the Mauriac plain left Aetius free to contemplate a forcible recovery of Britain, the Jutish pottery of Kent shows how real this danger was thought to be.

Our sources indeed do seem faintly conscious of the correct sequence of federate arrangements in Britain. It has not always been sufficiently recognized that they make this Kentish story a sequel to the general planting out of barbarian settlers *in orientali parte insulae*.[2] No dates for the preliminary manœuvres are given, and the evidence of the pottery suggests that the process had been going on far longer than the historical record implies.[3] And it is of interest also to recall hints preserved in Anglo-Saxon memory suggesting another feature in its final stages, this time dated only shortly before 450. In one version of the Anglo-Saxon Chronicle a British appeal for help to 'the rulers of the Angles' in 443 (correctly 446) immediately follows the failure of

---

[1] *Hist. Britt.* 31.

[2] *De Excidio* 23: *Hist. Eccles.* i. 15. Gildas distinguishes the first settlements *in orientali parte insulae* from the subsequent and more turbulent reinforcements. Bede, elaborating this distinction, calls the first group *Anglorum sive Saxonum gens* and only introduces Jutes with the second.

[3] I am in general agreement with C. F. C.

Hawkes's analysis of the literary references to the settlement of Kent, and the significance of the Vortigern/Hengist story in the wider context of European events at this time: see *Dark Age Britain* (1956), 91–6. But, for reasons which will be obvious to readers of these chapters, I cannot follow him in the claim that there was no Anglo-Saxon federate settlement in eastern Britain before 442.

a similar appeal to Rome, doubtless that reported by Gildas as 'the groans of the Britons' to Aetius in his third consulship. In the context of Vortigern's recorded fear of Roman intervention in British affairs the appeal to Aetius can only have come from circles hostile to him, perhaps those supporting Ambrosius. But an appeal to the Angles could well have come from Vortigern himself. While the Chronicle does not record the result of this appeal to the Angles, there is no reason why it should not here be preserving a scrap of genuine Northumbrian tradition.[1] There is indeed plenty of pure Angle and Anglo-Frisian pottery in Yorkshire, Lincolnshire, and East Anglia, which could well be the direct consequence of a fresh reinforcement to the northern settlers from the continental Angles at this time.[2] At this point however we pass into the next phase of the story, the phase in which sub-Roman Britain was finally overwhelmed by barbarian forces over which at long last it had entirely lost control.

[1] The annal appears only in MS. E of the Chronicle. This MS., though itself of early twelfth-century date, preserves for this period the only surviving version of the Northern Recension of the Chronicle that was kept going, probably at York, in the later Saxon centuries: see The Anglo-Saxon Chronicle, ed. D. Whitelock, D. C. Douglas, and S. I. Tucker (1961), xiv–xvii. It has generally been assumed, following C. Plummer and J. Earle, Two Saxon Chronicles Parallel (1899) ii. 9, that the whole of the 443 (E) annal was derived from what Bede says, Hist. Eccles. i. 13–14, about the failure of the appeal to Aetius. But Bede has no notice at this point of any consequent appeal to Anglian rulers, and there is no reason why it should be taken as a reference to the later account of Vortigern's dealings with Hengist, who is never described anywhere as an Angle.

[2] It may be relevant to recall the note attached to the name of Soemil in the Deiran royal pedigree preserved in Hist. Britt. 61 to the effect that 'he first separated Deira from Bernicia'. Soemil comes six generations above Edwin, who died in 633, and was therefore presumably flourishing in the mid fifth century. While the note is nonsensical as it stands, since Bernicia did not come into existence until after 547, it might preserve a confused memory of a revolt by Anglian foederati in Yorkshire at this time which first established a principality in the East Riding independent of whatever sub-Roman authority had succeeded in the north to the old command of the Roman Dux Britanniarum. Such a move would be a natural northern counterpart to the outbreak of the Kentish foederati in the south.

VII

THE SETTLEMENT OF ENGLAND

3. THE PHASES OF UNCONTROLLED SETTLEMENT, BRITISH RECOVERY, AND ANGLO-SAXON CONSOLIDATION

THE point has now been reached at which the nature of Germanic settlement in this country finally changes from a process taking place, however brutally, within the established framework of the old order, to one in which that order is either ignored and left to die away or, where it stands in the path of barbarian movements, is ruthlessly destroyed. It is the stage following what early writers termed the *Adventus Saxonum in Britanniam*, with its failure of the final attempt, traditionally located in Kent and the southeast, to absorb the barbarian menace by the time-honoured expedients of federate settlement.[1] The failure is pictured by the early sources in dramatic terms with the general uprising of all the settled barbarians and their destruction of Roman culture in the cities and the Church, the replacement in an orgy of blood and flames of what remained of the old world by the tentative and barbaric beginnings of the new.

It is to Gildas that we owe the essentials of this picture,[2] and there can be no doubt whatever that he was right. He was, after all, born less than fifty years later, when the British rally under Ambrosius Aurelianus had culminated about 500 at Mons Badonicus,[3] and his parents must have been in a position to tell him directly of what they had themselves seen and heard of the years of destruction. Moreover his witness can be checked from what is known independently of events in ecclesiastical and secular affairs. The British Church in lowland Britain, with its eloquent and well-educated bishops still busily debating Pelagianism with Germanus in urban surroundings, probably at

---

[1] See my article on the *Adventus Saxonum* in *Aspects of Archaeology*, ed. W. F. Grimes (1951), 221–42.

[2] *De Excidio* 23.

[3] Ibid. 26: see my discussion of the date in *Roman Britain and the English Settlements*, ed. 2 (1937), Appendix III, 460–1.

Verulamium, in the 440s,[1] disappears completely from history after accepting
a change in the method of calculating Easter in 455. British Christianity only
surfaces again after a generation or two of total obscurity, transformed out of
all recognition into the faith of wandering ascetics who struggle with lawless
chieftains in the spiritual and material isolation of the Celtic west. Sub-Roman
tyrants of the type of Vortigern, still painfully striving in the 440s to preserve
the urban society of the lowland *civitates* by reliance on the military protection
afforded by friendly barbarians, are overwhelmed by irreparable disaster and
translated in their own lifetime into legendary figures of Welsh mountain
folklore wholly remote from the rationalities of Roman life. Modern historians,
it seems to me, have no grounds whatever for accusing Gildas of melodramatic
exaggerations, for in the chaos which he describes these things were actually
taking place. All the basic assumptions and amenities of Roman and Christian
civilization vanished from lowland Britain while his parents were growing up
in the third quarter of the fifth century. It is not at all surprising that Gildas
should have exhausted the considerable resources of sixth-century rhetoric
in portraying the horrors of the time. He was viewing it with all the traumatic
experience of a displaced person, a cultured Christian refugee looking back with
bitter nostalgia to the vanished glories of the civilized past.

What signs are there, in the English pottery, of the period of chaos and
confusion when the federates broke loose from British control, probably soon
after 450, and completed the destruction of what remained of Roman Britain?
It must always be hazardous to seek traces of a political movement such as this
in the presence and distribution of artefacts of everyday use. In most communities the daily round of the living and the routine disposal of the dead may
continue little affected by the passage of armies. Even substantial movements
of population may leave few archaeological traces unless the newcomers have
a quite different cultural equipment. Nevertheless there are some novelties of
ceramic fashion which seem to be at least coincident in time with these events.

This is the period to which the elaborate Saxon *Buckelurnen* belong, and their
distribution may well be an indication of one aspect of this eruption. The
first point to notice is that they are found not only in the traditionally Saxon,
but also in the traditionally Angle areas. But, as was noted in Chapter III,[2] there
seems to be a distinction in the earlier phases of the movement represented by
Groups I–IV, between those who favoured *Buckelurnen* without feet and those
who preferred them with feet. The distribution of the former seems to fan

---

[1] Constantius, *Vita Germani* 26.   [2] p. 46, Appendix p. 142, and Map 4.

out from the Humbrensian area over the northern Midlands, while the latter appear to spread rather from East Anglia south-westward through Middle Anglia to the upper Thames valley and to have penetrated at quite an early stage as far as such Berkshire sites as Harwell and East Shefford. Though *argumenta ex silentio* are particularly vulnerable in discussing such distributions, it is perhaps significant that no normal early *Buckelurnen* with feet are recorded in the middle or lower Thames valley. Nor are there any in Kent and the south-east, where, as will be seen shortly, other forms prevailed.

It would seem therefore that the spread of *Buckelurnen* with feet is in fact the ceramic equivalent of the movement postulated many years ago by E. T. Leeds, on the strength of the distribution of the equal-armed and other fifth-century brooches of Saxon type. He took this as evidence for a Saxon penetration into northern Wessex and the Thames valley from the north-east along the Icknield Way route from Middle Anglia.[1] These groups of material are closely related to the *Buckelurnen*, for the equal-armed brooches and the early types of saucer brooches belong to exactly the same cultural complex. They spring from the same Saxon homelands between the Elbe and the Weser, and it is indeed surprising that Leeds did not use this obvious line of support from the pottery to reinforce his argument. But, while the movement is a real one, it does not, if the argument here developed carries conviction, represent the first incursion of Anglo-Saxons into the southern Midlands, as Leeds supposed. It seems to indicate a later wave of uncontrolled invasion, superseding, and liquidating, the earlier federate arrangements.

The point can be well illustrated by comparing the distribution of the *Buckelurnen* with that of the *stehende Bogen* urns from which, as has already been explained in Chapter III, they are the next typological development. As can be seen from Map 3 the *stehende Bogen* urns of the simplest, and typologically earliest, kind occur in three main areas, of which east Yorkshire and Lincolnshire, the Humbrensian area, is one; East Anglia, with an extension towards Cambridge, is another; and the Thames valley, with a notable concentration at Abingdon, is the third. As the style develops, all these areas are filled out with examples of more complex character, and in addition two or three fresh sites with pieces of this kind link together the Humbrensian and East Anglian regions around the southern and western margin of the Fens. Whether the latter belong just before or just after the final break between the Britons and the Saxons must remain uncertain.

[1] *History* x (1925), 97; *Ant. Journ.* xiii (1933), 229.

In marked contrast to this is the distribution of the earlier kinds of *Buckel-urnen*, Groups I–IV (Map 4(a)), which can be broadly dated in the second half of the fifth century. This shows no extension in the Humbrensian area, except for an outlier at Saltburn on the north Yorkshire coast, but a very heavy concentration in East Anglia, Middle Anglia, and in the upper Thames valley, which now forms a single continuous spread, with extensions into Warwickshire on one side and into Hertfordshire and the lower Thames valley on the other.

Part of this growth can no doubt be explained in terms of the reinforcement of the earlier communities and their natural extension into neighbouring areas. But it is worth noting that this was accompanied by a suggestive change in pattern, as though different political forces were now at work. Of the sites producing *stehende Bogen* urns nearly half are directly related, as we have seen, to Roman towns and to strategic points on the main roads connecting them. These include Caistor and Markshall in Norfolk, Heworth and Sancton in Yorkshire, Thurmaston near Leicester, and St. John's, Cambridge. But on the *Buckelurnen* map, while all these sites are still represented, there has been virtually no extension to their number, and they now constitute less than a quarter of the total. No less than twenty-seven additional sites, with no obvious relationship to the Roman administrative pattern, now appear for the first time, and, to anyone familiar with Romano-British affairs, the whole balance of the distribution has thus a different look. One could hardly have a neater demonstration of the change in political initiative. Uncontrolled seizure of the best land has replaced the concentration of barbarian settlement at points of strategic significance to the defence of Roman and sub-Roman Britain.

A further point may be noted. It looks as if conditions in the Humbrensian area may have followed at this time a somewhat different course from that taken in East Anglia and the Midlands. In the distribution of *stehende Bogen* urns no cultural distinction can be made between them. But while the older sites mostly continued everywhere into the *Buckelurne* period, there is no sign in Yorkshire and north Lincolnshire of a general land seizure by folk who favoured this type of pottery. The new non-Roman sites are all further south. This can mean only one thing. Newcomers from the Saxon lands between the Elbe and the Weser, while undoubtedly present, were not at all so strongly represented in the late fifth-century settlement of the Humbrensian area as they were further south. The links of Deira and Lindsey with the south Scandinavian culture that can be broadly termed Anglian are dominant in those regions from this time onwards. Such alien influences as can be recognized suggest connections rather with south than with north Germany. The pottery evidence is here in full accord with that of the brooches and other metal work.

In the south-east of Britain the corresponding eruption out of Kent is less clearly indicated. It may perhaps have left ceramic traces in the distribution of the horned or zoomorphic *Buckelurnen* on sites ranging from Northfleet and London to Alfriston and High Down in Sussex, with a related example at Feering on the Roman road from London to Colchester in Essex.[1] But the movement represented by the distribution of these urns may be related less to the initial outbreak than to the subsequent conquests of Aelle of Sussex which began, if the dating given in the Anglo-Saxon Chronicle is followed, in 477.

The evidence for pottery of the late fifth century from Essex is of considerable interest, because of the general dearth of early Anglo-Saxon material from all the region north and east of London. Actually there is rather more early pottery here than has been recognized, and it ties in neatly with Nennius's story that Hengist's last deal with Vortigern involved the surrender of Essex to him.[2] The contiguous sites at Linford and Mucking on the Thames estuary have already been noticed, in connection with the very early pedestal bowls found there, and there are other fragments from those sites that imply continuing fifth-century occupation.[3] There are fragments of several fifth-century pieces from Great Stambridge in the Prittlewell Museum at Southend, and from Little Oakley there are parts of further pots of this date from hut floors over-lying a Roman rubbish pit that was associated with a nearby villa. One sherd from Little Oakley is of especial interest because it is decorated with what appears to be part of a finger-tipped rosette of the kind noted on the late fourth-century *stehende Bogen* urns from Caistor-by-Norwich[4] and Brundall, so that occupation might have begun nearly as early as it did at Mucking. But the sherd is not large enough to make this certain. Finally there is the pedestal pot from Feering that derives from the horned urn series. Over the border in Hertfordshire parts of two or more fifth-century *Buckelurnen* have been found recently on an occupation site at Stevenage New Town,[5] while a cremation from Hertford itself was contained in a globular urn of Anglian type, datable probably about 500.[6] All this does not add up in terms of population

---

[1] See Map 6a and p. 48.
[2] *Hist. Britt.* 46.
[3] p. 88. See also *Ant. Journ.* xlviii (1968), 222–8.
[4] p. 72 and *Ant. Journ.* xvii (1937), 429, Fig. 1b.
[5] I owe knowledge of this site to the kindness

of Professor S. S. Frere.
[6] Hertford Museum GR 52/338131. I am indebted to Mr. A. G. Davies, Curator of the Hertford Museum, for information on this pot.

even to the contents of one small cemetery, but it does show that at several points in Essex and Hertfordshire there were groups of Saxons settled by the end of the fifth century at latest, and their presence is most readily explained as part of the general seizure of British territory that followed the final break-down of the federate system.

According to Gildas this period of destructive and uncontrolled Saxon advance was slowed down by the British revival under Ambrosius Aurelianus and finally halted altogether following a great slaughter of the invaders at an unidentified place called Mons Badonicus. He seems to place this in the year of his birth, some forty-four years before the date at which he was writing. Mount Badon cannot be exactly dated, but it must have been between 490 and 516, say about 500.[1] Gildas claims moreover that throughout his own lifetime, the forty-four years since Mons Badonicus, which must correspond roughly to the first half of the sixth century, there had been no further barbarian conquests, at least in the parts of Britain familiar to him. There are even hints in the later continental sources of some backwash of Anglo-Saxons out of Britain into north Germany early in the sixth century.[2] Some scholars have seen, in the not infrequent occurrence there and in the Low Countries of English-looking cruciform brooches and other objects of this date (including, one may add, some very English-looking pottery),[3] some archaeological indications of such a migration in reverse. This would most likely imply the evacuation of areas overrun but insecurely occupied in the first onrush, and the concentration of settlement in regions more thickly peopled and more firmly held. Can the distribution of sixth-century Anglo-Saxon pottery in Britain throw any light on this possibility? Does it reveal, for example, any areas of early settlement in which sixth-century material is lacking or sparsely represented, or which seem

[1] *De Excidio* 26. I have discussed the date in *Roman Britain and the English Settlements*, ed. 2 (1937), Appendix III, 460–1.

[2] Rudolf of Fulda in his *Translatio Sancti Alexandri*, written about 865, has a circumstantial account of the landing of Saxons from Britain at Hadeln, near Cuxhaven, during the war, about 531, between Theoderic king of the Franks and the Thuringians. A similar landing in this area is reported in the more fanciful account of Saxon origins given by Widukind of Corvey. Neither is a first-hand historical source for this period, but, as Widukind himself says, there was evidently an oral tradition (*fama*) among the Saxons themselves

of such a movement at this time. It may not be without significance that Widukind's story of the treacherous slaughter of Thuringian notables by the Saxon immigrants is almost exactly paralleled by Nennius's account of the similar treatment of Vortigern's notables by Hengist (*Hist. Britt.* 46). This is good evidence of a common Saxon origin for the tale, and of a close cultural association between the two peoples concerned, for there is no likelihood of any direct borrowing either way between the insular sources available to Nennius and the continental stories used by Widukind.

[3] See pp. 58–9 and the examples given in footnotes thereto.

to have suffered any hiatus or interruption or distortion in the normal development of ceramic fashions?

This is an inquiry demanding extreme caution, since what we are seeking
is negative evidence, and to claim to prove a negative archaeologically, in the
present state of our knowledge of sixth-century pottery, is of all things the
most risky and unwise. It could in any case be disproved by fresh discoveries
at any time. All one can do is to point to such areas as there may be where, in
our present knowledge, a normal pottery sequence is not immediately apparent.

What can be regarded, first of all, as constituting such a normal sequence?
It will in general show a continuous development from the forms that have been
seen as characteristic of the late fifth century. Thus the late Group V of the
Buckelurnen (Map 4(b)) in which stamped decoration plays a major part in the
designs, and finally swamps the older emphasis on plastic ornament, certainly
falls after 500, but probably before 550. The development of panel-style ornament on shoulder-boss pottery of Anglian antecedents is a feature of the same
period, the bossed series showing both rectangular and triangular designs falling,
for the most part, early in the sixth century and giving way later to the unbossed
varieties of this type, as plastic ornament of every sort goes out of fashion.
Biconical schemes, like shoulder-boss schemes, come to be more and more
involved in the growing popularity of stamped decoration: they are increasingly
found, as time passes, on vessels of less angular and more sagging contour, and
are more frequently used in combination with motives of different origin to
produce all sorts of hybrid and composite arrangements. Growing intercourse
between settled communities, however diverse their origin, may induce a fusion
of styles, and, though old local variations may persist, and new ones even arise,
they will do so against a background of increasing uniformity in ceramic fashion.

All the while, moreover, the percentage of inhumation against cremation
will be rising, especially in Middle Anglia and the southern Midlands. This
may be due in some cases to interruption in the use of a burial ground or to the
replacement of one group of people by another, or it may indicate no more than
a changing fashion in the ritual of burial. Whatever its cause it means, for the
student of this pottery, that more attention has to be paid to inhumation accessories and less exclusive weight given to the distribution of the later types of
cremation urns, except in those parts where cremation remained all but universal throughout the pagan period.

The inhumation accessories, however, follow in the main the fashions set
by the larger urns. Stamped ornament, generally in one or two horizontal

zones, is increasingly introduced on the hollow-necked or sharply biconical forms characteristic of the fifth century (Fig. 41). In some cases this may have occurred well before 500, as with the Stamford window-urn, but perhaps later in the case of that from Haslingfield.[1] It is difficult to be certain about such pieces of angular profile as those from Islip (Northants.), Howletts (Kent), and Cassington (Oxon.). Some stamped biconical accessories seem to echo in hand-made form the wheel-made Frankish *biconi* so common in the inhumation cemeteries of the Rhineland and the Low Countries, and appear in this sense analogous to the similar sixth- and seventh-century wares used by the Alamanni in south-west Germany. Such vessels as the East Shefford (Berks.) and Guildown (Surrey) pieces may thus owe something to the Frankish influences that affected south-eastern Britain through Kent in the sixth century: the chevron rouletting on the first, and the large criss-cross stamps on the second, would suggest this source for their inspiration. Others, however, like the little Cambridge pot of sagging form, reproduce in miniature the unbossed panel-style with stamped pendent triangles that was one of the characteristic Saxon fashions for the decoration of cinerary urns in the years following 550.

With these lines of development in mind we may ask what areas show a normal sequence of ceramic styles implying a continuous development through the sixth century, and which do not. Broadly speaking, the whole area covered by the great cremation cemeteries of eastern England presents a complete and unbroken range of ceramic fashions from at least the beginning of the fifth to the middle of the seventh centuries. This continuity is everywhere apparent, not least in some of the largest cemeteries adjacent to Roman towns. It is clearest in such places as Caistor-by-Norwich or Loveden Hill, where cremation persisted as the general practice from the beginning almost to the end. But even where the situation is complicated by a varying degree of preference for inhumation at different times, the pottery sequence in these parts generally shows no significant interruptions that could be correlated with major political change.

It is true that there may be differences in the extent to which new fashions

[1] See Fig. 41. Apart from its window, regarded by F. Roeder as an early feature unlikely to occur after 500 (*Röm.-germ. Kommission* xviii (1928), 149), the Haslingfield piece, with its rather sagging contour, might well belong to the sixth century. There is in fact no means of knowing how late the fashion for windowed pottery may have continued in the special circumstances of the English settlements. The Haslingfield vessel is, however, not the only English example known to me whose form and decoration suggest a later date. The recently discovered piece from Grave 59 at Willoughby-on-the-Wolds, Notts., for knowledge of which I am indebted to Mr. M. J. Dean, also looks like a sixth-century vessel.

and influences were accepted in different parts. East Yorkshire, for example, never seems to have adopted the stamped panel-style with such enthusiasm as did Middle Anglia. This style itself took rather different forms in East Anglia from those that were followed in the Cambridge region and further west. But it remains the case that every stage in the various developments that succeeded one another in the course of the sixth century can be illustrated from every cemetery with a sufficiently long series of urns to provide a fair sample.

One special feature of the east Yorkshire pottery, and especially of that from Sancton, in the sixth and early seventh centuries, has already been noted.[1] This is the unusual prevalence of vessels which echo in hand-made form the styles of pottery prevalent at this time in the Rhineland and south-west Germany. It is difficult to explain this phenomenon by direct influences from Kent, as it is reasonable to do in the comparable case of some inhumation accessories in south-eastern cemeteries discussed above.[2] At Sancton there is a whole group of hand-made *biconi* used as cremation urns, some with linear designs,[3] others with stamped ornament,[4] and displaying in their shape and decoration every degree of fusion and hybridization with the Anglian styles prevalent in the preceding age.[5] This feature, coupled with the fact that a number can be shown to be the products of a single workshop (see those on Fig. 42), suggests a local industry reflecting the influence of these unusual continental contacts. It has been suggested that one element in the Sancton community may have been derived from the Alamannic *laeti* known to have been settled somewhere in Britain in the third quarter of the fourth century.[6] If so, they must have kept in touch with their homeland, and presumably have been reinforced by fresh settlers from south-western Germany, where similar hand-made copies of Frankish *biconi* were popular in the period following the Frankish conquest of the Alamanni in the 530s.[7]

Nothing is known of the political situation in Deira in the second quarter of the sixth century which might provide an occasion for a fresh influx of settlers

---

[1] p. 39.   [2] p. 107.

[3] e.g. Sancton 3, 4, 5/54, 6, 7, 22, 137(b). An indication of the date of this group is given by the fact that 137(b) overlay, and had disturbed, an urn (150) of fifth-century type with *stehende Bogen* decoration.

[4] e.g. Sancton 1, 25, 108(b), 111(a), 112(a), 123. The urn from Catterick in the Bowes Museum at Barnard Castle is another Yorkshire example of this kind.

[5] e.g. Sancton 9(b), which, though of *biconus* form, is decorated in the stamped panel-style with bosses. See also 108(a) and 98(b) (2278 and 2293 on Fig. 4), where stamped biconical and late panel designs are used on this type of pottery.

[6] Ammianus Marcellinus xxix. 4, and see pp. 66 and 75.

[7] See my note in *Ant. Journ.* xlvii (1967), 49–50.

at that time. It is however worth noting that the traditional date for the first establishment of Ida and his people in Bernicia is 547. That some of them came from the southern part of the Humbrensian area seems likely from the place-name link between Lindsey and Lindisfarne.[1] This may perhaps indicate that the situation was still very fluid in those parts. However that may be, there is no ceramic evidence for any discontinuity of usage in the Sancton cemetery which could be associated with the British rally under Ambrosius Aurelianus at the beginning of the sixth century.

It is not in fact until we pass outside the main area of the early cremation cemeteries that various deviations from the normal pottery sequence can be observed, though by no means all of them need have anything to do with political events. In Kent, for example, there is little to carry on the Jutish or Anglo-Frisian pottery of Hengist's time much beyond the early years of the sixth century, to which no doubt the few examples of shoulder-boss bowls, and jars with simple linear ornament and occasional use of stamps, in the eastern cemeteries belong. This whole group of pottery is related to the same cultural phase as the group of early Kentish cruciform brooches,[2] and it ends, as they do, with apparent abruptness leaving no typological succession. There is virtually no panel-style stamped pottery in Kent, whether of the bossed or unbossed kind. It is true that in a few cemeteries in the north on the Thames estuary cremation continued to be practised, using urns of Saxon character, some of which are stamped and look to be quite late.[3] But this, for some reason, remained an isolated and backward area which had little to do with the development of Kentish culture as a whole.[4]

---

[1] See Ekwall's note on these names, s.v. Lindisfarne, in *Oxford Dictionary of English Place-Names* (1936): and my own discussion of the relations of Bernicia and Deira in the sixth century in *Roman Britain and the English Settlements*, ed. 2 (1937), 421.

[2] A fine early shoulder-boss urn of Anglo-Frisian type is that from Dover Gr. 87 for knowledge of which I am indebted to Miss V. I. Evison. The Kentish cruciform brooches are conveniently assembled by N. Åberg, *The Anglo-Saxons in England* (1926), 29–32.

[3] One of the Horton Kirby vessels (Maidstone Museum 40–1933), though not apparently used for cremation, is of this late kind, and so are several from Northfleet (the only place in Kent to have a relatively good sequence of sixth-century pottery), and at least one from Riseley. The late saucer

brooches from north Kent belong to this complex. There are a few pieces of sixth-century stamped pottery from elsewhere in Kent, such as Faversham (Ashmolean Museum, formerly Queen's College), Sarre, and Howletts (Fig. 41), but the number is extremely small.

[4] The backwardness and poverty of these settlements on the Thames estuary is difficult to understand if London was of any political or economic consequence in the first half of the sixth century, for they were very well placed to control any traffic passing up and down the Thames. That they did not apparently profit from this favourable situation is one of the stronger arguments for the view that there was a real break in the continuity of London's life at this time.

Elsewhere in Kent hand-made pottery of any kind seems to have been little used in the sixth century, and it is something of a puzzle to know what took its place for the main range of domestic purposes. The so-called bottle-vases, in wheel-made wares strongly influenced by Frankish technique, served only the specialized need for liquid containers, and there is surprisingly little in the way of imported Frankish *biconi*, or local imitations of them, even in cemeteries, such as Lyminge, which show a strongly Frankish character.[1] But, in spite of the total obscurity which veils the political history of Kent between the death of Aesc in 512 and the accession of Æthelberht in 560, there is no reason to suppose that the peace following Mons Badonicus did more harm to the invaders of Kent than to confine them for a generation or two to forced inactivity. It is, however, surprising that, if this were so, it should have produced so abrupt a break in the pottery sequence. In spite of the lack of positive evidence one can only guess that growing economic sophistication, brought about by close continental contacts, had the effect of driving pottery of any kind almost completely out of use.

This explanation is more difficult to accept in some of the regions bordering on Kent which do not appear to have shared its otherwise rich culture. Beyond the Thames, for example, in Essex and Hertfordshire, there is hardly any sixth-century pottery to follow the indications of Saxon occupation in the fifth century, which have already been recorded. I have not been able to detect any continuous ceramic sequence here to link the fifth century to the seventh.[2] It is possible to argue that, as the number of sites is so small and the material from them so scanty, the absence of sixth-century forms and decoration may be merely accidental. But these facts in themselves point an astonishing contrast with the situation in the cremation areas of East Anglia and the Midlands. North of Essex and west of Hertfordshire the situation is still more remarkable. In parts of east Suffolk and over most of Buckinghamshire there is virtually no Anglo-Saxon pottery on record at all until the last quarter of the sixth century.[3] If the ceramic evidence were alone in question the natural

[1] *Arch. Cant.* lxix (1955), 1–40.

[2] An urn from Heybridge and an accessory from Bulmer, both at Colchester, have Anglo-Frisian linear decoration like the Kentish series, perhaps datable around 500. There was also a stamped accessory from Bulmer and stamped fragments from Little Oakley and Mucking. The sherds from Bulmer Tye (*Med. Arch.* iii (1959), 284, Figs. 98 and 99) include a few that could be around 500, but seem mostly later. I know of no other certainly sixth-century pottery from Essex, unless the plain bowl from Plumberrow Mount, Hockley (*Trs. Ess. Arch. Soc.*, N.S. xiii (1913–15), 234, Pl. C), belongs here. A stamped accessory in the Hertford Museum (GR 52/3540) may come from Royston, Herts., but the provenance is dubious: I owe this information to Mr. A. G. Davies, Curator of the Hertford Museum. See additional note p. 118.

[3] This is probably the date of the stamped cremation urn from Winchendon, Bucks., now at Aylesbury, almost the only thing of its kind in the whole county.

conclusion to be drawn would be that these regions remained in British hands, and that at the time of the rally which culminated at Mons Badonicus the native forces based there were strong enough to overwhelm or eject most of the scanty Saxon settlements which had established themselves earlier in Hertfordshire and Essex. If something of this kind actually happened, it would help to explain the failure of Kent ever to establish effective cultural or political influence north of the Thames estuary. During the crucial half-century when such expansion might have taken place, the rulers of Kent may have been contained by superior British forces beyond the line of the river.

In the lower Thames valley west of Kent the position was quite different. Most of the sites which have produced Anglo-Saxon pottery in Surrey show a continuous series through the sixth century, and in at least two places, Mitcham and Ham, on the river close to Richmond, the presence of late fourth-century carinated pedestal bowls indicates occupation as early as anywhere in England. The ill-recorded cremation cemetery at Shepperton on the Middlesex bank produced a fine early *Buckelurne* of Group II,[1] and possibly a *stehende Bogen* urn[2] that could be even earlier. There is fifth-century pottery of Kentish type from Hanwell (Fig. 40). On the Surrey bank almost opposite Shepperton several other pieces, probably not much later than 500, have been found at Walton Bridge. Of the three major cemeteries in Surrey, two, Croydon and Guildown, have produced late *Buckelurnen* of Group V (the Croydon urn is on Fig. 24), and a piece like the accessory from Guildown (Fig. 37), which combines stamped ornament and a facetted carination, supports their evidence for the continuance of fashions of fifth-century type into the succeeding age. There is no reason to suggest that the conflicts culminating at Mons Badonicus had any effect on the Surrey Saxons except possibly to make them drive their roots more firmly into the land they had won.

This would not appear to have been so in Sussex. Here too there are clear signs of early settlement. The two largest cemeteries, at Alfriston and High Down, have produced examples of the fifth-century zoomorphic *Buckelurnen* whose south-eastern distribution has already been noted. There are also carinated bowls, both with and without facetted carination, and pieces with elaborate line-and-dot decoration which, like the hollow-necked bowl from High Down (Fig. 37), have a very Norwegian appearance. Whatever Aelle's origin may

---

[1] Illustrated in *Proc. Soc. Ant.*, 2nd ser. iv (1867–70), 119.

[2] Now in the Brentford Public Library: from an unrecorded site in Middlesex, Shepperton being perhaps the most likely.

have been, all this is in place with the traditional date for his conquest of Sussex between 477 and 491, and such a date is fully borne out by contemporary glasses and metal work from these coastal cemeteries.

But there appears to be no pottery in Sussex to link these early pieces with the late sixth- and seventh-century wares from Hassocks and such sites as Moulscombe, Pagham, Saddlescombe, or Glynde. Panel-style pottery of every kind is wholly absent, and there is no local variant to take its place. It is particularly significant that High Down, a prolific site where continuity might surely be expected, has produced examples of both the early and the late groups of pottery, but apparently nothing whatever in between. It is interesting in this context to recall that after the initial victories of Aelle and his sons, recorded in the Anglo-Saxon Chronicle between 477 and 491 (a record of his importance independently confirmed by Bede, who places him first in the list of Saxon overlords or Bretwaldas),[1] the political affairs of Sussex itself lapse into total obscurity. There is not even, as in most other parts of England, a continuous royal pedigree, and there is no means of knowing what genealogical links, if any, may have joined the obscure *subreguli* of late seventh-century Sussex charters with their illustrious predecessor, the Bretwalda Aelle. The gap in our knowledge begins exactly at the time of Mons Badonicus, and it seems to be a gap not only in literary evidence but also in the sequence of pottery. It is hard to resist the conclusion that the coast of Sussex, like Essex and Hertfordshire, may have been one of the regions which the victory of Mons Badonicus for a while restored to British control.[2]

Southern Hampshire and the Isle of Wight seem however to present yet another story. Apart from a few Anglo-Frisian pieces from the Island, and the recent finds at Portchester,[3] there is no early pottery at all, and in fact very little sign of Saxon settlement of any kind before the beginning of the sixth century. Until recently it would indeed have been impossible, owing to lack of material, to make any contribution from the ceramic angle to the story of Hampshire settlement. But the position has been altered by the excavation of a substantial mixed cemetery at Worthy Park, just north of Winchester, and the discovery of three urns from Fareham that probably came from a similar burial ground.[4]

[1] *Hist. Eccles.* ii. 5.
[2] I have not yet examined the material from Bishopstone, which has been stated to present a continuous series through the pagan period: *Sussex Express*, 13 Dec. 1968.
[3] This includes some early fifth-century pottery from a hut floor: information kindly supplied by Prof. B. Cunliffe.
[4] On the other hand the only pot from Winnal II (Winchester) is an undecorated beaker of seventh-century type: that cemetery evidently belongs to the Christian period.

Most of this material appears to belong to the sixth and early seventh centuries, and, though the quantity is not great, it would seem to constitute an unbroken series from about 500 onwards. It is thus remarkable for starting in the period of British recovery that followed Mons Badonicus, and for falling right across that period and the succeeding phase of renewed Anglo-Saxon expansion. The pottery from over forty cremations at Worthy Park is the most informative group, not only for its quantity but for the fact that, having been excavated in controlled conditions,[1] it has given most interesting information on the chronology of the site. The cremating folk at Worthy Park seem to have succeeded to, and perhaps overlapped with, a different group, the earliest of whose inhumed burials may slightly antedate the beginning of the sixth century. Towards the end of the occupation in the mid seventh, further inhumations took place, some of them disturbing cremations, although that rite was still being practised up to the end. This pagan custom can hardly have survived the establishment of Christianity in nearby Winchester in 648.

This sequence seems to rule out the possibility that the Worthy Park people originated in a controlled settlement concerned with the defence of Roman Winchester. But they could clearly be connected in some way with the traditional activities of Cerdic and his followers as recorded in the Anglo-Saxon Chronicle at the turn of the fifth and sixth centuries.[2] The early inhuming folk, though unfortunately leaving no significant pottery in their graves, appear to have south-eastern associations with Sussex or Kent, and their supersession by the cremating people could be coincident with the collapse of Aelle's Bretwaldaship. The earlier cremation urns, including Anglian globular types, a very decadent undecorated *Buckelurne*, and two examples of the bossed panel-style, suggest associations with Middle Anglia. The fact that cremation was practised on this scale at all in this part of England is most easily understood if an intrusive group arrived for some reason from an area where cremation was normal. In any event their establishment here at this time provides some archaeological support for the movement described in the early West Saxon entries in the Anglo-Saxon Chronicle: it looks as if this really was a corner of England in which the long standstill following Mons Badonicus was more

---

[1] By Mrs. S. C. Hawkes, to whom I am indebted for much information and for the opportunity to examine and comment on the pottery.

[2] Annals concerning Cerdic's operations in southern Hampshire fall in the Chronicle between 495 and 534, some being possibly doublets of others. The detailed chronology is unimportant for the present purpose: there is no reason to doubt that the settlement began here about this period.

honoured in the breach than the observance.[1] But there is no ceramic evidence for any Saxon advance, northwards across the Hampshire uplands or westwards into Wiltshire, before the standstill ended towards the middle of the century.

The valley of the upper Thames from Reading westwards, together with much of the country accessible from its tributaries, all the way from the Kennet to the Ock, had been partly under Saxon control at least since the phase of transition early in the fifth century. There are indications that it received a further influx of Germanic population in the phase of uncontrolled settlement that followed. That is certainly the conclusion to be drawn from the presence of *Buckelurnen* of Groups I–IV at Souldern, Osney, Abingdon, Harwell, and Wallingford, and from the pottery sequence as a whole at such places as Cassington, Frilford, Long Wittenham, or East Shefford. Then, if not earlier, the newcomers must have reached the Gloucestershire borders, as the little accessory with facetted carination from the Fairford cemetery shows (Fig. 37). The distribution of the earlier groups of *Buckelurnen* (Map 4(a)) suggests that the bulk of this invasion took the route from Middle Anglia south-west up the Ouse, and so down the Cherwell to the Thames. But the presence of such pottery also at Croydon (Surrey) and Shepperton (Middlesex) makes it possible that there could have been some movement up the main river as well.

It is interesting to note that, whereas the earliest cruciform and equal-armed brooches follow, as E. T. Leeds pointed out many years ago,[2] the route from Middle Anglia to the upper Thames, another certainly contemporary group of brooches, the earliest saucer brooches with five running scrolls, make a suggestive extension to this pattern. In addition to the same concentration in the upper Thames and a somewhat similar trail following the Cherwell, Ouse, and Nene valleys to Middle Anglia, there is also a substantial group in Sussex, notably at Alfriston and High Down, and others in Surrey, linking with the lower Thames.[3] This distribution covers very much the sort of area, with forces converging from north-east and south on the upper Thames, that might have been loosely comprised in the last quarter of the fifth century under the sway of the Bretwalda Aelle of Sussex. Indeed a combined distribution map of *Buckelurnen* Groups I–IV, the zoomorphic horned urns and other related types

[1] The only gap of any length in the sequence of warlike operations in the early West Saxon annals lies between the conquest of the Isle of Wight in 530 and the battle of Searobyrg in 552: this barely covers the second half of the period of general peace recorded by Gildas.

[2] *Ant. Journ.* xiii (1933), 239–41.

[3] See the distribution map of these brooches in *Surr. Arch. Coll.* lvi (1959), 92, Fig. 10.

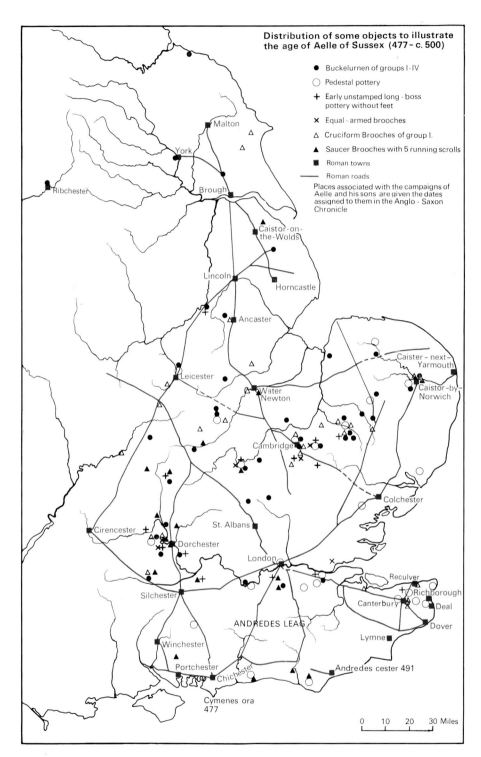

Distribution of some objects to illustrate the age of Aelle of Sussex (477 - c. 500)

- ● Buckelurnen of groups I-IV
- ○ Pedestal pottery
- + Early unstamped long - boss pottery without feet
- × Equal - armed brooches
- △ Cruciform Brooches of group I.
- ▲ Saucer Brooches with 5 running scrolls
- ■ Roman towns
- — Roman roads

Places associated with the campaigns of Aelle and his sons are given the dates assigned to them in the Anglo - Saxon Chronicle

Malton

York

Ribchester

Brough

Caistor-on-the-Wolds

Lincoln

Horncastle

Ancaster

Leicester

Caister - next - Yarmouth

Water Newton

Caistor-by-Norwich

Cambridge

Colchester

St. Albans

Cirencester

Dorchester

London

Silchester

Reculver

Richborough

Canterbury

Deal

ANDREDES LEAG

Dover

Lymne

Winchester

Portchester

Chichester

Andredes cester 491

Cymenes ora 477

0   10   20   30 Miles

MAP 8

of the south-east, the Group I cruciform brooches, the equal-armed brooches, and the saucer brooches with five running scrolls, may give as good a picture of the areas of Anglo-Saxon occupation towards the end of the phase of un-controlled settlement, on the eve of Mons Badonicus, as is ever likely to be obtainable from the material relics of the time (Map 8).

Such a brief empire, if it ever existed, would have fallen to pieces after Mons Badonicus. Is there any hint from the pottery of the time how this may have affected the upper Thames region and the links that had connected it with neighbouring lands? The contrast between the distribution of the latest (Group V) *Buckelurnen* and the earlier forms which must have been going out of fashion about the date of Mons Badonicus may provide one answer. It is remarkable that, whereas these urns continued in use over East and Middle Anglia, to a reduced extent on both sides of the Humber estuary, and, as we have seen, on two sites in Surrey, there are no examples at all in the valley of the upper Thames or those of its tributaries. Something seems to have happened there at the beginning of the sixth century to interrupt the normal development of these late *Buckelurnen*.[1]

This impression is strengthened by a consideration of the shoulder-boss and panel-style wares. It has been noted that the Cambridge region and Middle Anglia generally are the main centre for the development of stamped panel-style pottery, whether of the rectangular or triangular types which arose from the linear shoulder-boss tradition of Anglian and Anglo-Frisian antecedents. The bossed variety of the style, which mainly belongs to the early decades of the sixth century, occurs also, if less freely, in East Anglia, and Lincolnshire, over the watershed in the upper valley of the Warwickshire Avon, and even, as we have seen, in southern Hampshire. But it is hardly found at all in a normal form in the upper Thames region,[2] although the later unbossed variety with stamped pendent triangles, characteristic of the second half of the century, is exceedingly common there.[3] Once again there seems to be some sort of dislocation in the upper Thames sequence, though not perhaps in this case a complete interruption, if it is correct to think of the long-boss style as here

[1] Maps 4 (a) and (b) point this instructive contrast. It will not escape notice that it is closely matched by the contrast between the distribution, in these parts, of Group I and Group II cruciform brooches. While both types occur equally in Middle Anglia, Group I alone is represented south-west of Bedfordshire.

[2] Or indeed in Bedfordshire, which in this respect presents an unusual contrast to neighbouring Northamptonshire, which has at least eleven examples from seven separate sites.

[3] Of these Bedfordshire can show seven examples from three sites; Oxfordshire four examples from three sites (one on the Bucks. border in the Vale of Aylesbury); Berkshire eight examples from six sites.

taking the place of normal shoulder-boss pottery in the early sixth century. As has been noted already, this long-boss style, which has its main continental parallels in the Low Countries and the Rhineland, is found in some quantity, both in larger sizes and as small accessories, in the Thames valley cemeteries.[1] There is unfortunately little direct evidence for dating these vessels except on typological grounds and from their continental parallels.

In the valley of the Warwickshire Avon the earlier history is, on the pottery evidence, quite different from that of the upper Thames. In the Avon cemeteries, in spite of the presence of some bits of early metal work, there is scarcely any certainly fifth-century pottery.[2] But from about 500 the sequence of bossed panel-style through to unbossed pendent triangles is unusually well represented, and it is evident that, once the settlers had pushed across the watershed from Northamptonshire and Leicestershire about the beginning of the sixth century, they remained to develop, undisturbed in our period, the communities that cremated their dead in such cemeteries as Baginton, Stratford, and Bidford-on-Avon. The situation is in fact curiously similar to that revealed at Worthy Park in southern Hampshire.

After the middle of the sixth century the extension and consolidation of Anglo-Saxon power everywhere proceeded apace. This is the period in which many of the historic kingdoms of the heptarchy began to take recognizable shape. Bernicia, Deira, and Lindsey are being formed from the old Humbrensian block. East Anglia, Essex, and Kent, the last soon to emerge from its obscurity into the long and epoch-making reign of Aethelberht (560–616), are all consolidating or establishing their positions in the eastern counties. Sussex never regained the ascendancy that had made Aelle notable as the first Bretwalda, but that may have been largely because, to the west and north, there was springing up, under the energetic rule of Ceawlin, another mushroom empire which, however transitory its glory and however disastrous its immediate outcome, left a permanent legacy in the historic kingdom of Wessex.

The entries in the Anglo-Saxon Chronicle relating to Ceawlin fall between 556, when he first appears in partnership with Cynric at the battle of Beranbyrg (Barbury Castle on the Wiltshire Downs, south of Swindon), and 593, when his death is reported after a disastrous encounter at Wodnesbeorg on the Wansdyke north of the vale of Pewsey in the previous year. Between these dates he

---

[1] Figs. 38 and 39 and Map 6(b).

[2] The Group IV *Buckelurne* from Long Itchington is a possible exception. Otherwise the earliest

would seem to be the linear shoulder-boss urns from Baginton (Coventry Museum A/1014/6 and 34), both perhaps around 500.

and chieftains certainly related to him are recorded as defeating Aethelberht of Kent in 568 (a victory which probably carried with it an absorption of the Surrey Saxons), consolidating their hold on the upper Thames valley and the vale of Aylesbury in 571, capturing Gloucester, Cirencester, and Bath in 577, and striking up into north Oxfordshire or Warwickshire in 584.

This is not the occasion to discuss in detail the political significance of these terse and telegraphic notices of Ceawlin's career,[1] which are clearly intended as an *aide-mémoire* recalling the most dramatic incidents in a well-known and well-loved saga. But it is relevant to our purpose to note that his reign covers precisely the period in which the later phases of the panel-style, and particularly the unbossed variety with stamped pendent triangles, is the most characteristic ceramic fashion. The distribution of these wares is shown on Map 9. It cannot be claimed that the fashion originated in Ceawlin's own West Saxon territory, for the centre of its distribution pattern seems rather to lie in west Norfolk and west Suffolk, where its most notable practitioners, the Illington/Lackford potters, were based (Map 10). But it is found freely in almost every part of southern England known to have been the scene of his military activities.[2] It appears, as has been noted, at Worthy Park and Fareham in southern Hampshire, traditionally the first homeland of the West Saxon royal family. It becomes extremely popular in the Berkshire and Oxfordshire settlements in the upper Thames country from Reading, Theale, and East Shefford in the south and east to Souldern in the north and Frilford in the west. It spreads into the vale of Aylesbury, where examples come from Kingsey on the borders of Buckinghamshire, and further east in Bedfordshire at Dunstable, Kempston, and Moggerhanger. Other examples are on record from Hampnett in Gloucestershire,[3] from several sites in Northamptonshire, and, as has been noted, in the valley of the Warwickshire Avon. These areas seem almost tailor-made to fit the consequences of the recorded campaigns of 571, 577, and 584.

[1] See my 'Wansdyke and the Origin of Wessex' in *Essays in British History*, ed. H. R. Trevor-Roper, (1964), 1–28, for an attempt to assess some of the possibilities.

[2] The style is also found freely in areas such as east Norfolk, east Suffolk, and Lincolnshire, outside the known sphere of Ceawlin's direct influence. But Bede, by describing him as a ruler 'qui . . . cunctis australibus . . . provinciis quae Humbrae fluvio et contiguis ei terminis sequestrantur a borealibus, imperavit', implies that, like the other kings on the so-called Bretwalda list (*Hist. Eccles.* ii. 5), Ceawlin exerted authority over a much wider area than is suggested by the battles recorded in the Anglo-Saxon Chronicle.

[3] The Saxon warrior whose grave was cut through the Orpheus mosaic pavement at Barton, Cirencester, had with him a small stamped accessory (now in the Corinium Museum, Cirencester) quite appropriate in period to the campaign of 577, which was followed by Ceawlin's capture of Gloucester, Cirencester, and Bath.

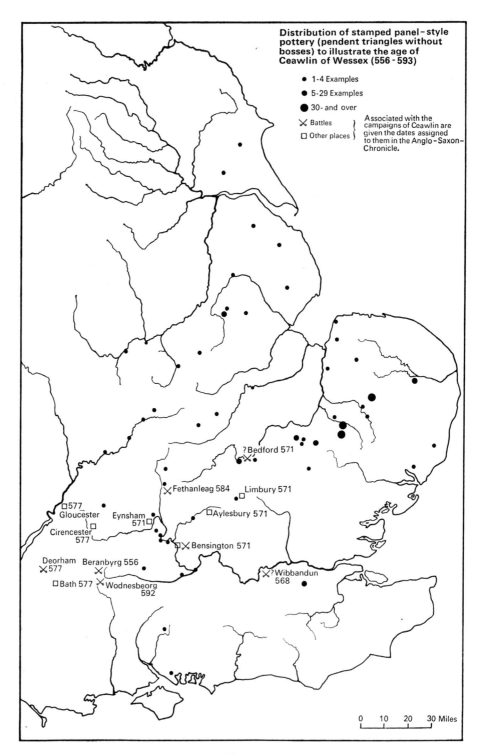

Distribution of stamped panel–style pottery (pendent triangles without bosses) to illustrate the age of Ceawlin of Wessex (556 - 593)

- • 1-4 Examples
- ● 5-29 Examples
- ⬤ 30- and over
- ✕ Battles
- □ Other places

Associated with the campaigns of Ceawlin are given the dates assigned to them in the Anglo–Saxon–Chronicle.

?Bedford 571

Fethanleag 584   Limbury 571

□577
Gloucester   Eynsham   □Aylesbury 571
            571□
Cirencester
577

Deorham   Beranbyrg 556
✕577
            ✕Bensington 571

            ✕?Wibbandun
                568

□Bath 577 ✕Wodnesbeorg
            592

0   10   20   30 Miles

Map 9

This is certainly as far as it is reasonable to go at present in seeking ceramic clues to the political confusion of the sixth century. Cautious heads may well exclaim that it is already going much too far. But it is sometimes worth while for a historian deliberately to press a new line of inquiry beyond the point of proof, to suggest ways in which old material may perhaps serve new purposes, and to leave to the future rather than to the present the judgement between a searchlight and a will-o'-the-wisp. It is time in any case to pass from what the pottery may, or may not, reveal of the complex course of political events, to the light which it can certainly throw on the social and economic arrangements of the folk who made and used it. These matters will engage our attention in the next and final chapter.

Additional Note to Chapter VII

p. 110.   The small stamped accessory recently published from Grave 102 at Mucking, Essex, is conveniently dated by the sixth-century square-headed brooches found with it: *Ant. Journ.* xlviii (1968), 210–30 and Fig. 4 a–c.

The important cemetery at Great Chesterford, Essex, not yet published, includes both fifth-century and late sixth-century graves, and may have a continuous intervening series. But it belongs geographically rather to the Cambridgeshire than to the Essex settlement area, and thus has little relevance to the situation in Essex. I am indebted to Miss V. I. Evison for information on this cemetery, and for permission to refer to the pottery before its publication.

VIII

SOCIAL AND ECONOMIC ASPECTS
OF THE SETTLEMENT

THERE are a great many ways in which the pottery of any primitive people can be expected to throw light on their habits and customs, their religious beliefs and artistic sensibilities, their economic conditions and their social arrangements. The strength of the light will obviously vary with the special circumstances applicable in each case. If there has been in the past a comparative neglect of this source of information on the Anglo-Saxon settlement of England, that has been mainly due to the peculiar conditions of the settlement itself. Such factors as the confusion in the Germanic world of the Continent before the movement took place, the disturbances caused to the social ties of tribal and family life by the very fact of an overseas migration, the varying types of burial rite which affect the quantity and availability of pottery in different parts of the country, and the general dearth of material from occupation debris, as distinct from cemeteries, must all severely restrict our understanding of everyday conditions, and limit our knowledge of the material equipment available to households of different social and economic standing. There has also been until lately the special difficulty involved in determining whether much of the pottery itself was made in the confused years at the beginning of the period or the more stable conditions of the later years of settlement. Yet in spite of all these difficulties, and the limitations which they necessarily impose, it should be possible to extract some information of interest on these aspects of pagan Anglo-Saxon life from the very considerable quantity of their pottery which has survived and is available for study. The subject is a very wide one, but it is still in its infancy. It can only be treated here in a superficial and preliminary manner, the aim being rather to indicate some possible lines of profitable inquiry than to attempt a definitive treatment, for which the time indeed has not yet come.

Since, as we have seen, the great mass of this material comes from cemeteries, it may be as well to say something first of all about the disposition of cemetery sites and the way they were arranged.[1] The relationship which many of the larger cremation cemeteries bear to Roman walled towns and the lines of communication between them has already been mentioned. These relationships were primarily determined by political rather than social or economic considerations, and no more need be said about that aspect of the matter. But it may be noted that, while it is very uncommon indeed to find Anglo-Saxon, any more than Roman, burials inside a town's walls, there are a good many cases where cemeteries are set on sites previously occupied by Roman buildings, whether in the immediate suburbs of towns as at Caistor-by-Norwich, a mile or two away from a town as at Girton, or right out in the countryside as at Lackford. In such cases it is not always clear whether the choice was deliberate or accidental, whether the Roman site had been recently inhabited, or was perhaps long deserted, when the burials began. But there are instances, of which Lackford is probably one, and several in the Thames valley, such as Frilford and Long Wittenham, are others, where an earlier Roman cemetery, perhaps centred on a local shrine of some kind, was itself the focus of pagan Saxon burials, sometimes on an extensive scale. In these cases some deliberate continuity, at least of association, perhaps sometimes of cult also, seems to be implied. At Frilford, for example, the Saxon burials appear to have been continuous with those of a Roman cemetery whose site was determined by a succession of ritual buildings beginning as far back as the pre-Roman Iron Age.[2]

The pagan Anglo-Saxons certainly showed themselves sensitive to the religious associations of a site even when it had long ceased to sustain an active cult. This had been true in their continental homes, where many of the great cemeteries such as the Galgenberg-bei-Cuxhaven, or Westerwanna itself, had been centred on prehistoric burial mounds of Neolithic or Bronze Age date. Many examples of this practice could be quoted in this country, of which Kirton Lindsey and Loveden Hill in Lincolnshire are typical. Abingdon is an interesting case, for there the cemetery, which lies on Thames flood-plain gravel,

---

[1] The best general account of the cemeteries is still that of G. Baldwin Brown (*The Arts in Early England* iii (1915), 114–91), and I have not thought it necessary to go into many matters that are fully discussed by him.

[2] *Oxoniensia* iv (1939), 1–70. Rather more instances are now known of individual Saxon objects being found in Roman villas, but in very few cases are these certainly associated with burials. A notable case is at Denton (Lincs.) where a Saxon warrior was buried centrally in a principal room of a villa, the ruins of which were evidently regarded as an appropriate funeral monument for him. It is possible that such occurrences may have been due to the real or imaginary association of the Roman buildings with religious cults. This seems, e.g., the most likely explanation of the use of the detached bath house at Furfooz, Belgium, as a burial place for Germanic *laeti*, for such detached bath houses are best understood as healing centres associated with sacred springs in Roman times. J. A. E. Nenquin, *La Nécropole de Furfooz* (1953).

overlies one of the Bronze Age concentric ring-ditches, so common in that subsoil, which may well have been as little noticeable superficially in the fifth century as it is now. Its significance indeed only came to light in the course of excavating the cemetery.[1] Here the juxtaposition might have been accidental, but the excavators thought not. In any case, one cannot help suspecting that the Anglo-Saxons, with their very keen nose for niceties of soil and contour, were probably as quick to note the significance of a crop-mark ring-ditch as any modern archaeologist. As so many later charter boundaries remind us, they were very ready to recognize as 'heathen burials' any apparent instances of human interference with the natural terrain that attracted their attention in the countryside.

The arrangement of burials within a cemetery frequently appears chaotic. There is not even the same general adherence to broad conventions of orientation, whether north–south or west–east, that often prove helpful to excavators of continental cemeteries of this age in distinguishing the relative date of several groups of inhumations. Some inhumation cemeteries, it is true, show a general inclination to one direction or another,[2] but variations from the norm are frequently so wide and numerous as to defy rational explanation. Presumably this is one consequence of the conditions in which the main migration to Britain took place after the middle of the fifth century, folk of different funerary practices being from that time so jumbled together that rigid adherence to hereditary custom in the new conditions may have seemed difficult to sustain or even to justify. It is not until the seventh century, when the growing influence of Christian practice permeated all levels of the population, that anything approaching a systematic adoption of west–east orientation, and a regular layout of the graves in the manner of the Merovingian *Reihengräber*, is found in the English cemeteries.[3]

[1] *Abingdon*, 9–10. Of the eight typologically earliest cremation urns, one (C 17) was inside the outer ring-ditch on the south-west side, as was also B 106, the inhumation with a *tutulus* brooch; three (C 5, C 38, C 64) were among the only six cremations found in the fill of the outer ditch itself, two being on the south-west and one on the north-west; one (C 22) was close outside it to the west; and the remaining three (C 67, C 74, C 76, all *stehende Bogen* urns) were further away to the south-west. Of the two inhumations with early accessories, one (B 111) was also in this latter area. The cemetery evidently began both inside and to the south-west of the outer ring-ditch; a fact which only becomes apparent from a typological analysis of the pottery.

[2] At Abingdon, for example, there was a strong preference from the start for west–east orientation. Worthy Park is a good instance of a completely chaotic arrangement, resulting in many disturbed, overlapping, and superimposed burials.

[3] This new type of Christian cemetery is discussed, in relation to those at Leighton Buzzard, by Miranda Hyslop in *Arch. Journ.* cxx (1963), 189–94. The date of the type is further discussed by Mrs. Hawkes, in connection with the Winnall II cemetery, in *Med. Arch.* xii, forthcoming.

This same lack of regularity and order seems generally to have prevailed in the mixed cemeteries where both cremation and inhumation burials were made in pagan times. That the two rites were often practised concurrently is evident from the many known instances of inhumations disturbing earlier cremations, and of cremations overlying earlier inhumations in the same cemetery. Nor, so far as the use of pottery was concerned, does there seem to have been any ceremonial objection to vessels from the same workshop being used for both rites. Two of the Girton potters, for example, certainly made both urns for cremation and small accessory vessels for use with inhumations, and ornamented them all alike with the same tools.[1] This fact, which, to the best of my knowledge, has not been stressed before, is the more remarkable because adherents of the two rites must have held somewhat different views on the nature of life after death, and must also have practised widely divergent funeral rituals. This is implied not only by the physical difference in the treatment accorded to the bodies, but by the different range of grave-goods interred with the remains. In both cases of course the dead were disposed of in their clothes, so that their usual ornaments and dress-fittings, brooches, beads, belt-buckles, and the like, were buried or burnt with them. But whereas weapons, spear, shield, and an occasional sword for men of noble rank, are found with male inhumations, such things are hardly ever found with cremations. On the other hand it was a common practice to place unburnt manicure sets—combs, tweezers, small shears, and so on—with the ashes in cremation urns, although such objects seldom, if ever, accompany unburnt bodies. Evidently the two rites carried with them quite different beliefs on the nature of the equipment that might be found useful to take with one on the journey to the next world. It is interesting to conjecture, but impossible to determine, what effect these differences of belief and ritual may have had on the social relations between families using the same cemetery, and so presumably belonging to the same community. Were mixed marriages between them tolerated, for example, and, if so, did the next generation follow paternal or maternal custom in these vital matters? Conditions in the mixed cemeteries suggest that such questions, aggravated by the confusion of the settlement, must have contributed to the uncertain and even agnostic attitude towards pagan beliefs, as recorded by Bede,[2]

---

[1] Examples of their work in both forms are illustrated in *Antiquity* xi (1937), 397, Fig. 9.

[2] The discussion at the court of Edwin of Northumbria which preceded the rejection of paganism (*Hist. Eccles.* ii. 13) turned largely on the general desire for certainty about the nature of life after death.

which made the ultimate adoption of Christianity both so rapid and so painless.

These considerations may seem to take us rather far away from the detailed study of the pottery which is our primary concern. It is, however, important not to neglect any sources of information which can throw light on the social conditions in which pottery was produced, and the relation between cremation and inhumation in the mixed cemeteries is certainly relevant to this matter. It is, for example, very unusual to find any part of the mixed cemeteries reserved for burials exclusively by one rite or the other. Here and there, it is true, there may be some partial segregation of this kind, as at Abingdon, where an area immediately to the west of the Bronze Age ring-ditch is occupied mainly by cremations.[1] Where this occurs, it may, of course, be due not so much to a conscious policy of segregation as to the lapse of time, an original group of early cremations being deliberately avoided by those making subsequent inhumations, or vice versa. But normally burials by the two rites seem to occur indiscriminately over the same ground in these mixed cemeteries, with as little apparent arrangement among the cremations as there is among the inhumations. In a few cases earlier excavators have claimed to find cremation urns set out regularly in rows, but in some of these instances the plans of later excavators in other parts of the same cemeteries have suggested that these orderly arrangements are more apparent than real.[2] It is at any rate clear that in most places individual graves were not marked, or at least were not marked in such a way that their positions remained permanently obvious. If they had been so marked there would not have been so many cases, as occur in almost all cemeteries, of earlier graves being disturbed by later burials, sometimes on several occasions.

What is occasionally observable in cremation cemeteries is a tendency for urns to be deposited in more or less tightly packed groups. Some of these are doubtless fortuitous, being produced by the chance deposit of a number of single urns at different times in close proximity to one another. But other groups of this kind are certainly deliberate, as, for example, where several urns set close together are surrounded by a single rough barrier of stones, or flints, or Roman tiles;[3] or where an urn may have one or more other urns set on its

[1] These however do not include the earliest group: see p. 122, fn. 1 above.
[2] This is the case at Sancton and at Newark: see T. Sheppard in *Hull Mus. Publns.* lxvi (1909), 51 and 68.
[3] As, e.g., with the Y 9 group at Caistor-by-Norwich, which consisted of at least five urns surrounded by large flints and a Roman tile. It had itself apparently disturbed one or two earlier urns.

shoulders in a way that makes it reasonably certain that they were all buried at the same time.[1] Instances of this kind are of course especially valuable for the evidence they provide for the contemporaneity of the pots.

It is of course possible that some groups of urns buried in close proximity to one another are not simultaneous burials, but successive interments in an area set apart for the use of a single family, or a chieftain and his household. Very little has so far been done to explore this possibility by examining the evidence of the urns themselves or their contents. In the nature of the case it would be very difficult to be certain that any groups of urns not buried simultaneously owed their proximity to one another to such a cause, but it would clearly be a more probable explanation in cases where the urns concerned were themselves similar in character or appeared to be the products of one workshop.[2] At Brighthampton, for example, two of the unusual pots with stamped long-boss decoration and a peculiarly distinctive omphaloid base (Fig. 38)—obviously made by the same hand—were found in the graves of a man and woman buried 'in close proximity' to one another.[3] This is a line of inquiry which would certainly repay more detailed investigation.

It is at this point that the questions naturally arise, who made this pottery, and what do we imply by asserting that two or more vessels are obviously the products of a single hand, a single workshop, or related workshops? In most primitive societies the making of domestic pottery is women's work, and, in so far as each household may be presumed to have supplied its own needs for the usual sets of undecorated pots and pans, the products of such a domestic industry will rarely be sufficiently distinctive for the work of individual hands to be recognizable. Nor will the output of any one housewife extend far beyond her own immediate surroundings, or be so substantial that many examples

[1] The N 17 group at Caistor-by-Norwich was of this kind. The main urn, containing adult bones, had N 16, containing a child cremation, and the lower part of another urn, containing adult bones, set on its shoulder. This could well represent a simultaneous family burial of man, woman, and child, victims perhaps of an accident, an epidemic, or a blood-feud.

[2] A group like that comprising Sancton 129–31, 139, 140, 144–5, set close together but certainly not all contemporary, could be so interpreted. Of this group of seven, the earliest (129) is a very large shouldered urn, with broken down *stehende Bogen* ornament, and the remainder are un-

decorated, but one (139) contained a large comb of early type, and one (144) the crescentic foot of a small-long or hybrid cruciform brooch, probably of the type of that from Feering, Essex, (N. Åberg, *The Anglo-Saxons in England* (1926), 58, Fig. 94) of the early sixth century. One or two of the others could well be still later in date. Another such group is that comprising Illington 68–71 which includes pieces both early and late in the pagan period.

[3] J. Y. Akerman, *Second Report of Researches . . . at Brighthampton* (1859), Graves 24 and 27 (reprinted from *Arch.* xxxviii). This is clearly a case of contemporary or near-contemporary burial.

could be expected to survive. It is probable that most of the domestic un-decorated wares, both from settlement debris and from the poorer interments in our cemeteries, were produced in such do-it-yourself conditions. Although here and there a group of such pots in one place may appear—as, for example, do some of those from Ruskington (Lincs.)[1]—so like one another in form and fabric as to justify the suspicion that they may have been made by one hand, there is no reason to regard them as the products of a professional potter, let alone a commercial industry.

But the position does seem to be different in the case of much of the decorated pottery. Not only does the mere fact of decoration imply a conscious intention to produce an attractive effect, however simple and rudimentary it may be, but there is the possibility of striking a personal and individual note in the use of even a limited number of easily made tools, and within a restricted range of possible designs. In the material from even the smallest cemeteries it is generally easy to find at least one pair of pots that, by applying the simplest criteria, such as the use of identical stamps and individual tricks in the handling and spacing of linear ornament, can be demonstrated as the work of one potter.[2] The larger cemeteries can mostly show a number of such pairs of pots that are clearly the work of one hand.[3]

Even these cases, however, are probably still examples of a purely domestic industry, each family producing within its own circle what pottery is required, whether for household needs, or for more special occasions such as a funeral, but rarely if ever allowing its products to find their way, by gift or sale, into a wider circle. Where, as often happens with these single pairs, they are found not merely in the same cemetery, but close together in one part of it, the case for thinking that only a domestic industry, based on the unit of single house-holds, is involved, is of course the strongest.

To pass beyond this stage it is necessary, I think, to demonstrate either that the pots themselves show a specially professional touch (and this is bound to involve subjective considerations that are hardly susceptible to proof) or that they occur in cemeteries some distance apart. A group of four or five or more pots from one cemetery that are linked in this way may still indicate only a domestic industry, for some domestic potters may have catered for large house-holds or may have produced pots of one pattern for some time. A number of

---

[1] *Arch. Journ.* cviii (1952), 90, Fig. 10. 4–9.

[2] e.g. the cases noted by me from North Luffenham (Rutland), Brighthampton (Oxon.), East Shefford (Berks.), in *Antiquity* xi (1937), 392, Pls. I and III: or Brundall (Norfolk) in *Norf. Arch.* xxvii. 191, Figs. 1, 3, and 4.

[3] One of the few possible exceptions is South Elkington (Lincs.): see *Arch. Journ.* cviii (1952), 63.

the potters whose work has been recognized at Girton,[1] Caistor-by-Norwich,[2] or Sancton[3] are in this category.

Now all these craftsmen[4] seem to have worked only for one cemetery. In the present state of our knowledge, therefore, it is probably safest to treat them as prolific examples of domestic production. But it may well be that several of them, especially those whose work shows the undefinable quality of a certain professional finish, were in business in a small way, disposing of their surplus wares among friends and neighbours who admired their style but lacked the industry or expertise to imitate them.[5] Then as now, there was no hard and fast line to be drawn between the activities of a craftsman working primarily to meet the needs of his own household, and one who found it both pleasant and profitable to cater for his neighbours' requirements as well as his own. In the handiwork of these Anglo-Saxon potters of the sixth century it is thus possible to recognize the early stages of a specialized industry, growing out of a more primitive domestic economy.

With the appearance of workshops whose products are found in several places we come much nearer to the world of manufacture for a wider market than that of friends and neighbours. Already in 1937 I was aware of some links of this kind between the cemeteries of the Cambridge region, and I published examples of the work of the same potters occurring both at Girton and Newnham, and at Girton and St. John's.[6] These three cemeteries are not more than a few miles apart, and the folk who used them, as I have suggested earlier, may have had a similar origin in the last days of Roman or sub-Roman Britain.[7] Doubtless they were well acquainted with one another as established neighbours in the sixth century when these pots were made, and the links which they imply could well be of a personal nature—gifts, the outcome of marriage ties and the

[1] e.g. the three potters, some of whose work is shown in *Antiquity* xi (1937), 397, Fig. 9 and Pl. II.

[2] e.g. Potter I, who made elaborately stamped and bossed urns, parts of ten of which survive: Potter II, who favoured unbossed panel-style urns, of which at least seven are known: or Potter IV, of whose work we have at least six urns showing bossed panel-style designs with a horizontal treatment of the panels.

[3] e.g. the potter, five of whose products are on Fig. 42.

[4] A possible exception is Potter I at Caistor-by-Norwich, a very professional-looking performer, to whose rather elaborate work there are some suggestive, if not wholly convincing, parallels at one or two cemeteries in Leicestershire and Northamptonshire. Thurmaston 62, in particular, could well have come from this workshop.

[5] The Girton potter, five examples of whose work I discussed and illustrated in *Antiquity* xi (1937), 392–3, and Fig. 6, is a case in point. Whereas in 1937 the work of this potter was only known at Girton, further specimens have since been recognized both at the Barrington A cemetery and at St. John's.

[6] *Antiquity* xi (1937), 395–7, Figs. 8 and 9.

[7] pp. 74–7.

like. On the other hand they may imply the existence of a specialized trade serving customers in more than one place. Perhaps already there was a central market of some kind in Cambridge itself where household goods from the surrounding villages could be exchanged. If so it must have operated on a system of barter, for there was no Anglo-Saxon coinage in the sixth century.[1]

But there are some links of this kind that take us much further afield. The cemeteries of Northamptonshire, like those around Cambridge, have several local potters whose work can be recognized not only at one but at several sites. The focus of this activity in the sixth century seems to lie at Kettering, where the products of several potters, including one with a distinctive style, involving the use of long bosses running up through horizontal stamped decoration on the neck, are conspicuous.[2] Another Kettering potter's work is also found at Barton Seagrave,[3] and there are further connections between both these cemeteries and those of Islip and Newton-in-the-Willows. But more interesting is the evidence for contact between the Northamptonshire and Cambridge groups. Thus two potters who worked for Girton seem to have left specimens of their handiwork also at Little Weldon and at Newton-in-the-Willows.[4] Yet another who made a fine stamped *Buckelurne* for Girton used the same three stamps (of which one is very unusual) on an urn of quite different and much simpler character at Kettering. But even more remarkable is the long-distance link between two late stamped *Buckelurnen*, one from Lackford in west Suffolk and the other from Thurmaston, north of Leicester, shown on Fig. 45. These two elaborately decorated vessels, one of which has diagonal zoomorphic bosses with stamps for eyes, share three identical stamps, two of which, the large, slightly whirling rosette, and the little 'ladybird', are most unusual and distinctive. Lackford and Thurmaston are fully eighty miles apart, not counting the need for a wide detour around the Fens, and no other urns by this highly original potter are known in the country between them.[5]

---

[1] It has been suggested that the small bronze coins of the later Empire, of which great quantities must still have been around on Roman sites, may have served the Anglo-Saxons as a token currency at this time. But I know of no proof that they were so used.

[2] Fig. 43, and Pl. 7.   [3] Fig. 44, top row.

[4] Fig. 44, middle and bottom rows. The Girton/Little Weldon potter was probably responsible also for one of the Kettering urns (Northampton D 327/54-5). The combination of concentric circle stamps with simple biconical designs of this character is found at a number of other cemeteries, such as Castle Acre and Dersingham, Norfolk (*Norf. Arch.* xxvii. 184, Pls. 3. 1 and 12. 2), Loveden Hill (58/137, with a Group II cruciform brooch), and Lackford (50. 148). But none of these urns, though very similar in treatment, can be safely attributed to this potter.

[5] There is a possibility that one or two urns in Lincolnshire may be attributable to this potter, which, if it could be proved, would extend the distribution still further. But I have not yet been able to establish the certain identity of their stamps.

It will be seen that most of these instances of the wide distribution of a potter's work belong to the sixth century when stamped decoration was most popular, and it is therefore possible to rely on the use of identical stamps to prove the common origin of several pots. It might also be supposed that the development of the industry from the domestic to the commercial stage, which some of these instances imply, would require some period of time, perhaps a generation or two after the main migration into Britain had taken place. There is no doubt some truth in this, and most of the instances probably date later rather than earlier in the sixth century.[1] But there are more cases than have been generally recognized of two or more fifth-century pots sufficiently individual in style to make attribution to a single workshop fairly certain. Most of these groups appear on a single site only[2] and may therefore belong to the phase of domestic manufacture. But there is at least one case where this is not so. It concerns a Sancton potter, of whose existence I was already aware in 1937, when I drew attention to the presence there of three fifth-century *Buckelurnen*, all, as I then put it, 'clearly the work of one rather original hand'.[3] One was in the Ashmolean Museum at Oxford,[4] the other two at Hull,[5] and one of the latter was so badly restored that it was difficult at first to appreciate its likeness to the others. The common features shared by these vessels are their sharply biconical form emphasized by long slashed bosses on the upper part, the panels between which contain three circular bosses and a variety of freehand designs including S-shaped serpents, swastikas, and *stehende Bogen* motifs, all carried out in light tooling. Since then, at least three others have turned up in the post-war excavations at Sancton, and, more interesting still, a seventh product of this workshop is South Elkington 110, from a site some forty-six miles away across the Humber estuary on the Lincolnshire Wolds.[6] A neater link between the two main groups of the *Humbrenses*, as seventh-century writers still called the folk settled on both sides of the great river,[7] it would be hard to imagine.

It would be going too far to argue from this one case that there was a big business in *Buckelurnen* among all these Humbrensian peoples in the fifth

[1] But not the Lackford/Thurmaston potter of Fig. 45, who must surely have made these elaborately stamped *Buckelurnen* before 550.

[2] e.g. the large early bowls of Plettke's Type C from Caistor-by-Norwich (M1, N56): but these could possibly be imports.

[3] *Antiquity* xi (1937), 394–6.

[4] *Arch.* xlv (1880), Pl. XXXIII. 1.

[5] One is illustrated in *Hull Mus. Publns.* lxvi and lxvii (1909), 59–61 and Pl. VIII. 18.

[6] Six of these urns are on Fig. 46. The South Elkington piece, which is less elaborate than most of the others, has also been illustrated in *Arch. Journ.* cviii (1952), 52, Fig. 14.

[7] See my article on 'The Teutonic Settlement of Northern England' in *History* xx (1935), 250–62.

century, but the circumstances are sufficiently suggestive to justify a special watch for ceramic connections between the Yorkshire and Lincolnshire cemeteries. Other links of the kind can certainly be found. On Fig. 47, for example, are three urns from Heworth and Sancton (Yorks.) and West Keal (Lincs.), all decorated in the same way and showing a similar, if not identical, stamp. If they are not from a single workshop, one can only say that three Humbrensian minds, two in Yorkshire and one in Lincolnshire, had a strangely similar thought.

It may be asked at this point whether there are any instances of the same potter having worked both in England and on the Continent, or of the products of the same workshop being found on both sides of the North Sea. The second possibility is clearly the more likely, and it is indeed probable that some of the corrugated Anglian pottery from Caistor-by-Norwich may have come from the same sources as those which supplied the cemeteries of Schleswig and Fünen. Some of these Caistor vessels are in fact almost exact doublets of continental Angle pieces, but the lack of specific decorative features, other than the rather mechanical corrugation, makes it impossible to claim a common origin in the same workshops.[1] There is, however, one rather elaborately ornamented pot whose decoration, though unfortunately fragmentary, is sufficiently distinctive to link it, with some plausibility, to a continental workshop at least two of whose urns are known from the cemeteries of Hammoor and Sørup, the latter site being in the heart of Angeln itself.[2]

An even more remarkable case concerns the potter of an elaborate Group I *Buckelurne* from the Saxon cemetery of Wehden-bei-Lehe, north-east of Bremerhaven at the mouth of the Weser.[3] This piece has the very unusual, indeed all but unparalleled, feature of being decorated with well-modelled plastic representations of a human face, set between diagonally slashed vertical bosses on the upper part of the pot. When sorting through the large quantity of potsherds in the Norwich Castle Museum that derived from disturbed cremations at Markshall, close to Caistor-by-Norwich, I came across two pieces of a large *Buckelurne* with unusual decoration that reminded me of this

---

[1] The point might be settled by analysing the composition of the clay. But see p. 136.

[2] Caistor B 2. The Hammoor urn, also incomplete, is 164: Genrich (1954) Tafel 50. 5. I owe knowledge of the Sørup piece to the kindness of Dr. D. K. Raddatz. The special features shared by these three urns, apart from their shape and general design, are the similar 'two-decker' corrugation on the upper part, horizontal and vertical strips being laid over continuous horizontal corrugation, and the fact that the numerous shoulder-bosses are alternately plain and feathered. The Caistor piece, being a size smaller than the other two, has no circular bosses in the upper panels.

[3] *Wehden*, Tafel 23. 58.

Wehden urn. A further search revealed a third piece which, in conjunction with the other two, comprised the greater part of a face treated in almost exactly similar fashion to those on the Wehden urn.[1] It was moreover from a pot of similar design, since enough was preserved of the adjacent decoration to make the general arrangement certain. There can be no doubt whatever that the Markshall urn was made by the same hand that formed that from Wehden, for the resemblance between them is too close to permit any other conclusion. It is of course impossible to say whether the English piece was brought over from Germany, or the German piece from England, or whether the craftsman made one for Wehden before joining the migration to England, and the other for Markshall after settling in Norfolk. Some differences of detail might suggest that the Markshall piece, being slightly more elaborate, is the later. It is however worth noting that both this Saxon link between Wehden and Markshall, and the Angle link between Hammoor/Sørup and Caistor, concern pots of early *Buckelurne* type which belong to the period of uncontrolled settlement in the second half of the fifth century. Since Caistor and Markshall are no more than a mile apart they afford the strongest possible proof that folk both from Angle Schleswig and from the Saxon communities on the lower Weser were arriving side by side in these years on this part of the Norfolk coast.

Such early links are of the greatest rarity. It remains to go forward a hundred years and consider the two most interesting workshops that produced stamped pottery in East and Middle Anglia in the second half of the sixth century. The first is the Animal Stamp workshop whose products are known from Caistor, and possibly from Markshall in east Norfolk,[2] on one side, and from Lackford in west Suffolk on the other. This is a case where it is wiser to speak of a workshop than of a potter, for, although all the pots concerned share so many unusual and distinctive features as to make them immediately recognizable, and their common origin obvious, the stamps used on them are similar rather

---

[1] Markshall LXX. The nose is still missing. On both pots the faces are modelled as circular bosses surrounded by two lines, the hair is indicated by vertical or diagonal lines separated by one (Wehden) and two (Markshall) horizontal lines from the face, the mouth is drawn by one (Wehden) and two (Markshall) curved lines drooping at the corners, and there is in each case a dimple on the chin. The eyes, simple finger-tips at Wehden, are given an internal circle for the pupil at Markshall. On the Wehden urn there are two small circular bosses with nipples, suggesting breasts, below the face, so that the figure is evidently intended to be female: this part of the Markshall pot is unfortunately not preserved.

[2] The sherds with animal stamps from Markshall XI and XCI unfortunately show too little of the decorative scheme to make it certain whether they belong to this workshop or to urns of the type of Caistor N83 and Lackford 48, 248 (*Lackford*, Fig. 31), which also have animal stamps, but neither swastikas nor cabling, and seem to belong to a different school.

than identical. The characteristics of this workshop are the use, in combination, of animal stamps, swastika stamps, both simple and complex, and cabled patterns composed of curved or S-shaped stamps set close together. All these features can be seen on an urn from Lackford[1] and on two from Caistor-by-Norwich, one being represented only by fragments.[2]

The date of this workshop is of some interest. The Caistor urn has a sharply biconical form and prominent bosses on the carination which give it an archaic appearance. But there are good grounds for the belief that these features are deliberately archaistic and that it was made quite late in the pagan period, perhaps even after 600. T. C. Lethbridge, in discussing the Lackford example,[3] pointed out the close resemblance which the animal stamps and developed swastikas bear to the drawing of similar motifs in the seventh-century Book of Durrow, and this is true also of the cabled patterns associated with both. The backward-looking or -biting beasts are particularly close in feeling. Moreover the Caistor urn formed part of a composite burial that had disturbed an earlier cremation, and included several urns of notably decadent decoration and late associations.[4]

Quite different in character is the work of the so-called Illington/Lackford potter,[5] by far the most prolific and commercialized of all the late sixth-century workshops in Middle Anglia. Here is the one instance at present known of a workshop that turned out large numbers of pots in standard sizes and shapes, and decorated, with only minor variations of detail, in two or three standard styles. Already in 1937 I had called attention to the very professional quality of three urns in the Ashmolean that came from Lackford and West Stow Heath in Suffolk, and carried an identical scheme of decoration, executed with the same two stamps, and differing only in size.[6] Since then the huts of the West Stow Heath village have produced sherds from at least fifty vessels,[7] Lethbridge has illustrated about a dozen more from his excavations at Lackford,[8] and Knocker has found over twenty-five at Illington, where more than a quarter

---

[1] *Lackford*, Fig. 31. 48, 2487.
[2] Caistor E7 and W30.
[3] *Lackford* 21.
[4] Besides E7, the burial included E8, E10, and E11. E8 shows elaborate random stamping (using five stamps), and archaizing features of small solid bosses and irregular stamped *stehende Bogen*. E10 and E11 were made by a potter who also used random stamping and a thoroughly loose and decadent treatment of traditional designs.

[5] Termed the Icklingham potter by Lethbridge (*Lackford* 15), but it seems best to use the names of the two cemeteries that have produced most products of this workshop.
[6] *Antiquity* xi (1937), 391 and Pl. I, Fig. 3.
[7] I am greatly indebted to Mr. Stanley West for the opportunity to examine the pottery from his excavations at West Stow Heath.
[8] *Lackford*, Figs. 17, 18, 22.

of all the stamped pottery excavated was supplied from this source. Others have been noted from St. John's and Little Wilbraham (Cambridge) and Rushford (Norfolk), the last being recognizable from an eighteenth-century drawing, so distinctive is the style.[1] Altogether nearly a hundred specimens are known.

The Illington/Lackford workshop deserves a monograph to itself,[2] and it is not possible here to do more than call attention to some of its more interesting aspects. Its products fall into three main types, of which the commonest is decorated with multiple close-set necklines interspersed with one or two zones of stamps above pendent swags—*hängende Bogen*—or triangles filled with stamps. The execution is always sharp, clear, and precise, almost mechanical in its regularity, and most of the pots are of the same form, with wide mouths and a somewhat sagging profile. Examples of this style come from Illington, Lackford, Rushford, West Stow Heath, and Little Wilbraham. The second main type carries the same arrangement of close-set necklines and stamps, but omits the pendent swags. This group is at present confined to Illington. There are also a few minor variants.[3] Finally there are a few much larger urns, including one from Lackford, one from St. John's, Cambridge, and parts of at least three from West Stow Heath, which are decorated in a much more elaborate manner with slashed collars, vertical slashed bosses, and, in two examples, swastikas in relief, accompanied by a profusion of stamped ornament, including several of the stamps most commonly used on the standard types.[4]

The workshop favoured a comparatively limited range of stamp-types, of which a raised cross-in-circle (like a button), a St. Andrew's cross, and a concentric circle with blob centre are the most frequently used. These, with three or four others less commonly found, constitute its basic repertoire. A number of slight variants in these types show that several similar, but not quite identical, tools were available to produce each form of impression. One of these tools, for the St. Andrew's cross stamp, has fortunately been picked up as a surface find at West Stow Heath and is now in the Moyses' Hall Museum at Bury St. Edmunds. It is most beautifully made out of a tine of red-deer antler, from

[1] 'An account of Roman Urns and other Antiquities found in England', 1754 (MS. in the Maidstone Museum): apparently by Rev. G. Burton of Elveden, Suffolk. This is one of the earliest collections of Anglo-Saxon pottery drawings known in this country. The urn is no. 7 of the eighteen drawn by Burton. The Little Wilbraham example was also first noticed by me from the illustration of it in R. C. Neville, *Saxon Obsequies* (1852), Pl. 25, top left.

[2] I hope to discuss the matter thoroughly in the forthcoming publication of the Illington cemetery.

[3] Such as *Lackford*, Fig. 18, 48, 2478, and 49, 3 which include a zone of linear chevrons. An example from Lackford in private hands shows this arrangement but omitting the stamps. The main varieties are here illustrated on Fig. 48.

[4] *Lackford*, Fig. 18, 48, 2475. Both types of these elaborate urns are shown on Fig. 48.

which four regular flakes have been sliced to leave at the narrow end a flat surface on which the cross die has been neatly carved.[1]

From the typological point of view it would be natural to date the activity of this workshop in the second half of the sixth century, for one main group of its products consists of straightforward examples of the stamped panel-style, with pendent swags or triangles and no bosses. The form of the vessels with their rounded contour and tendency to a wide mouth is also typical of that period. This dating is happily confirmed from the fragment of a florid square-headed brooch of that date found in one of the Lackford urns.[2] At Illington a slightly earlier date is suggested by a Group II/III cruciform brooch found in one of these urns with pendent triangles, which was itself associated with a plain urn containing a Group II cruciform brooch.[3] But such associations are consistent with a date around 550, since the pot is likely in any case to be later than the objects it contains. Whether it will be possible to establish any distinction of date between the urns with pendent swags and those with horizontal decoration only, is doubtful, since none of the latter have so far been found accompanied by datable objects. It is, however, clear that the exceptionally large urns from Lackford, West Stow Heath, and St. John's, in spite of their slashed bosses and relief decoration, which hark back to earlier fashions, should be treated as broadly contemporary with the rest. Like the animal-stamped urn (E7) from Caistor, they owe their archaic features to what seems to have been the normal tendency among Anglo-Saxon craftsmen, who harked back to older fashions in decoration when confronted with a demand for something of special magnificence to grace an unusual or important occasion.[4]

It will be seen from Map 10 that although the products of this prolific workshop are found on a number of sites in west Suffolk, west Norfolk, and Cambridge, the area they cover is not so extensive as might be expected. They do not seem to have penetrated either to Caistor[5] and Markshall on the east, or

---

[1] See Pl. 8. I am grateful to Mr. Edwardson, Curator of the Moyses' Hall Museum for permission to illustrate this tool. I have not yet been able to make a complete conspectus of the stamps known to have been used by this workshop, a task which would require amongst other things a detailed confrontation of the Lackford urns at Cambridge with the Illington series at Norwich. Some difference of emphasis certainly exists between the two main groups: the concentric circle stamps, for example, which are very common on the Lackford urns, do not seem to have been used at Illington.

[2] *Lackford*, Fig. 17, 50, 126.

[3] Illington 101 and 102.

[4] The same point has been noted by me in connection with one of the Girton potters. *Antiquity* xi (1937), 397–8 and Fig. 9. At West Stow Heath the sherds of elaborately decorated pots came from the same hut-floors as those of simpler types.

[5] Caistor P27 is very similar in style to the work of the Illington/Lackford potter, but does not seem to come from this workshop.

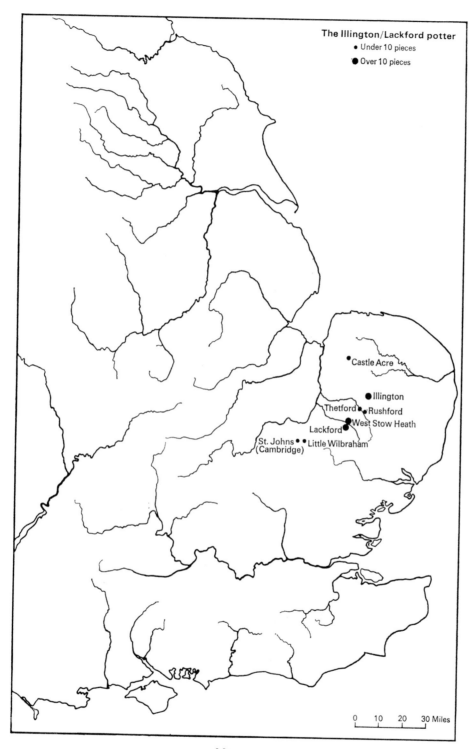

The Illington/Lackford potter
  • Under 10 pieces
  ● Over 10 pieces

● Castle Acre

● Illington

Thetford ● Rushford
      ● West Stow Heath
Lackford ●
St. Johns ● ● Little Wilbraham
(Cambridge)

0   10   20   30 Miles

Map 10

into Northamptonshire or Bedfordshire to the west and south. The question naturally arises whether they were all made at one place from which the finished goods were distributed to the communities using these various cemeteries, or whether the potters travelled around this region with their tools making urns on the spot as and when they were wanted.

One clue to this might be the composition of the clay. In an effort to determine whether the clay used is all of one local type or displays differences that might indicate several sources of supply, the Oxford University Research Laboratory for Archaeology kindly undertook in 1962 the spectrographic analysis of sample sherds from pots of this group found at Illington and at Lackford respectively. The results of this experiment are suggestive, but unfortunately inconclusive. The varying proportions of trace-elements, especially calcium and sodium, and to a lesser extent magnesium and titanium, found in the samples, do suggest a significant difference in the composition of the material from which the two groups were made. But the groups themselves are not very uniform in composition, and there seem to be one or two marked divergences from the norm which occur in both groups. The significance of this is not apparent. It is possibly due only to the sample being too small to provide a proper norm, but abnormalities could arise not from the original composition of the clay, but from its being made up and fired in different conditions. It would be necessary to conduct extensive pot-making experiments before one could be certain what these conditions were: even with pots of such standard quality as those produced by the Illington/Lackford workshop, conditions of manufacture and firing were probably very primitive and by no means uniform for different batches of pots. Although the evidence is not conclusive, it does on the whole support the notion, suggested by the minor differences of style between the several local groups, that the operations of this workshop were not all conducted from a single centre.[1]

It remains to consider whether the decoration of this pottery, so useful to us in establishing typological sequences and identifying the work of particular craftsmen, was intended to convey anything but a purely decorative effect. This is a topic of great fascination, over which it is easy for the imagination to run riot. It is only possible here to draw attention briefly to one or two aspects of it that would repay more detailed study. At first sight it may seem obvious

[1] I am greatly indebted to Dr. E. Hall and his staff, especially Mrs. E. E. Richards, for conducting these preliminary experiments and for their very helpful interest in the problem.

that a purely decorative intent was uppermost in a craftsman's mind in devising the patterns of his stamps. It has long been recognized that many of the commoner stamps such as the cross-in-circle, star-in-circle, or various criss-cross designs, can be very easily made by shaping the end of a stick and cutting notches on it.[1] Moreover, pottery was occasionally ornamented by stamped impressions, made with bits of brooches or other objects, where no purpose except the purely ornamental could have been intended.[2]

But some of the designs, even such simple and common forms as concentric circles and rosettes, certainly represent objects of ritual or magical significance familiar in northern mythology,[3] and sometimes associated with the worship of particular gods. As we have seen, there are urns, such as those decorated by the Sancton/Elkington potter,[4] on which freehand drawings of swastikas, serpents, and various other devices have been set with obvious intent. In a few cases an apparent confrontation between swastikas and serpents or dragons is portrayed.[5] This group can be clearly associated with the cult of Thor, or Thunor, whose particular symbol the swastika was, and whose combat with the Cosmic Dragon or Serpent, representing the forces of evil and destruction, was a familiar tale in the mythology of Germanic peoples. Decoration of this kind is clearly pictorial and religious in character. It is intended, like the stained glass of mediaeval churches, to act as a kind of visual aid in recalling to an illiterate people the more memorable tales of gods and heroes.

It is indeed no accident that the cult of Thor is so strongly in evidence on our funeral pottery, for it was particularly concerned with the great events of human life, birth, marriage, and death, and with the ceremonies of burial. While his power covered both inhumation and cremation rituals, Thor's

---

[1] Criss-cross stamps are sometimes referred to as 'textile stamps' from the notion that the impression could be produced by holding a coarse cloth over the end of a stick. Felicity Pearce has shown (*Antiquity* xl (1966), 217 and Pl. XXXV) that the normal criss-cross effect could not be so produced. She has, however, also shown that one of the stamps on Lackford 49, 19 was made by a (probably pottery) die on which the pattern of a coarse textile was impressed before baking.

[2] I have mentioned earlier (p. 81 fn.) the vessel from Wingst, near Cuxhaven, decorated with impressions of the spring of a fourth-century brooch. Among English examples Loveden Hill 59/150 has impressions from a late cruciform brooch. T. Sheppard suggested that some of the stamps on

Sancton urns were made with Roman signet rings (*Hull Mus. Publns.* lxvi (1909), 64, 70). Bird bones were also used, and a Lackford urn carries impressions of a pony's tooth (*Lackford*, Fig. 27, 50, 68B). Many other unusual stamps are doubtless due to chance employment of any object that came to hand.

[3] The use of concentric circles and rosettes as solar symbols has a very long history, going back at least to the Bronze Age in Scandinavian and north European art.

[4] Fig. 46.

[5] e.g. *Lackford*, Fig. 8, 49, 4; Illington 69. A close continental parallel is a sherd from the Hoogebeintum *terp* at Leeuwarden.

special association with fire through his command over thunder and lightning, and the working of metal, gave him an unrivalled authority as the protector of a cremating people and of the urns in which they deposited the ashes of their dead.[1]

Even more prominent than the swastika symbol of Thor, and often appearing by itself on our urns, is the serpent or legless dragon, the 'wyrm' of Anglo-Saxon vocabulary. It is the creature that forms the zoomorphic bosses of the south-eastern group of *Buckelurnen* and it is also represented in freehand drawings, often in a kind of shorthand, by an S-curve that may, or may not, have an eye at one end to indicate its character.[2] Examples are on Fig. 49. It would seem that in these cases the serpent combines the role of what Mrs. Davidson has recently termed 'a natural image for devouring death and in particular for the greedy fire swallowing up the dead man and his treasures',[3] and that of the guardian of the dead and his tomb deposit, as the dragon guards the treasures of the burial mound in the final dramatic scenes of the Beowulf story. To surround an urn with 'wyrm' drawings was thus both a symbolic and a prophylactic exercise. At one and the same time it symbolized the destruction wrought by death, and provided the burial with some degree of magic protection against disturbance, to secure it indeed not only against contemporary tomb-robbers but also against the prying curiosity of the modern archaeologist.[4]

But Anglo-Saxon potters soon found that it was not essential to portray these notions in plastic bosses or freehand drawings. They could as well be represented in a more mechanical form by the use of stamps of the appropriate shape. This is most commonly seen in the rosette stamps which come to symbolize in little the freehand rosette designs so common on pottery of the fourth and early fifth centuries.[5] But it is also the explanation of the 'S' or reversed 'S' stamps that are one of the most frequently used of all categories. That they are intended to represent the prophylactic 'wyrm' is clear from a number of

---

[1] H. R. E. Davidson, *Gods and Myths of Northern Europe* (1964), 83, 158, 205.

[2] Continental examples are *Westerwanna* i. 1322, or one from the Beetgum *terp* at Leeuwarden: in this country, *Lackford*, Fig. 28, 48, 2473 or West Keal (Lincs.), Fig. 49.   [3] Op. cit. 159.

[4] This is the meaning of the continuous procession of running 'wyrms' shown on such continental urns as *Wehden*, Tafel 21. 92, or the English examples on Fig. 49. It will be seen that on the Caistor example (1539) the procession is interrupted by what may well be intended to represent the burial mound which is the object of the

serpent's care. In the two Sancton examples (2279 and 66) the zoomorphic character is almost lost in a series of overlapping curves, easily represented as a simple cable pattern. The same stylization is apparent on Norwegian examples like that from Linnestad i Ramnes (Vestfold). *Oslo Universitetets Oldsakssamlings Arbok* (1961), 21, Fig. 9.

[5] A good example of the transition from the one method to the other is the late stamped *Buckelurne* illustrated in *Ant. Journ.* xvii (1937), Pl. XCI(*a*), where stamps which are themselves rosettes are used to build a rosette pattern around the circular bosses.

instances in which zoomorphic features, an eye at one end, or hairs down the back, are retained.[1] By peppering a pot with stamps of this form, however lacking in zoomorphic verisimilitude, it was felt that something had been done to safeguard it and its contents from disturbance. It is more than probable that other types of stamps carried some similar significance which is no longer apparent to us.

There is however no doubt about the interest of one further group of symbols on our urns which has recently been identified by Dr. Fennell in the course of investigating the runic inscription on the Loveden Hill urn, A. 11/251. This is not the place to discuss the significance of this, or any other, genuine group of runes to be found on objects of this period. But the search for comparable material has led to the realization that, along with a few deceptive inscriptions made up of bogus runes,[2] and some other meaningless groups of lines that may or may not have been so intended, there are also cases where individual runes appear on Anglo-Saxon urns, either drawn freehand or in the form of stamps. In particular the '↑' rune is occasionally used in this way, both on the Continent[3] and in this country.[4] There seems little doubt that, where this is done, the intention was to indicate a special devotion to the god Tiw or Tig, for whose worship in pagan Anglo-Saxon times there is evidence in such place names as Tuesley (Surrey), Tewin (Herts.), and Tysoe (War.), as well as in the allocation of a weekday, Tuesday, to his special protection. Tiw is apparently identical with Seaxneat, the eponymous ancestor of the Saxon people, from whom the kings of the East Saxons claimed descent: as a god of war he belongs to an earlier mythological stratum than Woden, to whom most of the other Saxon royal pedigrees go back, and his cult would thus be particularly in place in the first stages of the invasions.[5]

The appearance of runes on Anglo-Saxon pottery, while in itself of great interest from the literary point of view, is exactly on a par with that of the other meaningful symbols which have been discussed above. All alike had a magical or religious significance to those who worked them into their designs.

[1] The 'wyrm' stamps on *Lackford*, Fig. 30, 50, 47 have a head at both ends.

[2] e.g. those on *Lackford*, Fig. 27, 49, 36: and Caistor XII.

[3] e.g. *Westerwanna* i, Tafel 37, 270 and Tafel 183, 1406: *Altenwalde*, Tafel 17, 152. *Galgenberg*, Tafel 8, 5 seems to carry this usage back to the earlier centuries A.D.

[4] Three cases have been noted by Dr. Fennell at Loveden Hill (62/C8/305, C1/298, and 61/B17/279C). There are at least four at Caistor-by-Norwich: see Fig. 50 (1). The other Caistor pieces on Fig. 50 (1), 1701 and 1703, and all those on Fig. 50 (2), are perhaps better described as carrying rune-like signs than true runes. I am grateful to Dr. R. I. Page for guidance on this difficult matter.

[5] H. R. E. Davidson, op. cit. 60.

In their use of such motifs as rosettes, swastikas, serpents, and their various combinations—swastikas, for example, can readily be produced by super-imposing two 'wyrm' stamps at right angles to each other[1]—the Saxon potters were drawing on a stock of ancient symbols full of meaning and of mysterious power. This was an activity very similar to that being performed by the rune-masters, who used the alphabetical signs of the *futhorc* to convey ideas in an only slightly more sophisticated way. Both alike were engaged in a sort of picture-writing, making permanent and potent the thoughts of men by means which might have developed, had the course of history run differently, into an original type of ideographic script.[2]

In so far as these developments were still expressed in terms of freehand draw-ing, there was nothing especially original about them from the technical point of view. They remained, so to speak, in the manuscript stage. But the employ-ment of stamps in the decoration of pottery, and particularly the occasional use of such stamps to carry individual runes, made possible discoveries of a most exciting and far-reaching kind. If any Anglo-Saxon potter had decided, as he well might, to have individual stamps made not only for '↑' but for all the runes of the *futhorc*, and had then collaborated with the local rune-master in applying them in meaningful order to his cremation urns, he would have done something that no one else thought of doing for a thousand years. He would have invented the technique of printing by movable type. It is fascinating to speculate on the consequences for the whole history of Europe which could have followed this transition from manuscript writing to a printing technique had it been made in this simple way in the fifth or sixth century A.D. As things turned out, of course, the Anglo-Saxon peoples fell quickly under the spell of Rome and abandoned in favour of the Roman alphabet their tentative essays towards the original development of writing, just about the time that they gave

[1] As, e.g., on *Lackford*, Fig. 30, 50. 47. This relationship of the 'wyrm' and swastika symbols is of course of very great antiquity in the history of the Indo-European peoples. It goes back at least to the second millennium B.C. in India, appears along with rosettes and other familiar symbols later used by Anglo-Saxon potters, on Greek vases of the Geometric period, and so enters the com-mon stock of Greco-Roman decorative motifs. For a striking instance of the combination, in an inscription apparently of the third century from the temple of Belen in the Vivarais, see E. Salin, *La Civilization mérovingienne* i (1949), 22, Fig. 1.

[2] Professor Charles Thomas has recently sug-gested that the signs used on the Pictish symbol stones were intended to convey ideas in a some-what similar manner: *Arch. Journ.* cxx (1963), 31–97. Even such a sophisticated character as Isidore of Seville was still fascinated by the mysteri-ous power of writing to convey thought. He writes: 'litterae autem sunt indices rerum, signa verborum, quibus tanta vis est, ut nobis dicta absentium sine voce loquantur.' *Etymol.* I. iii. I. Illiterate Anglo-Saxon potters were trying to ex-press such ideas when they decorated their wares with runes or something like them.

up pagan forms of burial and the use of cremation urns. But this rather startling thought may be left perhaps as a fitting conclusion to this study of Anglo-Saxon pottery. It may suggest that the subject is not so wholly barren and so wholly unrewarding as has sometimes been supposed. It may indeed have many worthwhile, and some almost sensational, contributions to make to our knowledge of the settlement of England.

APPENDIX

List of *Buckelurnen* on which the statistics given on p. 46 are based. For their distribution see Map 4

THIS list does not claim to be complete, but it includes the great majority of English *Buckelurnen*, classified according to the principles mentioned on p. 45. Many different types are thus covered in each group, but straightforward shoulder-boss urns of the kinds discussed in Chapter IV are excluded. I have not given the precise figures for each group in the text, partly because there is room for some difference of opinion about the inclusion or exclusion of marginal cases, partly because the totals constantly require modification to remedy omissions or add fresh discoveries,[1] partly because the line separating Group V from Groups III and IV is necessarily subjective and somewhat arbitrary, and partly because, in the case of fragmentary urns, there is sometimes a doubt whether a footstand or footring was present or not. In spite of these uncertainties, the relative numbers in the groups, and their distribution, have some interest. References to museum registrations and to published illustrations are given where known, and a note is made of datable associated objects in the few cases where such are on record.

I. BUCKELURNEN with feet, decorated with linear or line-and-groove designs, with or without finger-tipping and/or dots: but without stamps.

BEDS. Luton	Luton 45/41/27	*Ant. Journ.* viii (1928), Pl. XXXVII, 1
BEDS. Sandy	BM 37. 11–11. 9	*Ant. Journ.* xxxiv (1954), Pl. XXI, *b*
BEDS. Sandy	BM 37. 11–11. 8	*Ant. Journ.* xxxiv (1954), Pl. XXI, *c* (both as from Ickwellbury, Beds., but corrected to Sandy in *Ant. Journ.* xxxvii (1957), 224)
CAMBS. Little Wilbraham	Cambridge 48. 1249	R. C. Neville, *Saxon Obsequies* (1852), Pl. 28
CAMBS. St. John's	Cambridge	*Ant. Journ.* xxxiv (1954), 207, Fig. 3, 2
CAMBS. St. John's	Cambridge	*Ant. Journ.* xxxiv (1954), 207, Fig. 3, 1

[1] Since these lists were compiled, the excavations at Newark have produced examples of Group II and Group V which are not included here, but have been added to the Maps. Examples of Groups I, II, and V are now recorded from the West Stow Heath village, Suffolk. I have also noted a Group II urn from St. John's, Cambridge, at Wisbech; and Loveden Hill 60/206 should be added to Group V.

HUNTS. Somersham	Cambridge 36 D. 1	*Ant. Journ.* xxxiv (1954), Pl. **XXI**, *a*
LEICS. Thurmaston	Leicester, Thurmaston 12, 18, and 19 (parts of three urns)	
LINCS. Loveden Hill	Lincoln, Loveden Hill A6/246	Fig. 22
NORFOLK Caistor-by-Norwich	Norwich, Caistor C1 and Y38 (two urns)	
NORFOLK Castle Acre	Norwich 47. 10	*Norf. Arch.* xxvii, Pl. 2. 7
NORFOLK Markshall	Norwich 51. 949 (base missing, but a foot can be presumed, after *Wehden*, Tafel 23. 58, which appears to be by the same potter)	See p. 130–1
NORTHANTS. Milton	Northampton D20/1947	Fig. 22
SUFFOLK Lackford	Cambridge 50. 54	*Lackford*, Fig. 1
SUFFOLK Lackford	Cambridge 48. 2288	*Lackford*, Fig. 1
SUFFOLK Lackford	Cambridge 48. 2491 (with a Group I cruciform brooch)	*Lackford*, Fig. 2
SUFFOLK Lackford	Cambridge 50. 178B (a degenerate example, found with part of a large late square-headed brooch, and zoomorphic wrist-clasp)	*Lackford*, Fig. 17
YORKS. Heworth	York	*Ant. Journ.* xxxiv (1954), 207, Fig. 3. 4
No provenance	Cambridge 48. 1292	

It is probable that BERKS. Abingdon C3, *Abingdon*, Fig. 4, was another, but not enough is preserved of the decoration to be sure.

II. BUCKELURNEN with similar decoration to those of Group I but without feet.

BEDS. Kempston	Bedford P4 3778	
BEDS. Kempston		Only known from sketch by T. E. Elger in Bedford Museum records
BERKS. Abingdon	Ashmolean, Abingdon C48 and C82 (two urns)	*Abingdon*, Fig. 4; and Pl. II
BERKS. Wallingford	Ashmolean 1939. 446	Fig. 23
HERTS. Stevenage	Hitchin (parts of two, possibly three, vessels, only one of which can be shown to be without a foot)	
LANCS. Ribchester	Ribchester (no base preserved)	
LANCS. Site unknown	BM 52 4–29. 2	*Horae Ferales*, Pl. **XXX**. II
LEICS. Thurmaston	Leicester, Thurmaston 68	
LINCS. Baston		*Arch. Journ.* xx (1863), 30, Fig. 1
LINCS. Elkington	Lincoln, Elkington 93, 110, and 147 (three urns of which the last has no base preserved)	*Arch. Journ.* cviii (1952), Figs. 14 and 15
LINCS. Loveden Hill	Lincoln, Loveden Hill 57/34	Fig. 23
LINCS. Loveden Hill	Lincoln, Loveden Hill 62/D10/319	
LINCS. Loveden Hill	Lincoln, Loveden Hill C1/298	

LINCS. Loveden Hill	Lincoln, Loveden Hill 62/B32/294	
LINCS. Loveden Hill	Lincoln, Loveden Hill D7/316	
LINCS. Loveden Hill	Lincoln, Loveden Hill D3/333	
MIDDX. Shepperton		*Proc. Soc. Ant.*, 2nd ser. iv (1868), 119
NORFOLK Caistor-by-Norwich	Norwich, Caistor M28	
NORFOLK Caistor-by-Norwich	Norwich, Caistor X24	
NORFOLK Caistor-by-Norwich	Norwich, Caistor W11 (no base preserved)	
NORFOLK Caistor-by-Norwich	BM 70 12–6. 1	
NORFOLK Markshall	Norwich, Markshall LXXXIV (no base preserved)	
NORFOLK Markshall	Ashmolean, Markshall 1820	
NORFOLK North Elmham	BM SL385	*Horae Ferales*, Pl. XXX, Fig. 7
NORFOLK North Runcton	King's Lynn	*Norf. Arch.* xxvii, Pl. 7, 1
OXON. Souldern	Cambridge	W. Wing, *Antiquities and History of Steeple Aston* (1845), 74
RUTLAND North Luffenham	Oakham School (two urns)	Fig. 23
SUFFOLK Culford	Ipswich 1920–85–4	*V.C.H. Suffolk*, Pl. III, Fig. 2
SUFFOLK Ingham	London, Society of Antiquaries (with annular bronze brooch)	
SUFFOLK Lackford	Cambridge, Lackford 49. 6 (with bone comb and comb case)	*Lackford*, Fig. 1
SUFFOLK Lackford	Cambridge, Lackford 50. 90 (with bone comb)	*Lackford*, Fig. 1
SUFFOLK Lackford	Cambridge, Lackford 50. 25	*Lackford*, Fig. 1
SUFFOLK Lackford	Cambridge, Lackford 50. 27	*Lackford*, Fig. 3
SUFFOLK Lackford	Cambridge, Lackford 50. 191	*Lackford*, Fig. 3
SUFFOLK Lackford	Cambridge, Lackford 49. 16	*Lackford*, Fig. 9
SUFFOLK Lackford	Cambridge, Lackford 48. 2492A	*Lackford*, Fig. 9
SUFFOLK Lackford	Cambridge, Lackford 50. 100	Not illustrated
SUFFOLK Lackford	Cambridge, Lackford 49. 56	Not illustrated
YORKS. Sancton	Hull, Sancton 10	*Hull Mus. Publns.* lxvii (1909), Pl. 4, Fig. 10
YORKS. Sancton	Hull, Sancton 18	*Hull Mus. Publns.* lxvi (1909), Fig. 18
YORKS. Sancton	Hull, Sancton W1	Fig. 46
YORKS. Sancton	Hull, Sancton 191 (with iron knife, tweezers, etc.)	
YORKS. Sancton	Hull, Sancton 95 (with bronze tweezers, shears, and knife)	Fig. 46
YORKS. Sancton	Hull, Sancton 9a (with half a bone comb)	Fig. 46

Yorks. Sancton	Hull, Sancton 200	
Yorks. Sancton	Ashmolean 1886–114.	

III. BUCKELURNEN with feet, and with restrained use of stamps

Berks. East Shefford	BM 93 7–16. 25 ⎫	*Antiquity* xi (1937), 392, Pl. III,
Berks. East Shefford	BM 93 7–16. 26 ⎭	Fig. 5
Berks. Harwell	Ashmolean 1955. 464	*Oxoniensia* xxi (1956), 31, Fig. 11
Norfolk Caistor-by-Norwich	Norwich, Caistor M48 (b)	
Norfolk Shropham	BM 56 6–27. 9	*Horae Ferales*, Pl. XXX, 12
Northants. Newton-in-the-Willows	Kettering 132	Fig. 24
Notts. Newark	Newark (formerly Hull 32)	*Ant. Journ.* xvii (1937), 429, Fig. 1(a)
Oxon. Osney	Ashmolean	*Ant. Journ.* xxxiv (1954), 207, Fig. 3. 3
?Suffolk[1] Fakenham Heath	Ipswich R1920 85. 5	*V.C.H. Suffolk* i (1911), 334, Pl. III, Fig. 1
?Sussex[2] Lancing	Worthing	
Yorks. Heworth	York, Heworth 21	

IV. BUCKELURNEN without feet, and with restrained use of stamps

Berks. Abingdon	Ashmolean, Abingdon CX (no foot preserved)	*Abingdon* 12, Fig. 4 and Pl. II
Cambs. Girton	Cambridge D24. 41	
Kent Northfleet	BM 1947. 2. 1 (no foot preserved)	*Ant. Journ.* xxxviii (1948), 187, Fig. 1
Lincs. Loveden Hill	Lincoln, Loveden Hill 37 (no foot preserved)	
Norfolk Caistor-by-Norwich	Norwich, Caistor A8	
Norfolk Rushford	Norwich	*Norf. Arch.* xxvii, Pl. 8, 3
Northants. Kettering	Kettering 84	
Suffolk Lackford	Cambridge 48. 2282 (with two Group I cruciform brooches)	*Lackford*, Fig. 2
Suffolk Lackford	Cambridge 50. 53	*Lackford*, Fig. 9
Surrey Croydon	BM 95 3–15. 4	Fig. 24
War. Long Itchington	Warwick A21 (A)	
Yorks. Heworth	York, Heworth 14	
Yorks. Heworth	York, Heworth 22	
Yorks. Saltburn	Middlesbrough (no foot preserved)	
Yorks. Sancton	Ashmolean	*Arch.* xlv (1880), Pl. XXXIII, 1

V. BUCKELURNEN with or without feet, and with free or exuberant use of stamps

Beds. Kempston	BM 91 6–24. 24	Fig. 24
Beds. Kempston	Bedford	*Coll. Ant.* vi (1868), Pl. XLI

[1] It has been suggested that this urn may come from the Norfolk Fakenham, in which case it may well belong to the adjacent Pensthorpe cemetery. *Norf. Arch.* xxvii. 202.

[2] The location is uncertain, as it came from a miscellaneous collection: the urn may come from a workshop in the east Midlands.

BEDS. Sandy	Cambridge D. 14. 124	*Ant. Rutup.*, Tab. X
CAMBS. Girton	Cambridge D. 24. 42 ⎫	*Antiquity* xi (1937), 392, Pl. II
CAMBS. Girton	Cambridge ⎬	
CAMBS. Girton	Cambridge (two others, un-numbered)	
CAMBS. Little Wilbraham	Cambridge 48. 1209	R. C. Neville, *Saxon Obsequies* (1852), Pl. 29
CAMBS. Little Wilbraham	Cambridge 48. 1218	*Saxon Obsequies*, Pl. 26
CAMBS. Linton Heath	Cambridge 48. 1284	
CAMBS. St. John's	Cambridge	Fig. 48
LEICS. Thurmaston	Leicester, Thurmaston 88	Fig. 45
LINCS. Elkington	Lincoln, Elkington 186	*Arch. Journ.* cviii (1952), 56, Fig. 16
LINCS. Kirton Lindsey	BM 80 6–20. 1	*Arch. Journ.* cviii (1952), Pl. III, 1
LINCS. Loveden Hill	Grantham 71	*Arch. Journ.* cviii (1952), 78, Fig. 5, 1
LINCS. Loveden Hill	Lincoln, Loveden Hill 11	
LINCS. Loveden Hill	Lincoln, Loveden Hill 59/151 (with two bone combs)	
LINCS. Loveden Hill	Lincoln, Loveden Hill 59/150 (stamped with foot of Group III/V cruciform brooch)	
LINCS. Loveden Hill	Lincoln, Loveden Hill 60/197	
LINCS. Loveden Hill	Lincoln, Loveden Hill 57/101	
LINCS. Stamford	Burghley House	*Arch. Journ.* cviii (1952), 94, Pl. III, 3
NORFOLK Caistor-by-Norwich	Norwich, Caistor P16	
NORFOLK, Castle Acre[1]	Norwich, Castle Acre 54	
NORFOLK North Elmham	BM	*Ant. Journ.* xvii (1937), Pl. XCI (*a*) (as from Lincolnshire)
NORFOLK North Elmham		drawing by W. Stukeley in *Soc. Ant.*, MS. 265, fo. 14. (*Ant. Journ.* xxvii (1947), 49 and Pl. XIII *b*.)
?NORFOLK North Elmham	BM OA233 (no certain location)	
NORTHANTS. Kettering	Kettering 2	*Ant. Journ.* x (1930), 255
SUFFOLK Lackford	Cambridge, Lackford 50. 23	*Lackford*, Fig. 3
SUFFOLK Lackford	Cambridge, Lackford 49. 7	*Lackford*, Fig. 19
SUFFOLK Lackford	Cambridge, Lackford 50. 33	*Lackford*, Fig. 30
SUFFOLK Lackford	Cambridge, Lackford 50. 51A	Not illustrated
SUFFOLK Lackford	Cambridge, Lackford 48. 2475	*Lackford*, Fig. 18
SUFFOLK Mildenhall	Bury St. Edmunds	Fig. 24
SUFFOLK Redgrave	Bury St. Edmunds	
SURREY Croydon	BM 95 3–15. 5	
SURREY Guildown	Guildford (no foot preserved)	
WAR. Baginton	Coventry A/1014/3	
WAR. Baginton	Coventry	
YORKS. Sancton	Hull, Sancton 94	

[1] Not shown on Map 4 (b).

NOTE ON THE ILLUSTRATIONS

THE vessels illustrated have been chosen with the object of providing the widest possible range of varieties within the general scheme of classification here proposed. Since this principle has made it necessary to use drawings derived from various sources, it has not been possible to present them all in the same way or with identical standard conventions. In particular, the irregularities of workmanship normal in hand-made pottery are more clearly indicated in some drawings than in others. Where sections are not shown this is sometimes because complex decoration has required the full elevation of the pot for its effective display, sometimes because a shattered vessel has been restored in such a way that a correct section is no longer obtainable, and sometimes because at the time of drawing an urn still retained its original contents of burnt bones, or even earth, making access to its interior inconvenient or impossible. But sections are not normally very significant with this type of hand-made pottery, whose thickness is far from uniform and whose rims and base angles normally lack careful moulding and may vary considerably from point to point on the same pot. Where significant features can only be shown in section, as in the case of pedestal or footring bases, sections are provided wherever possible.

The pots are uniformly shown at 1:4 scale: stamps, where drawn separately, are at 1:2, except where otherwise indicated. The numbers to the left of each pot are there to facilitate reference to the descriptions, where they will be found repeated. These numbers are those given to the individual drawings in my unpublished *Corpus Vasorum Anglo-Saxonicorum*, and have no significance in any other context. It should be noted in particular that they are neither Museum registration numbers nor site-find numbers, and they should not be used in correspondence with Museums or excavators, to whom they would be meaningless. Whenever possible both the find-spot and the present location of each illustrated piece, with its number in the relevant collection, if any, is placed at the head of its description, Museum registration numbers being added in brackets, where known. To save space, references to previous publication have been omitted.

The detailed descriptions of each vessel are provided in an attempt to suggest a standard method for describing this kind of pottery. Form, fabric, and ornament are covered successively, the individual elements of the decorative scheme being indicated from the neck downwards. If some uniform, but not unduly rigid, conventions of this sort can be generally adopted it should be possible to convey an accurate idea of the shape, appearance, and decoration of even the most elaborately ornamented pots on occasions when illustration is not possible. More precision than is here attempted is obviously desirable in the description of fabrics. Unfortunately it is at present impossible to provide exact and intelligible descriptions of the material composition and firing of the vessels, owing to the lack of a generally accepted standard in the use of technical terms in this field.

Fig. 1. *Plain biconical urns*

2004 YORKS., SANCTON (Ashmolean Museum 1886–1294)
Sharply biconical urn with flaring rim: well-made reddish ware with smooth dark surface.

1380 LINCS., LOVEDEN HILL 58/81 (Lincoln Museum)
Biconical urn with broad base and short upright rim: brown ware.

1784 NORFOLK, CAISTOR-BY-NORWICH Y 33 (Norwich Museum)
Biconical urn with very short upright rim: rough grey ware.

1776 NORFOLK, CAISTOR-BY-NORWICH X 5 (Norwich Museum)
Biconical urn with wide mouth and upright rim: smooth brown ware. This vessel inclines to the hollow-necked type (Fig. 2)

2027 BERKS., ABINGDON C 57 (Ashmolean Museum 1934–356
Biconical urn with everted swollen rim: brick-red/black ware.

2045 BERKS., FRILFORD (Ashmolean Museum 1886–1403)
Biconical urn with short everted rim: smooth dark brown/buff ware.

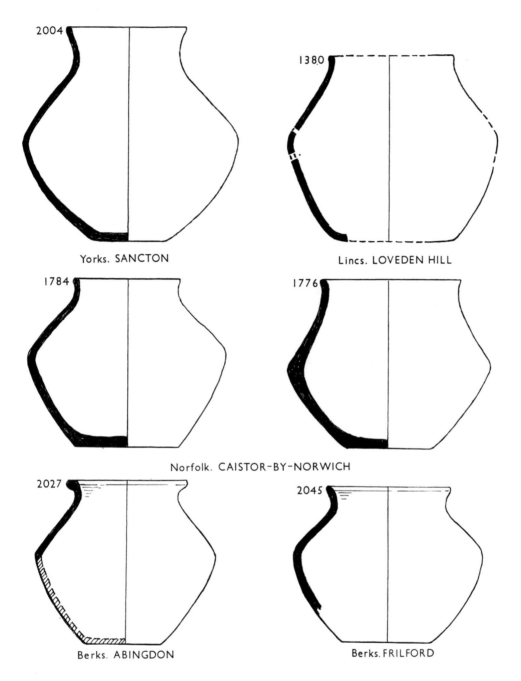

2004 Yorks. SANCTON

1380 Lincs. LOVEDEN HILL

1784 Norfolk. CAISTOR-BY-NORWICH

1776

2027 Berks. ABINGDON

2045 Berks. FRILFORD

Fig. 2. *Plain hollow-necked urns*

1760 NORFOLK, CAISTOR-BY-NORWICH M 53 (Norwich Museum)
Urn with tall concave neck, flat-topped upright rim, and sharply carinated shoulder: smoothed grey/brown ware.

1761 NORFOLK, CAISTOR-BY-NORWICH Y 12 (Norwich Museum)
Urn with tall concave neck, upright rim, and sharply carinated shoulder: heavy grey ware.

1506 NORFOLK, MARKSHALL VI (Norwich Museum)
Urn with tall concave neck and broad carinated shoulder. Rim missing.

1935 NORFOLK, MARKSHALL XVIII (Norwich Museum)
Urn with concave neck, upright rim, and sharp carination.

2015 YORKS., SANCTON (Ashmolean Museum 1886–1317)
Urn with slightly hollowed neck and flaring rim: smooth reddish-brown ware.

1257 LINCS., LOVEDEN HILL 58/98a (Lincoln Museum)
Urn with hollow neck and upright rim.

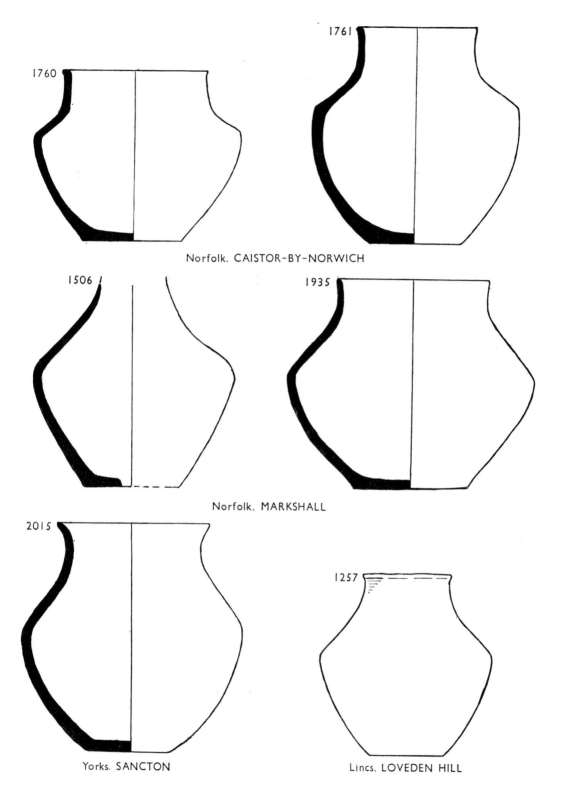

1760

1761

Norfolk. CAISTOR-BY-NORWICH

1506

1935

Norfolk. MARKSHALL

2015

1257

Yorks. SANCTON

Lincs. LOVEDEN HILL

Fig. 3. *Plain sub-biconical urns*

2161 NORFOLK, ILLINGTON 226 (Norwich Museum)
Sub-biconical urn with short upright rim: smooth reddish-brown/black ware.

1328 LINCS., LOVEDEN HILL 60/193 (Lincoln Museum)
Tall ovoid urn with very short upright rim: wipe marks visible on surface.

2012 YORKS., SANCTON (Ashmolean Museum 1886–1316)
Sub-biconical urn with short everted rim: sandy dark-brown ware.

1072 WAR., MARTON A 58 (County Museum, Warwick)
Sub-biconical urn with wide mouth and swollen upright rim, almost round-bottomed: smooth grey ware.

740 NORTHANTS., NEWTON-IN-THE-WILLOWS (Kettering Museum 133)
Sub-biconical urn with short everted rim: smooth brown/grey ware.

745 NORTHANTS., KETTERING (Kettering Museum 7)
Sub-biconical urn with short everted rim and sagging base: smooth brown/grey ware.

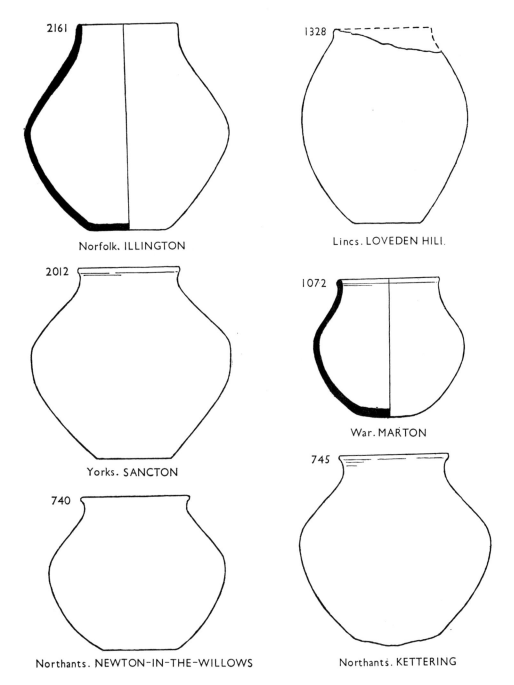

2161

Norfolk. ILLINGTON

1328

Lincs. LOVEDEN HILL.

2012

Yorks. SANCTON

1072

War. MARTON

740

Northants. NEWTON-IN-THE-WILLOWS

745

Northants. KETTERING

Fig. 4. *Plain shouldered urns*

SCALE: Pottery 1:4; Brooch 1:4

1808 NORFOLK, CAISTOR-BY-NORWICH M 46 (Norwich Museum) Wide hump-shouldered urn with short deeply hollowed neck and well-moulded everted rim (reminiscent of Romano-British): smooth red/brown/buff ware.

914 SUFFOLK, LACKFORD HE 91 (Cambridge Museum of Arch. and Eth.)
Wide-mouthed hump-shouldered urn with short upright rim, found with a cruciform brooch of Åberg Group II: brown ware.

1139 LINCS., WEST KEAL, Hall Hill 9 (Lincoln Museum)
Wide-mouthed shouldered urn with upright rim and sagging base: smooth brown ware.

1333 LINCS., LOVEDEN HILL 59/183 (Lincoln Museum)
Wide sloping-shouldered urn with short upright rim.

1990 BERKS., LONG WITTENHAM (British Museum 75 3-10. 17)
Shouldered urn with narrow hollow neck and everted rim: smooth grey/brown ware.

693 LINCS., ELKINGTON 172 (Lincoln Museum)
Shouldered urn with everted rim.

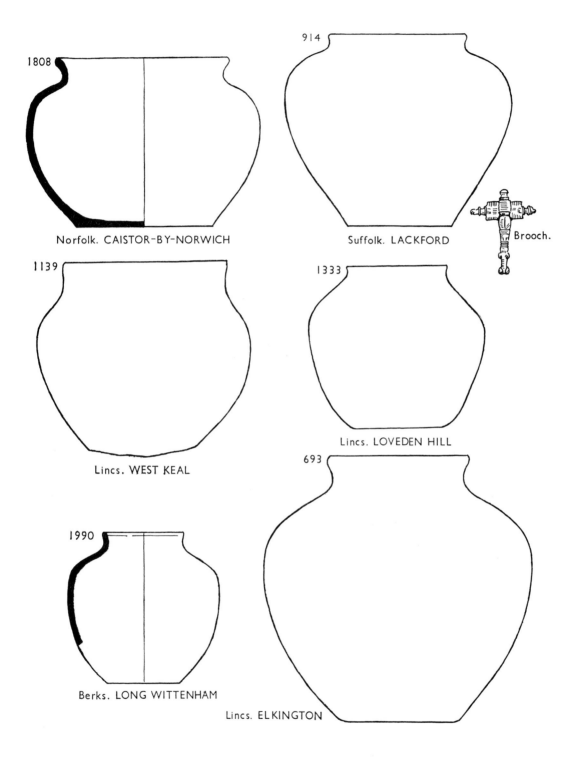

1808

Norfolk. CAISTOR-BY-NORWICH

914

Suffolk. LACKFORD

Brooch.

1139

Lincs. WEST KEAL

1333

Lincs. LOVEDEN HILL

1990

Berks. LONG WITTENHAM

693

Lincs. ELKINGTON

Fig. 5. *Plain bowls*

SCALE: Pottery 1:4; Tweezers 1:3

807 NORTHANTS., MILTON (Northampton Museum D 407/1954–5)
Sub-biconical round-bottomed bowl with slightly everted rim: smooth brown ware.

1193 HANTS, WORTHY PARK Cr. 11
Sub-biconical bowl with narrow base and short upright rim.

2170 NORFOLK, ILLINGTON 273 (Norwich Museum)
Globular bowl with short slightly everted rim: dark-grey ware varying to pink on surface.

500 LINCS., CAYTHORPE (Nottingham Castle Museum 99. 65)
Globular bowl with very short upright rim and rounded base: soft black ware.

1471 LINCS., FONABY Gr. 29 (Scunthorpe Museum)
Tub-shaped bowl with slightly everted rim and sagging base.

1949 KENT, NORTHFLEET (Maidstone Museum)
Small sub-biconical bowl with upright rim.

1149 HANTS, FAREHAM (Cumberland House Museum, Portsmouth)
Small rounded bowl with sharply everted rim. The underside of the base is inscribed with broad grooves in the shape of a cross.

1766 NORFOLK, CAISTOR-BY-NORWICH Y 17 (Norwich Museum)
Sharply biconical bowl with everted rim: smooth polished grey/black ware.

2052 CAMBS., HASLINGFIELD (Ashmolean Museum 1886–1362)
Small shouldered bowl with upright neck and everted rim: pinkish buff ware with dark patches on surface.

1992 BERKS., LONG WITTENHAM (British Museum 75 3–10. 19)
Carinated bowl with short everted rim: smooth dark grey/black ware, once burnished.

900 SUFFOLK, LACKFORD (Cambridge Museum of Arch. and Eth. 50–50)
Sharply carinated biconical bowl with hollow neck and round bottom, found with bronze tweezers: burnished brown ware.

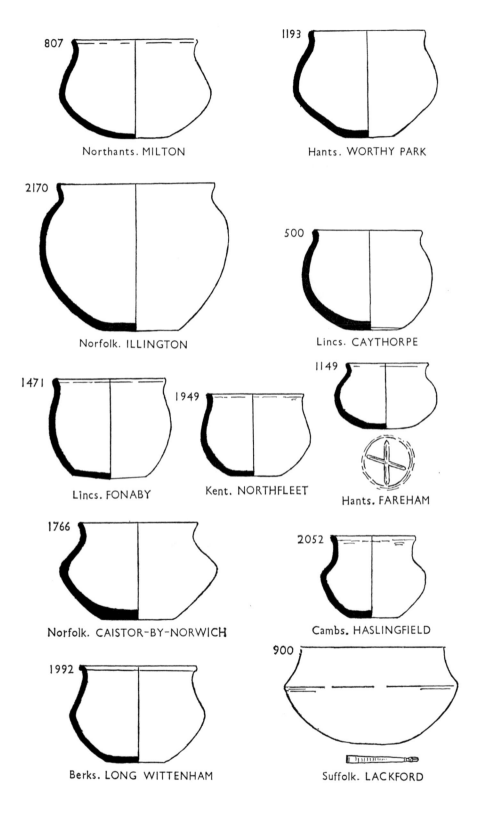

807 Northants. MILTON

1193 Hants. WORTHY PARK

2170 Norfolk. ILLINGTON

500 Lincs. CAYTHORPE

1471 Lincs. FONABY

1949 Kent. NORTHFLEET

1149 Hants. FAREHAM

1766 Norfolk. CAISTOR-BY-NORWICH

2052 Cambs. HASLINGFIELD

1992 Berks. LONG WITTENHAM

900 Suffolk. LACKFORD

Fig. 6. *Plain accessory vessels*

SCALE 1:4

1252   LINCS., LOVEDEN HILL 57/31 (Lincoln Museum)
Small biconical vessel with slightly everted rim and rounded base.

501   LINCS., CAYTHORPE (Nottingham Castle Museum 99. 62)
Small biconical vessel with everted rim: hard sandy/grey ware.

478   LINCS., GREETWELL (Lincoln Museum)
Small biconical vessel with tall neck and flaring rim: rough grey ware, rather hard and well made. From the Greetwell Roman villa.

1061   NORFOLK, GRIMSTON (King's Lynn Museum)
Small sharply carinated biconical vessel with wide mouth and everted rim: thick smooth dark ware, once burnished.

2073   CAMBS., BARRINGTON A (Ashmolean Museum 1909–277)
Wide-mouthed biconical vessel with slightly everted rim: hard smooth dark ware, well made.

475   LEICS., BREEDON-ON-THE-HILL (Derby Museum)
Small biconical vessel with sharp carination, hollow neck, everted rim, and angled base: grey ware, well made.

2083   BERKS., EAST SHEFFORD (British Museum 93 7–16. 29)
Small biconical vessel with everted rim: rough red/brown ware.

2048   BERKS., FRILFORD (Ashmolean Museum 1930–51)
Small sharply carinated biconical bowl with short everted rim: brown ware burnished yellow: very well made.

1062   BERKS., BLEWBURTON HILL (Reading Museum)
Sub-biconical vessel with upright rim: hard dark-grey ware.

2002   BERKS., LONG WITTENHAM (British Museum 75 3–10. 20)
Small sharply carinated biconical bowl with everted rim: smooth dark ware, perhaps once burnished.

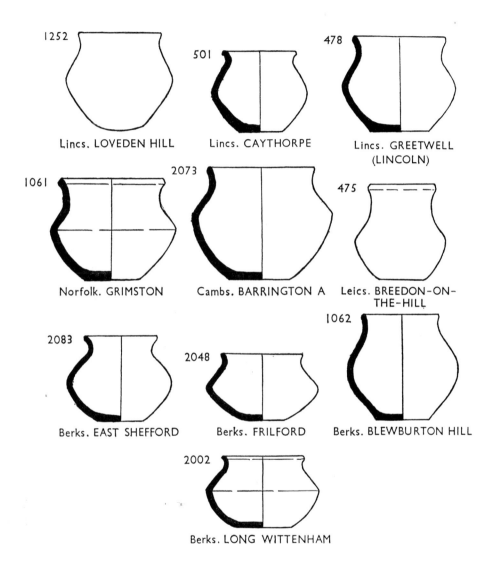

1252
Lincs. LOVEDEN HILL

501
Lincs. CAYTHORPE

478
Lincs. GREETWELL
(LINCOLN)

1061
Norfolk. GRIMSTON

2073
Cambs. BARRINGTON A

475
Leics. BREEDON-ON-
THE-HILL

2083
Berks. EAST SHEFFORD

2048
Berks. FRILFORD

1062
Berks. BLEWBURTON HILL

2002
Berks. LONG WITTENHAM

Fig. 7. *Plain globular urns I*

SCALE 1:4

2191 NORFOLK, ILLINGTON 125 (Norwich Museum)
Globular urn with short upright rim: coarse thick burnished black/fawn ware.

1936 NORFOLK, MARKSHALL IV (Norwich Museum)
Wide-mouthed globular urn with short upright rim.

621 LINCS., ELKINGTON 25 (Lincoln Museum)
Small globular urn with short upright rim and round bottom: dark-brown ware.

555 LINCS., LOVEDEN HILL NE 4 (Lincoln Museum)
Globular urn with short upright rim: coarse dark grey/black ware.

1974 BEDS., KEMPSTON (British Museum 75 6–2. 1)
Globular urn with slightly everted rim, the lower part much restored heavy black ware, once burnished.

1947 KENT, NORTHFLEET 1 (Maidstone Museum)
Globular urn with tall upright rim.

1046 KENT, RISELEY (Dartford Museum 1937/8. 2)
Small globular urn with sharp upright rim and sagging base: reddish-brown/black ware.

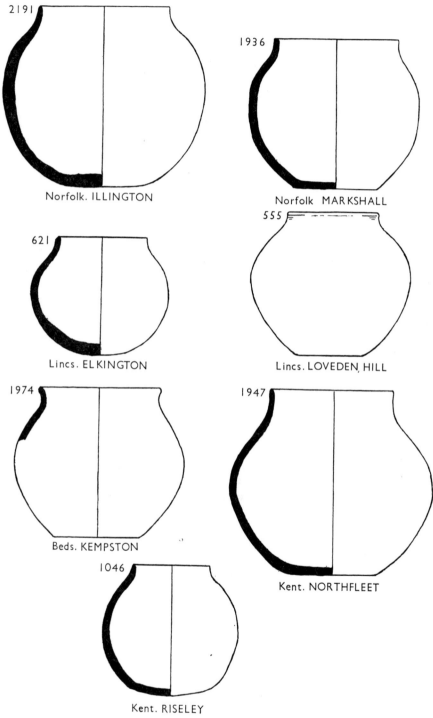

2191 Norfolk. ILLINGTON

1936 Norfolk MARKSHALL

621 Lincs. ELKINGTON

555 Lincs. LOVEDEN HILL

1974 Beds. KEMPSTON

1947 Kent. NORTHFLEET

1046 Kent. RISELEY

Fig. 8. *Plain globular urns II*

2172　NORFOLK, ILLINGTON 277 (Norwich Museum)
Globular urn with tallish everted rim: hard black/reddish-brown ware.
A hole has been cut in the centre of the base.

1777　NORFOLK, CAISTOR-BY-NORWICH G 1 (Norwich Museum)
Wide-mouthed globular urn with everted rim: rough grey/brown ware.

738　NORTHANTS., NEWTON-IN-THE-WILLOWS (Kettering
Museum 133)
Small globular vessel with short everted rim and round bottom: smooth
dark-grey ware.

692　LINCS., ELKINGTON 170 (Lincoln Museum)
Globular urn with everted rim and round bottom: dark-brown ware.

2029　BERKS., ABINGDON C 50 (Ashmolean Museum 1934–375)
Globular urn with everted rim and round bottom: smooth burnished
greyish-pink ware: well made.

2046　BERKS., FRILFORD (Ashmolean Museum 1886–1408)
Small globular vessel with slightly everted rim and rounded base: smooth
brown ware.

1048　KENT, RISELEY (Dartford Museum 1937/8. 4)
Small globular vessel with slightly everted rim and round bottom: smooth
reddish-brown/black ware.

2069　KENT, HOWLETTS (British Museum 1918 7–8. 30)
Small globular vessel with everted rim and sagging base: heavy rough
grey ware.

1056　KENT, FARNINGHAM (Dartford Museum 12)
Globular vessel with everted rim and rounded base: grey/black ware.

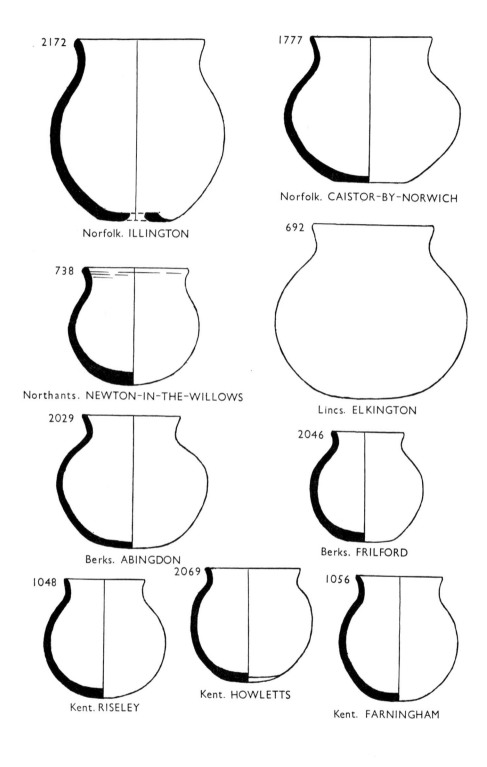

2172 Norfolk. ILLINGTON

1777 Norfolk. CAISTOR-BY-NORWICH

738 Northants. NEWTON-IN-THE-WILLOWS

692 Lincs. ELKINGTON

2029 Berks. ABINGDON

2046 Berks. FRILFORD

1048 Kent. RISELEY

2069 Kent. HOWLETTS

1056 Kent. FARNINGHAM

Fig. 9. *Plain vessels with tall narrow necks*

SCALE: Pottery 1:4; Seax 1:4

562 LINCS., LOVEDEN HILL NE 11 (a) (Lincoln Museum)
Beaker-shaped vessel with ovoid body, tall neck, and flaring rim: rough dark-brown ware.

2173 NORFOLK, ILLINGTON 278 (Norwich Museum)
Globular vessel with tall conical neck and flat base, rim missing: burnished black/red/fawn ware.

1058 RUTLAND, BARROW, near Cottesmore, 2
Low-shouldered vessel with tall conical neck: gritty red/buff ware, once burnished.

1157 BEDS., LEIGHTON BUZZARD Site II Grave 29
Low-shouldered vessel with tall hollowed neck: hard dark-grey ware.

1074 WAR., BURTON DASSETT A 237 (County Museum, Warwick)
Shouldered vessel, lower part missing, with tall hollow neck and everted rim: hard leathery dark ware, once burnished. Found with a seventh-century *seax*.

2272 NORTHANTS., CRANSLEY (British Museum 82 6–22. 2)
Sub-biconical urn with tall neck, slightly everted rim, and five very slight hollow bosses set low on the belly: smooth dark-brown ware.

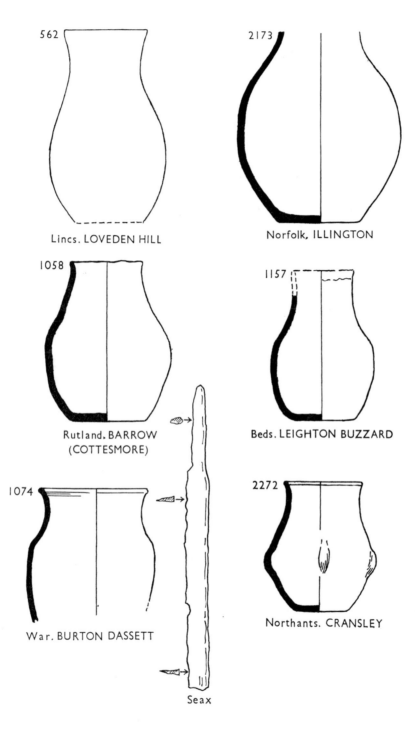

562   Lincs. LOVEDEN HILL

2173   Norfolk, ILLINGTON

1058   Rutland. BARROW
(COTTESMORE)

1157   Beds. LEIGHTON BUZZARD

1074   War. BURTON DASSETT

2272   Northants. CRANSLEY

Seax

Fig. 10. *Plain domestic wares I: small crude accessories*

2051 CAMBS., HASLINGFIELD (Ashmolean Museum 1886–1355)
Small wide-mouthed pot of irregular form and very crude workmanship:
coarse gritty grey ware, once smoothed.

2049 CAMBS., HASLINGFIELD (Ashmolean Museum 1886–1354)
Small tub-shaped pot of irregular form, with slightly incurved rim: smooth
dark ware.

1948 KENT, NORTHFLEET 12 (Maidstone Museum)
Wide-mouthed tub-shaped pot of irregular form.

481 LINCS., LACEBY (Lincoln Museum)
Small wide pot with near-upright sides and flat base: dark-brown ware with
black inner surface.

2037 BERKS., ABINGDON B 51 (Ashmolean Museum)
Bell-shaped pot with wide mouth, flaring rim, and round bottom; very
irregular in form: red/buff ware, with smooth black surface.

2082 BERKS., EAST SHEFFORD (Ashmolean Museum 1955–361)
Hemispherical bowl with very uneven rim: smooth dark brown ware.

2050 CAMBS., HASLINGFIELD (Ashmolean Museum 1886–1356)
Miniature tub-shaped pot of irregular form: thick coarse grey/brown ware.

1568 NORFOLK, CAISTOR-BY-NORWICH N 95(b) (Norwich Museum)
Miniature barrel-shaped pot with incurved rim and round bottom.

2089 OXON., BRIGHTHAMPTON 43 Urn 4 (Ashmolean Museum 1966–
93)
Miniature globular pot with incurved rim and flat bottom: crude
black ware, poorly made.

1050 KENT, RISELEY (Dartford Museum 1937/8. 6)
Small bell-shaped pot with wide mouth, flaring rim, and round bottom:
black ware.

1522 LINCS., CAYTHORPE (Nottingham Castle Museum 99. 63)
Small wide-mouthed globular bowl with sagging base: thick dark sandy
ware.

1057 RUTLAND, BARROW, near Cottesmore, 1
Wide-mouthed globular bowl with rounded base: gritty dark-grey ware.

1478 LINCS., FONABY US 57 (Scunthorpe Museum)
Wide-mouthed globular bowl with rounded base.

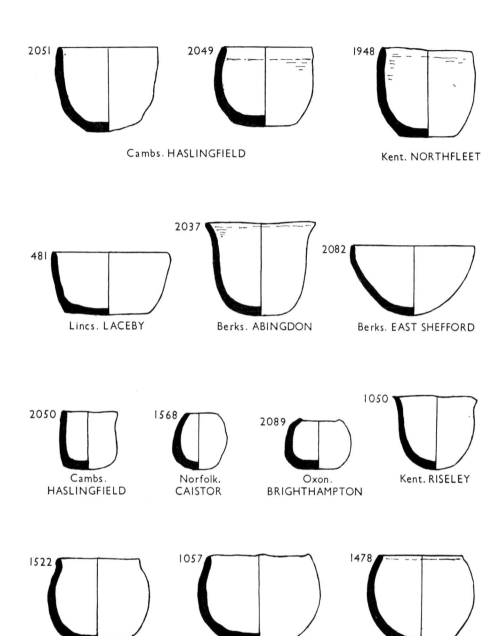

2051 Cambs. HASLINGFIELD

2049

1948 Kent. NORTHFLEET

481 Lincs. LACEBY

2037 Berks. ABINGDON

2082 Berks. EAST SHEFFORD

2050 Cambs. HASLINGFIELD

1568 Norfolk. CAISTOR

2089 Oxon. BRIGHTHAMPTON

1050 Kent. RISELEY

1522 Lincs. CAYTHORPE

1057 Rutland. BARROW (COTTESMORE)

1478 Lincs. FONABY

Fig. 11. *Plain domestic wares II: wide-mouthed cook-pots*

1144 LINCS., WEST KEAL, Hall Hill 17 (Lincoln Museum)
Wide-mouthed cook-pot with upright rim.

1482 LINCS., FONABY US 58 (Scunthorpe Museum)
Sub-biconical cook-pot with slightly everted rim.

2190 NORFOLK, ILLINGTON 101 (Norwich Museum)
Wide-mouthed cook-pot with flat topped upright rim: smooth red/brown
ware.

1311 LINCS., LOVEDEN HILL 59/173 (Lincoln Museum)
Wide-mouthed shouldered cook-pot with slightly everted rim.

1156 BEDS., LEIGHTON BUZZARD Site II Grave 30
Small wide-mouthed cook-pot with everted rim: soft brown ware.

1045 KENT, RISELEY (Dartford Museum 1937/8. 1)
Beaker-shaped cook-pot with wide mouth and irregular rim: brown/black
ware.

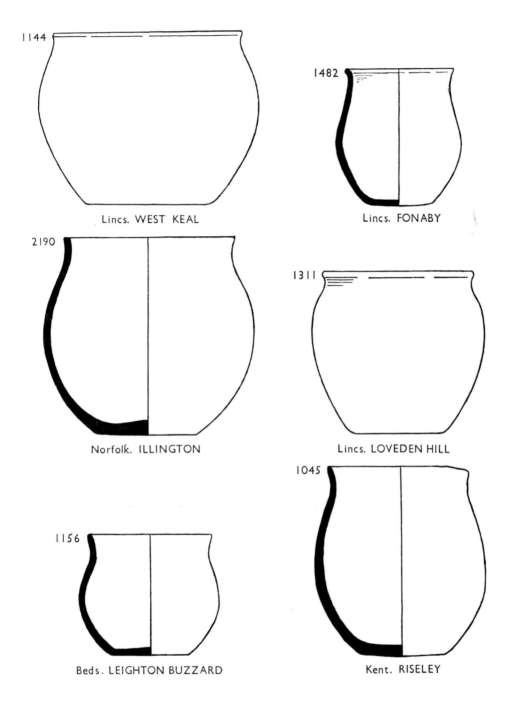

1144   Lincs. WEST KEAL

1482   Lincs. FONABY

2190   Norfolk. ILLINGTON

1311   Lincs. LOVEDEN HILL

1156   Beds. LEIGHTON BUZZARD

1045   Kent. RISELEY

Fig. 12. *Plain domestic wares III: cook-pots with lugs*

SCALE 1:4

1977 BEDS., KEMPSTON (British Museum 91 6–24. 30)
Globular vessel with everted rim and well-made footring, smooth dark-brown/buff ware.
On the belly are three very small narrow vertical lugs, partly countersunk by being pinched up from outside; they would not support a cord and are of no practical use.

2043 BERKS., FRILFORD (Ashmolean Museum 1409–1886)
Wide-mouthed vessel with everted rim and thick solid footstand: reddish-brown/black ware.
On the shoulder are three solid applied lugs.

783 NORTHAMPTON (Northampton Museum D 299/1954–5)
Small wide-mouthed vessel with thickened rim and flat applied footstand: rough dark ware with smoothed surface.
About half-way up the sides are three pierced applied lugs.

2154 NORFOLK, ILLINGTON 154 (Norwich Museum)
Wide-mouthed vessel with upright walls and thick solid footstand with sagging base: thick rough brown/grey ware.
About two-thirds of the way up the sides are three pierced applied lugs.

1153 BEDS., LEIGHTON BUZZARD Site I Grave 10
Small crudely made vessel with wide mouth, short everted rim, and rather angular shoulder: rough dark ware.
Just below the shoulder are three pierced lugs.

2034 BERKS., ABINGDON B 51 (Ashmolean Museum)
Small wide-mouthed vessel with sharply everted rim and low footring: coarse black ware, very crudely made.
On the shoulder are three small pierced applied lugs.

1109 BERKS., BLEWBURTON HILL Burial 11 (Reading Museum)
Small vessel with widely splayed sides on a low footring: dark grey ware.
On the sides are three large pierced lugs.

799 NORTHANTS., HOLDENBY (Northampton Museum D 311/1954–5)
Vessel with widely splayed sides on a low footring: rough grey/brown ware.
Slightly over half-way up the sides are three pierced lugs.

278 CAMBS., ST. JOHN'S (Cambridge Museum of Arch. and Eth.)
Sub-biconical vessel with wide mouth and everted rim: heavily made rough brown/red ware.
On the belly are three pierced lugs.

349 KENT, NORTHFLEET 7 (Maidstone Museum)
Wide-mouthed vessel of rounded form with everted rim: hard leathery rough dark-grey ware.
On the belly are three pierced lugs.

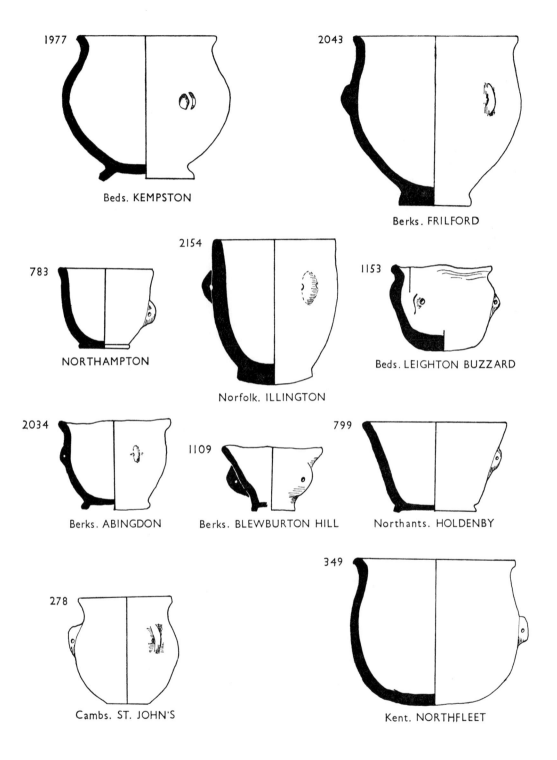

1977 Beds. KEMPSTON

2043 Berks. FRILFORD

783 NORTHAMPTON

2154 Norfolk. ILLINGTON

1153 Beds. LEIGHTON BUZZARD

2034 Berks. ABINGDON

1109 Berks. BLEWBURTON HILL

799 Northants. HOLDENBY

278 Cambs. ST. JOHN'S

349 Kent. NORTHFLEET

Fig. 13. *Plain urns with bosses*

SCALE 1:4

117   YORKS., ?BROUGHTON, near Malton, 28 (Yorkshire Museum, York)[1]
Shoulder-boss bowl with slightly everted rim: rough pitted brown ware.
On the shoulder are eight hollow bosses.

975   SUFFOLK, LACKFORD TDY 39 (Cambridge Museum of Arch. and Eth. 50. 85A)
Sub-biconical urn with slightly everted rim.
On the belly is a row of widely spaced bosses.

90   YORKS., HEWORTH 20 (Yorkshire Museum, York)
Shoulder-boss urn with hollow neck and strongly but roughly moulded lip: pitted grey ware.
On the shoulder are twenty hollow bosses.

1419   LINCS., LOVEDEN HILL 58/99 (i) (Lincoln Museum)
Shoulder-boss urn with tall, conical neck and short everted rim: dark-brown ware.
On the shoulder is a row of hollow bosses.

211   CAMBS., GIRTON (Cambridge Museum of Arch. and Eth.)
Tall biconical urn with narrow neck and short everted rim: hard smooth brown ware.
On the belly are four hollow bosses.

978   SUFFOLK, LACKFORD WDY 43 (Cambridge Museum of Arch. and Eth. 50. 36)
Tall biconical urn with upright rim.
On the shoulder is a row of bosses.

---

[1] Mr. G. F. Willmot, F.S.A., Keeper of the Yorkshire Museum, kindly informs me that the attribution to Broughton, near Malton, is dubious. The urn probably came from an unidentified site on the East Yorkshire Wolds.

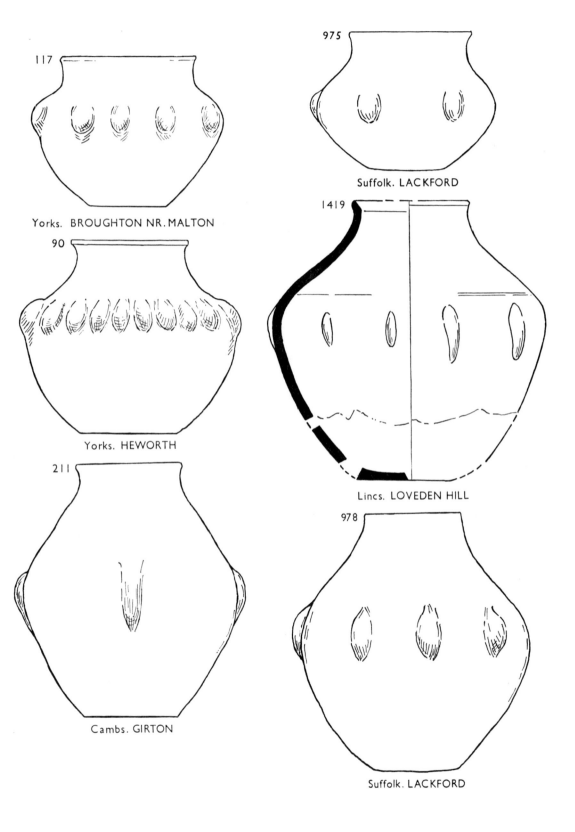

117 Yorks. BROUGHTON NR. MALTON

90 Yorks. HEWORTH

211 Cambs. GIRTON

975 Suffolk. LACKFORD

1419 Lincs. LOVEDEN HILL

978 Suffolk. LACKFORD

Fig. 14. *Horizontal linear ornament*

SCALE 1:4

1269 LINCS., LOVEDEN HILL 58/84 (Lincoln Museum)
Wide-mouthed sub-biconical urn with everted rim.
Decorated with six close-set horizontal lines below the neck.

464 LEICESTER (Leicester Museum)
Biconical urn with everted rim: burnished black ware, well made.
Decorated with four strong horizontal lines just above the maximum dia-
meter.

686 LINCS., ELKINGTON 164 (Lincoln Museum)
Round-shouldered bowl with sharply everted rim: dark-brown ware.
Decorated with three horizontal lines on the shoulder.

243 CAMBS., GIRTON (Girton College)
Small globular, round-bottomed vessel with everted rim: smooth black/
grey ware, rather roughly made.
Decorated with three sharp horizontal lines on the shoulder, between which
are two bands of broad shallow tooling.

2102 PETERBOROUGH (British Museum 79 9–27. 1)
Small biconical bowl with everted rim: smooth black ware, well made,
probably once burnished.
Decorated with four firm horizontal lines above the carination.

2105 NORFOLK, PENSTHORPE (British Museum 53 10–29. 2)
Large bowl with sharply carinated shoulder and hollow neck: heavy grey
ware, once burnished.
Decorated with two broad shallow grooves at the base of the neck.

866 SUFFOLK, LACKFORD HB 1 (Cambridge Museum of Arch. and
Eth. 49. 580)
Large sub-biconical urn with everted rim: grey/brown ware, burnished.
Decorated with four horizontal lines above the maximum diameter between
the inner two of which lies a flat feathered collar.

2112 NORFOLK, ILLINGTON 279 (Norwich Museum)
Sub-biconical urn with short slightly everted rim: hard, sandy, blue-grey
ware, mottled dark brown/fawn.
Decorated with four bands of four/six horizontal lines, two above and
two below the maximum diameter. A cross has been inscribed on the underside of the base.

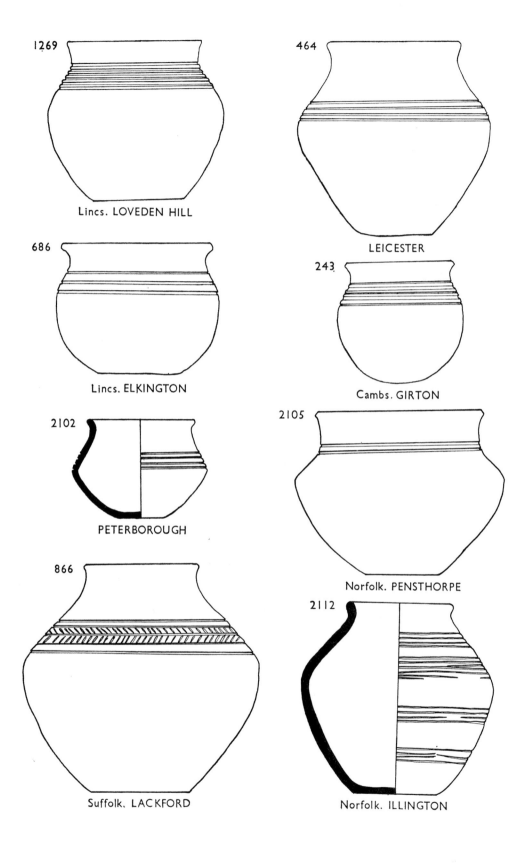

1269 Lincs. LOVEDEN HILL

464 LEICESTER

686 Lincs. ELKINGTON

243 Cambs. GIRTON

2102 PETERBOROUGH

2105 Norfolk. PENSTHORPE

866 Suffolk. LACKFORD

2112 Norfolk. ILLINGTON

Fig. 15. *Horizontal linear ornament with stamps*

SCALE: Pottery 1:4; Stamps 1:2

840 RUTLAND, NORTH LUFFENHAM (Leicester Museum)
Wide-mouthed biconical vessel with slightly everted rim: corky red-brown ware.
Decorated with two bands of three sharp horizontal lines on the neck, between which is a row of stamps. One stamp is used.

2205 NORFOLK, ILLINGTON 122 (Norwich Museum)
Small round-bottomed urn with wide mouth and upright rim: smooth red/fawn ware.
Decorated with three sharp horizontal lines on the neck, below which is a row of stamps, another line, and another row of stamps. Two stamps are used.

209 CAMBS., GIRTON (Cambridge Museum of Arch. and Eth.)
Biconical bowl with everted rim: smooth grey ware.
Decorated with two sharp necklines, below which are three rows of deeply impressed stamps extending across the carination, each row demarcated by a sharp line. Three stamps are used.

1176 NORFOLK, SHROPHAM (British Museum 56 6–27. 5)
Large biconical urn with tall neck and everted rim: polished black/brown ware, well made.
Decorated with four necklines, below which are three solid collars, each decorated with alternate groups of dots and slashing. Between the collars are two horizontal rows of stamps. Below the third collar are three more horizontal lines and another row of stamps, placed just above the carination. Two stamps are used.

384 BEDS., KEMPSTON (Bedford Museum, D 2 3727)
Biconical urn with hollow neck and short everted rim: hard black ware, once burnished.
Decorated with five groups of three/four necklines between which are four rows of stamps, covering the whole upper half of the pot. Three stamps are used.

1123 LEICS., SAXBY (Leicester Museum 350. 1952)
Biconical urn with tall upright neck: smooth grey ware.
Decorated with five groups of two/three horizontal lines between which are four rows of stamps, covering the whole upper half of the pot. On the carination are three slight hollow bosses. Three stamps appear to have been used.

797 NORTHANTS., HOLDENBY (Northampton Museum D 293/1954–5)
Wide biconical urn with sharply angled base and short narrow neck with upright rim: polished black ware, very well made.
Decorated with seven groups of two/three strong horizontal lines between which are six rows of stamps, extending from the neck to below the carination. Three stamps are used.

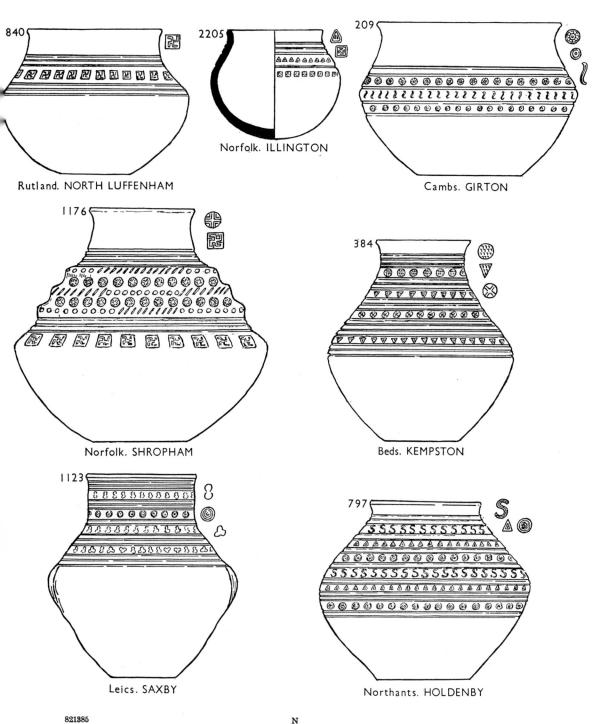

840

Rutland. NORTH LUFFENHAM

2205

Norfolk. ILLINGTON

209

Cambs. GIRTON

1176

Norfolk. SHROPHAM

384

Beds. KEMPSTON

1123

Leics. SAXBY

797

Northants. HOLDENBY

Fig. 16. *Biconical linear ornament I*

SCALE 1:4

1356 LINCS., LOVEDEN HILL 60/222 (Lincoln Museum)
Sharply biconical urn with slightly everted rim.
Decorated with five close-set necklines above a band of three-line chevrons
extending to the carination.

1322 LINCS., LOVEDEN HILL 59/164 (a) (Lincoln Museum)
Biconical urn with tall hollow neck, rim missing.
Decorated with at least seven close-set necklines above a double zone of
interlocking chevrons composed of irregular groups of three/four diagonal
lines extending to the carination.

1632 NORFOLK, CAISTOR-BY-NORWICH Y 40 (Norwich Museum)
Biconical urn with upright rim: dark-grey/brown ware, once burnished.
Decorated with two firm lines on the neck above a zone composed of groups
of diagonal lines set at right angles to one another, giving an overall basketry
pattern. Below are three more horizontal lines above the carination.

1649 NORFOLK, CAISTOR-BY-NORWICH M 49 (a) (Norwich Museum)
Biconical urn, rim missing: smooth brown/buff ware.
Decorated with two zones of two-line chevrons separated by two tooled
lines and demarcated top and bottom by a single line, the latter lying on
the carination.

1626 NORFOLK, CAISTOR-BY-NORWICH P 15 (Norwich Museum)
Wide-mouthed biconical vessel with short everted rim: hard very well
made smooth grey/brown ware.
Decorated with a zone of three-line chevrons demarcated above by three
and below by four firmly tooled lines. On the sharp carination is a line of
nicks, above a zone of continuous three-line swags. All the decoration is
executed with unusual precision and regularity.

2330 YORKS., SANCTON 4 (Hull Museum)
Wide-mouthed biconical urn with short everted rim.
Decorated with a zone of two-line chevrons demarcated above and below
by four horizontal lines, the lowest of which lies on the carination.

1979 BEDS., KEMPSTON (British Museum 91 6–24. 32)
Biconical urn with tall hollow neck and slightly everted rim: red/brown
ware.
Decorated with a zone of single-line chevrons, demarcated above and below
by a single thin sharp line, the latter lying on the carination. In the lower
triangle of the chevrons a vertical line extends from the base about two-
thirds of the way up the zone. The pattern is irregular.

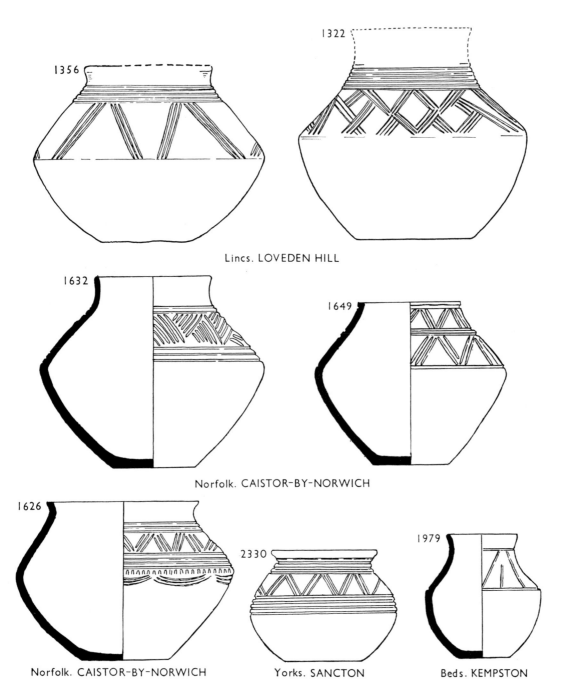

1356

1322

Lincs. LOVEDEN HILL

1632

1649

Norfolk. CAISTOR-BY-NORWICH

1626

2330

1979

Norfolk. CAISTOR-BY-NORWICH

Yorks. SANCTON

Beds. KEMPSTON

Fig. 17. *Biconical linear ornament II*

SCALE 1:4

662 LINCS., ELKINGTON 112 (Lincoln Museum)
Tall sub-biconical urn with everted rim.
Decorated with three necklines below which is a zone of three/four-line chevrons each with
groups of vertical lines in the centre of the lower triangle. In each half of the lower triangle
is a small two-line chevron containing three short vertical strokes. There is a similar group
of vertical strokes at the top of each upper panel of the main chevron zone. Below the main
zone are two horizontal lines on the maximum diameter.

1885 NORFOLK, CAISTOR-BY-NORWICH E 12 (Norwich Museum)
Globular urn with narrow hollow neck and everted rim: rough sandy-red ware.
Decorated from shoulder to rim with a random scheme of lightly drawn lines and jabs,
partly arranged in a series of narrow vertical panels with horizontal bars, and demarcated
below by a horizontal line.

1972 BEDS., KEMPSTON (British Museum 91 6–24. 29)
Small globular wide-mouthed accessory with short everted rim: light-buff/brown ware,
neatly made.
Decorated with a zone of three-line chevrons, demarcated above and below by three horizontal lines.

1178 NORFOLK, SHROPHAM (British Museum 56 6–27. 7)
Sub-biconical urn with hollow neck and everted rim: polished black ware.
Decorated with a zone of single-line chevrons bordered above and below by three strong
horizontal grooves.

13 SUSSEX, ALFRISTON (Barbican House, Lewes)
Round-shouldered round-bottomed bowl with everted rim: smooth dark-grey ware.
Decorated with two lightly tooled lines on the neck, below which is a zone of four-line
chevrons, bordered by a single line on the maximum diameter. At the base of the lower
triangle of each chevron is a horizontal or slightly curved line.

1022 SURREY, WALTON-ON-THAMES (British Museum 1928 2–11. 1)
Shouldered bowl with slightly everted rim: rough grey/brown ware.
Decorated with a zone of single-line chevrons between two lines on the neck, below which
is a larger zone of four-line chevrons, demarcated below by a single line rather below the
maximum diameter. The decoration is carried out in very faintly scratched lines and is
barely visible.

1640 NORFOLK, CAISTOR-BY-NORWICH M 39 (Norwich Museum)
Biconical urn with narrow neck and everted rim: fine smooth grey ware, rather thin-
walled.
Decorated with a single lightly tooled neckline, below which are large irregular three-
line chevrons, some of which have one or two vertical lines in the upper and lower triangles:
below the carination are wide two-line swags, rather out of step with the chevrons above.

2118 NORFOLK, ILLINGTON 165 (Norwich Museum)
Tall barrel-shaped urn with upright neck, rim missing: slightly corky fawn/grey ware, once
burnished.
Decorated with a flat plain collar, below which is a narrower flat slashed collar demarcated
by single lines. Below is a zone of pairs of lines arranged in irregular chevrons and verticals
bordered below by a single firm line. The decoration is carelessly executed.

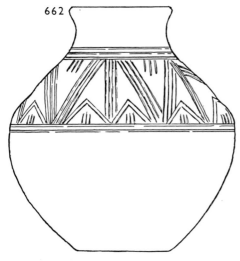

662

Lincs. ELKINGTON

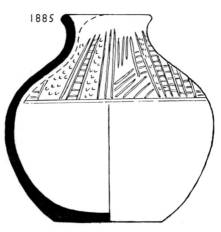

1885

Norfolk. CAISTOR-BY-NORWICH

1972

Beds. KEMPSTON

1178

Norfolk. SHROPHAM

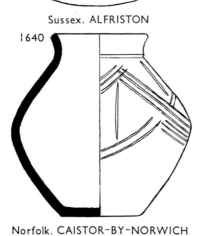

13

Sussex. ALFRISTON

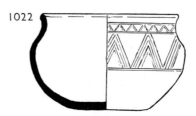

1022

Surrey. WALTON-ON-THAMES

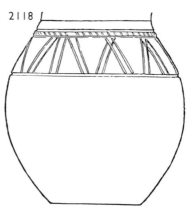

1640

Norfolk. CAISTOR-BY-NORWICH

2118

Norfolk. ILLINGTON

Fig. 18. *Biconical linear ornament with stamps I*

SCALE: Pottery 1:4; Stamps 1:2

2018 YORKS., SANCTON (Ashmolean Museum 1886–1319)
Sub-biconical urn with hollow neck and everted rim: smooth dark ware.
Decorated with two narrow flat slashed collars, between which is a row
of stamps. Below is a zone of three-line chevrons in wide shallow grooves,
bordered below by three horizontal grooves, between the lower two of
which is another row of stamps. One stamp is used.

2253 NORFOLK, ILLINGTON 240 (Norwich Museum)
Globular urn with short upright rim: smooth hard slightly corky light-
fawn ware, varying to red/brown and black, once burnished.
Decorated with four necklines below which is a wide zone containing at
top and bottom a row of stamps: these rows are interrupted by groups of
diagonal lines forming disjointed chevrons. One stamp is used.

39 BERKS., ABINGDON C 38 (Abingdon Museum)
Biconical urn with hollow neck and everted rim.
Decorated with two necklines above a band of three-line chevrons. Below
are two horizontal lines between which is a row of dots, and below this a
wide band of three-line chevrons, the lower triangles containing groups of
three vertical lines, and the upper a group of four dots. The decoration is
demarcated below by two horizontal lines, between which is another row
of dots.

453 KENT, HOWLETTS Grave 14 (British Museum 1936 5–11. 47)
Shouldered urn with hollow neck and everted rim: smooth dark-grey ware.
Decorated on the neck with a zone of four-line chevrons demarcated above
and below by three sharp lines: the triangles are outlined by sharp dots and
there is a vertical line of dots in each. Below the shoulder is a similar zone
of chevrons and dots left open below.

246 CAMBS., GIRTON (Girton College)
Biconical urn with wide mouth and slightly everted rim: grey ware.
Decorated with three fine necklines, above a row of stamps and two more
necklines. Below is a wide zone of single chevrons bordered by two
horizontal lines on the carination. The upper triangles of the chevrons are
filled with stamps, and there is a single row of stamps at the base of the
lower triangles. One stamp is used.

776 NORTHANTS., KETTERING (Northampton Museum D 329/
1954–5)
Shouldered urn with hollow neck and slightly everted rim: smooth red/
brown ware.
Decorated with a zone of three-line chevrons, demarcated above and below
by three firm lines, below which is another zone of three-line chevrons
demarcated below by one line. All the triangles of both chevron zones are
filled with a random arrangement of stamps. Two stamps are used.

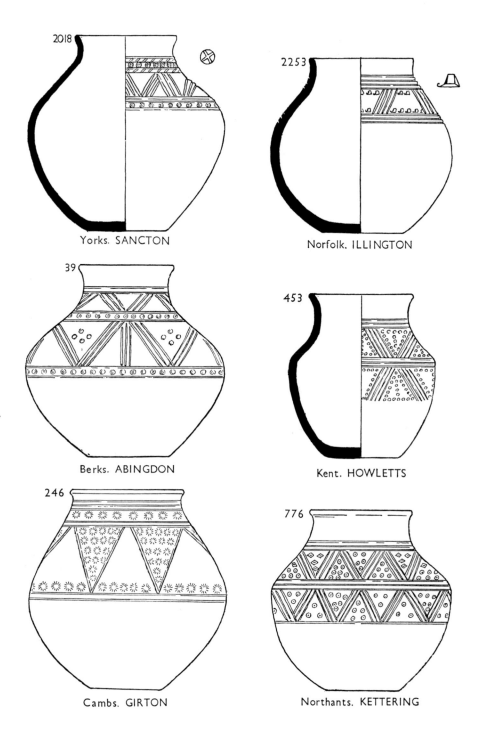

2018

Yorks. SANCTON

2253

Norfolk. ILLINGTON

39

Berks. ABINGDON

453

Kent. HOWLETTS

246

Cambs. GIRTON

776

Northants. KETTERING

Fig. 19. *Biconical linear ornament with stamps II*

SCALE: Pottery 1:4; Stamps 1:2

1280 LINCS., LOVEDEN HILL 58/116 (Lincoln Museum)
Ovoid urn with wide mouth and upright rim, base missing.
Decorated with three necklines above a zone divided into vertical panels by groups of two vertical lines, and demarcated below by two horizontal lines on the maximum diameter. The panels are filled with vertical rows of stamps. One stamp is used, though in some rows half only is impressed.

2250 NORFOLK ILLINGTON 39 (Norwich Museum)
Sub-biconical urn with wide slightly hollowed neck, rim missing: hard smooth dark-grey ware.
Decorated on the neck with a zone, bordered above and below by one horizontal line and divided into panels by single vertical lines, carelessly applied. Some of the panels remain empty, others are filled with random stamping. One stamp is used (possibly from the knob of a cruciform brooch?).

827 RUTLAND, MARKET OVERTON G 5 (Oakham School Museum)
Small sub-biconical accessory with hollow neck and slightly everted rim: rough red/brown ware.
Decorated with a zone of four-line chevrons, demarcated above by two and below by three horizontal lines. The whole space between the chevrons is filled with rows of stamps. One stamp is used.

431 HUNTS., WOODSTON (Peterborough Museum)
Small sub-biconical accessory with everted rim: rough dark-grey ware.
Decorated on the maximum diameter with a zone demarcated above and below by a single scratched line, and containing single-line chevrons, the lower triangles being filled with small pin-point jabs. The decoration is rather carelessly applied, and clearly decadent in character.

380 KENT, SARRE (Maidstone Museum)
Small sub-biconical accessory with upright rim: smooth brown ware.
Decorated with a zone of single-line chevrons demarcated above and below by a single line. The whole space between the chevrons is filled with stamps. One stamp is used.

311 CAMBS., ST. JOHN'S (Cambridge Museum of Arch. and Eth.)
Biconical bossed urn with wide mouth and everted rim: smooth grey ware.
Decorated with three faint necklines from which hang two-line pendent swags filled with rows of stamps. Below are three further horizontal lines, interrupted by four slight bosses outlined on each side by two vertical lines. One stamp is used.

322 CAMBS., LITTLE WILBRAHAM (Cambridge Museum of Arch. and Eth. 27. 1817)
Wide-mouthed biconical urn with upright rim: rough red/brown ware.
Decorated with one horizontal row of stamps on the neck, and another on the carination. Between these lies a chevron zone in stamps only, the lower triangle being filled with stamps. There are no guiding lines. One stamp is used.

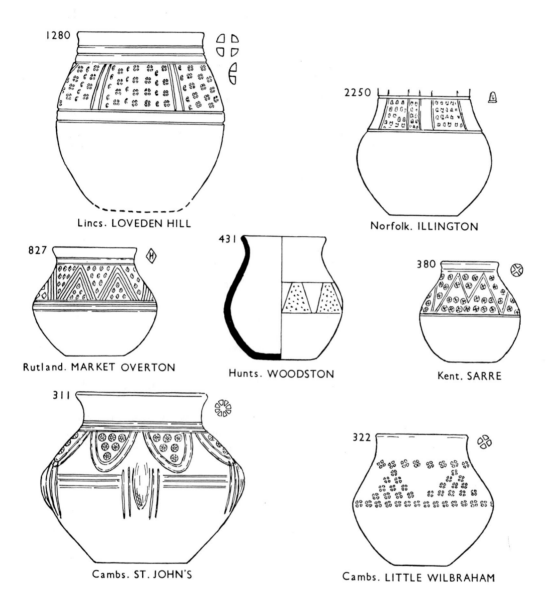

1280

Lincs. LOVEDEN HILL

2250

Norfolk. ILLINGTON

827

Rutland. MARKET OVERTON

431

Hunts. WOODSTON

380

Kent. SARRE

311

Cambs. ST. JOHN'S

322

Cambs. LITTLE WILBRAHAM

Fig. 20. *Biconical linear ornament with* stehende Bogen

SCALE 1:4

2003 YORKS., SANCTON (Ashmolean Museum 1886–1312)
Sharply biconical urn with everted rim: hard dark ware, mottled red.
Decorated with four necklines above a row of dots and three more necklines. Below is a zone, demarcated below by two lines on the carination,
containing three-line *stehende Bogen* between which, and below each, are
vertical lines of dots; the latter bordered by groups of vertical lines. Below the
carination are continuous three-line chevrons.

70 YORKS., SANCTON (Ashmolean Museum 1886–1323)
Biconical shoulder-boss urn with hollow neck, rim missing: dark ware.
Decorated with three grooved necklines above a zone of two-groove
stehende Bogen, below which are two further grooves and twenty-two
hollow bosses on the carination.

2117 NORFOLK, ILLINGTON 169 (Norwich Museum)
Sub-biconical urn with wide mouth and short everted rim: slightly burnished
fawn/dark-brown ware.
Decorated with three sharp necklines above a zone of multilinear *stehende
Bogen*. Below is a single firm line, above continuous multilinear chevrons
untidily drawn, and reaching to the maximum diameter.

1179 NORFOLK, SHROPHAM (British Museum 56 6–27. 6)
Biconical urn with hollow neck and slightly everted rim: burnished black/
brown ware.
Decorated with two wide grooves on the neck, below which is a zone of
three-groove *stehende Bogen*, above continuous four-groove chevrons. There
is irregular use of horizontal lines and of large dots in some of the triangles
between the chevrons.

1448 LINCS., LOVEDEN HILL 59/164 (Lincoln Museum)
Sub-biconical urn with upright neck.
Decorated with three strong grooves on the neck, below which is a zone,
demarcated below by three further lines on the maximum diameter, and
divided by groups of three vertical lines, between which are three diagonal
lines. Below is a row of small two-line *stehende Bogen*.

653 LINCS., ELKINGTON 94 (Lincoln Museum)
Wide-mouthed shouldered urn with everted rim and sagging base: dark-
brown/black ware.
Decorated on the neck with a row of one-groove *stehende Bogen*, above a
flat slashed collar, below which are two-line hanging swags alternating
with two-line chevrons pointing alternately up and down.

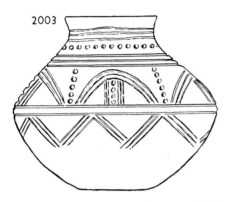

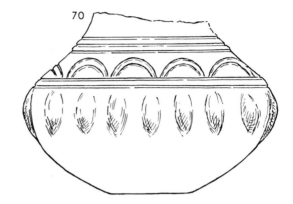

Yorks. SANCTON

Norfolk. ILLINGTON

Norfolk. SHROPHAM

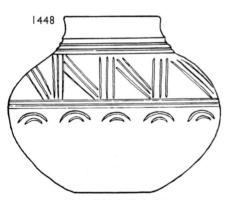

Lincs. LOVEDEN HILL

Lincs. ELKINGTON

Fig. 21. Stehende Bogen *designs*

SCALE 1:4

715 MIDDX., ?SHEPPERTON (Layton Collection P. 307, Brentford Public Library)
Sub-biconical urn with wide mouth and everted rim: grey ware.
Decorated with three broad horizontal grooves on the neck above large three-groove *stehende Bogen*.

341 LINCS., Site unknown (Newcastle Museum, 1810. 9)
Large biconical urn with wide mouth and everted rim: rough grey ware.
Decorated with six broad corrugated grooves on the neck below which are ten single-groove *stehende Bogen*, each covering one large dimple.

339 NORFOLK, CASTLE ACRE (Newcastle Museum 1890. 20)
Small biconical urn with everted rim: red/brown ware.
Decorated with six close-set fine necklines, below which are three-line *stehende Bogen*, each covering a group of three fine vertical lines.

2032 BERKS., ABINGDON C 64 (Ashmolean Museum 1935–397)
Small biconical urn with everted rim: slightly smoothed gritty dark-buff/orange ware.
Decorated with five necklines, below which are small single-line *stehende Bogen*.

1470 LINCS., FONABY Grave 8 (Scunthorpe Museum)
Small globular wide-mouthed urn, with bead rim and sagging base.
Decorated with two roughly drawn necklines above irregular single-line *stehende Bogen*.

1114 LEICS., THURMASTON 2 (Leicester Museum)
Large hollow-necked biconical urn with upright rim: buff/grey ware.
Decorated with four firm necklines, above a flat slashed collar, depending from which are vertical strips of two-line chevrons between two vertical lines. In the intervening panels are two-line *stehende Bogen*, each covering a group of vertical lines, in the centre of which is a vertical strip of feathering. This urn contained part of a Group I cruciform brooch.

2023 YORKS., SANCTON (Ashmolean Museum 1886–1318)
Biconical shoulder-boss urn with narrow neck and flaring rim: smooth dark ware.
Decorated with three firm necklines, below which are four two/three-line *stehende Bogen*, each covering an oval hollow boss outlined with two or three vertical lines or occasional groups of diagonals.

715

Middx.?SHEPPERTON

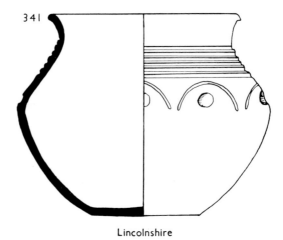

341

Lincolnshire

339

Norfolk. CASTLE ACRE

2032

Berks. ABINGDON

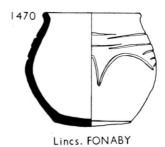

1470

Lincs. FONABY

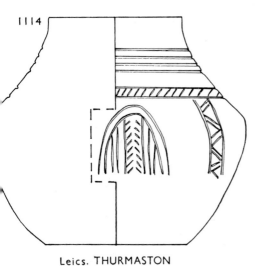

1114

Leics. THURMASTON

2023

Yorks. SANCTON

Fig. 22. Buckelurnen *of Groups I and III*

SCALE: Pottery 1:4; Brooch 1:4

2944 BEDS., LUTON (Luton Museum 45/41/27)
Wide shouldered *Buckelurne* of Group I with upright neck, slightly everted rim, and moulded footring: smooth brown/black ware.
Decorated with a raised collar carrying diagonal and chevron lines and demarcated above and below by a groove and two lines. On the shoulder are four vertical and four horizontal oval bosses set alternately and each carrying a different design in groups of diagonal and chevron lines.

56 OXON., OSNEY (Ashmolean Museum)
Shouldered *Buckelurne* of Group III with conical neck and well-moulded footring, rim missing: smooth dark ware.
Decorated with a flat collar carrying continuous single-line chevrons and three dots in each triangle. On the shoulder are five plain hollow bosses alternating with vertical bosses carrying different designs in lines, dots, and a few impressions of a stamp. Passing below the plain bosses and above the decorated bosses is a continuous raised cable decorated partly with slashed lines and partly with lines and dots. Below the bosses is a single horizontal line. One stamp is used.

852 SUFFOLK, LACKFORD (Cambridge Museum of Arch. and Eth. 48. 2491)
Globular *Buckelurne* of Group I with conical neck, slightly everted rim and moulded foot-stand: brown/black ware, burnished.
Decorated on the neck with a deep groove demarcated above and below by a fine line. On the shoulder are diagonal bosses forming continuous chevrons from the upper points of which depend narrow vertical bosses, all being demarcated on both sides by a groove between two fine lines. This urn contained a Group I cruciform brooch.

1175 BEDS., SANDY (British Museum 37. 11–11. 9). (*Ant. Journ.* xxxiv (1954), Pl. XXI b as from Ickwellbury, Beds., but corrected to Sandy in *Ant. Journ.* xxxvii (1957), 224.)
Biconical *Buckelurne* of Group I with tall hollow neck, everted rim and well-moulded footring: smooth black ware, once burnished.
Decorated with two necklines above three raised collars of which the second is slashed. On the carination are four horizontal oval bosses outlined and split horizontally with a groove and two lines: a continuous raised cable slashed with line and groove forms arches over these bosses: in the spandrels above it are round plain bosses.

808 NORTHANTS., MILTON (Northampton Museum D20/1947)
Biconical *Buckelurne* of Group I with well-moulded footring, rim missing: smooth grey ware, once burnished.
Decorated with three broad grooves on the neck: on the carination are seven diagonal hollow bosses, demarcated on each side with a single line and slashed alternately with diagonal and longitudinal lines.

1417 LINCS., HOUGH-ON-THE-HILL (Loveden Hill A6/246) (British Museum)
Biconical *Buckelurne* of Group I with narrow neck and slight footring, rim missing: brown ware.
Decorated with four raised collars of which the second is finger-tipped, and the third slashed with pairs of lines. On the carination are vertical hollow bosses demarcated on each side with two lines alternating with horizontal oval bosses surrounded and split horizontally with two lines. Over each oval boss is a *stehende Bogen* boss slashed diagonally with pairs of lines and demarcated above by two lines and below by a single line.

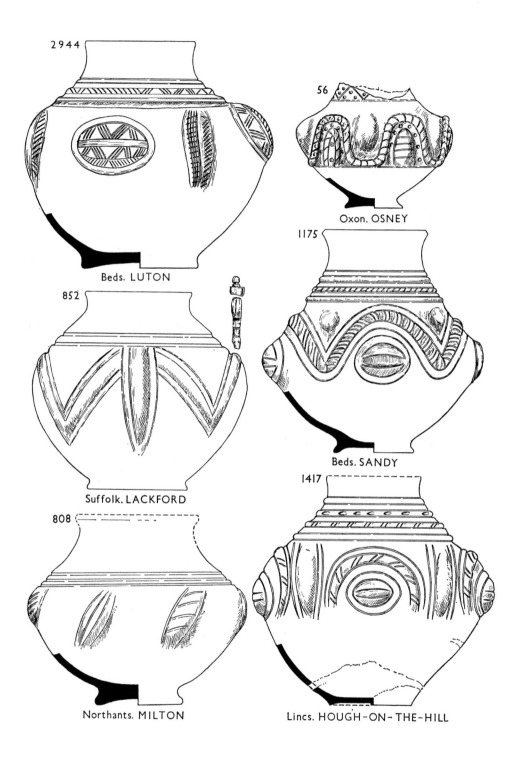

2944

Beds. LUTON

56

Oxon. OSNEY

1175

Beds. SANDY

852

Suffolk. LACKFORD

808

Northants. MILTON

1417

Lincs. HOUGH-ON-THE-HILL

Fig. 23. Buckelurnen *of Group II*

128 YORKS., SANCTON 10 (Hull Museum)
Biconical *Buckelurne* with tall hollow neck and everted rim: smooth dark-grey/brown ware.
Decorated with a raised finger-tipped collar, below which are four oval bosses on the carination,
each covered with raised, finger-tipped *stehende Bogen* bosses, broken at the top. In the intervening panels are small round bosses set level with the top of the main bosses.

1268 LINCS., LOVEDEN HILL 57/34 (Lincoln Museum)
Shouldered *Buckelurne* with wide hollow neck and slightly everted rim.
Decorated with six close-set necklines below which are *stehende Bogen* bosses each covering
three oval bosses which are demarcated by groups of vertical lines. In the intervening panels are
groups of two oval bosses also demarcated by groups of vertical lines.

1664 NORFOLK CAISTOR-BY-NORWICH M 28 (Norwich Museum)
Shouldered *Buckelurne* with low conical neck and slightly everted rim: smooth soft brown
ware, poorly fired.
.Decorated with four grooves on the neck, below which are ten hollow shoulder-bosses,
alternately vertical and horizontal, each covered by three-line *stehende Bogen*.

2086 BERKS., WALLINGFORD (Ashmolean Museum 1939–446)
Shouldered *Buckelurne*, rim missing: smooth thick brown/grey ware.
Decorated with at least two wide grooves on the neck, and eight hollow shoulder-bosses,
alternately round and vertical, each covered by one wide *stehende Bogen* groove.

841 RUTLAND, NORTH LUFFENHAM (Oakham School Museum)
Shouldered *Buckelurne* with everted rim: smooth dark ware, extremely well made. Decorated
with a raised collar on the neck below which are three sharp necklines. On the shoulder are
eight oval hollow bosses, alternately vertical and horizontal, between which are small round
bosses. The vertical bosses are demarcated with groups of vertical lines, and the horizontal
bosses by groups of both vertical and horizontal lines: some of both kinds carry a row of small
nicks on their long axes. The treatment varies in detail from panel to panel. Below the bosses
are four/five-line chevrons.

2042 BERKS., ABINGDON C 82 (Ashmolean Museum 1935–414)
Large biconical *Buckelurne* with upright neck, mostly restored, and sagging base: slightly
smoothed grey ware.
Decorated with three raised collars, the lowest of which is slashed with alternate groups of
vertical and horizontal lines. The two upper collars may have been decorated in the same way.
Below is a horizontal row of dots above continuous single-line chevrons, carelessly drawn.
On the carination are ten large hollow bosses alternately vertical and round, the long bosses
decorated with a central vertical row of dots, with horizontal slashing on each side, the round
bosses with a surrounding circle of dots and two lines of dots across the centre to form a cross.

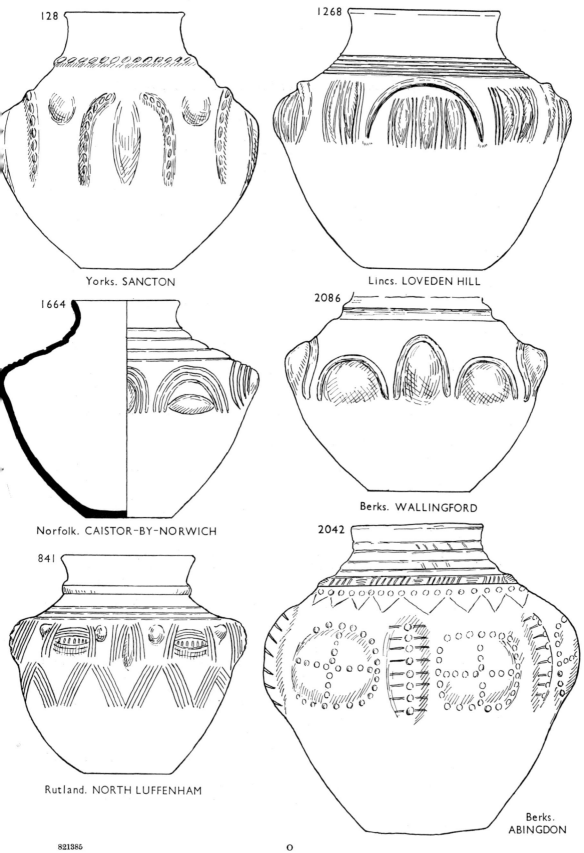

128 Yorks. SANCTON

1268 Lincs. LOVEDEN HILL

1664 Norfolk. CAISTOR-BY-NORWICH

2086 Berks. WALLINGFORD

841 Rutland. NORTH LUFFENHAM

2042 Berks. ABINGDON

Fig. 24. Buckelurnen *of Groups III, IV, and V*

SCALE: Pottery 1:4; Stamps 1:2

1180 NORFOLK, SHROPHAM (British Museum 56 6–27. 9)
Buckelurne of Group III with solid flat footstand, narrow neck, and everted rim: well-made dark-grey ware, once burnished.
Decorated with four necklines, between the second and third of which is a flat slashed collar. Below are alternately long vertical bosses and *stehende Bogen* bosses, each covering a small round boss. The long bosses and *stehende Bogen* bosses are alternately feathered and stamped; the round bosses are surrounded by a circle of stamps with one in the centre to form a rosette. One stamp is used.

744 NORTHANTS., NEWTON-IN-THE-WILLOWS (Kettering Museum 132)
Small *Buckelurne* of Group III with footring and upright rim: smooth ware, black above the collar, light orange-red below.
Decorated with four light but firm necklines above a row of stamps, and a raised slashed collar. On the maximum diameter are fourteen solid oval bosses, alternately vertical, each carrying three vertical lines, and horizontal, each carrying a cross. A horizontal line of stamps fills the space over the horizontal bosses. Two stamps are used.

393 BERKS., HARWELL (Ashmolean Museum 1955–464)
Small *Buckelurne* of Group III with low pedestal foot, narrow neck, and everted rim: burnished black ware.
Decorated with four necklines above a raised slashed collar. On the maximum diameter are four large round bosses with applied slashed strips around and crossed over them, meeting in a central knob. Between the large bosses are smaller oval vertical bosses outlined by three vertical lines. An irregular horizontal line of stamps fills the space over the vertical bosses. A horizontal line runs below the decorated zone. One stamp is used.

335 SURREY, CROYDON (British Museum 45 3–15. 4)
Buckelurne of Group IV, rim missing: rough red/brown ware.
Decorated with at least four necklines, above a horizontal row of stamps. Below, long vertical slashed bosses outlined by two vertical lines alternate with *hängende Bogen* bosses also outlined by two lines. Within each of the latter is a small round boss outlined by two lines and crossed by a single horizontal line. Below each of these is a slashed chevron covering a triangle of stamps. One stamp is used.

1012 SUFFOLK, MILDENHALL (Bury St. Edmunds Museum)
Buckelurne of Group V with conical neck and everted rim: rough buff ware.
Decorated with a row of stamps bordered above by two and below by three strong necklines. On the shoulder are four pairs of vertical bosses, variously decorated with slashing, vertical lines, and vertical rows of stamps. Between these are four horizontal bosses, also variously decorated with lines and stamps, each covered by two-line *stehende Bogen* outlined above by a row of stamps. A horizontal row of stamps runs over the vertical bosses and is interrupted by the stamps over the horizontal bosses. Seven stamps are used.

328 BEDS., SANDY (Cambridge Museum of Arch. and Eth. Dep. 14. 124)
Buckelurne of Group V with conical neck and everted rim: smooth dark-brown ware, well made.
Decorated with three sharply incised lines, a raised collar slashed in four-line chevrons, and a horizontal row of stamps demarcated above and below by two lines. Below are four large *stehende Bogen* bosses outlined above by two lines. Each boss carries a line of stamps and covers a long vertical boss, outlined with two lines and feathered. Between the main bosses is a small round boss outlined by three lines, with a circle of stamps upon it. Three stamps are used.

1983 BEDS., KEMPSTON (British Museum 91 6–24. 24)
Buckelurne of Group V with narrow neck and everted rim: smooth dark ware, well made.
Decorated with three firm lines on the neck, above a small zone of two-line chevrons, the upper triangles filled with a group of three firm dots. Below this are two rows of stamps demarcated by horizontal lines. On the shoulder are six *stehende Bogen* bosses, each covering a small round boss. Between the main bosses are two-line pendent triangles, each containing a round boss with a triangle of dots on each side of it. Two stamps are used.

1180

Norfolk. SHROPHAM

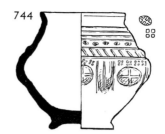

744

Northants. NEWTON-IN-THE-WILLOWS

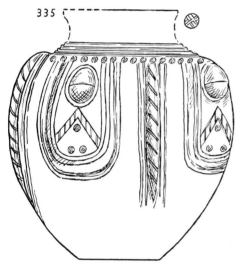

335

Surrey. CROYDON

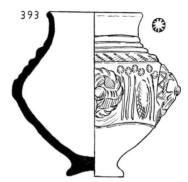

393

Berks. HARWELL

1012

Suffolk. MILDENHALL

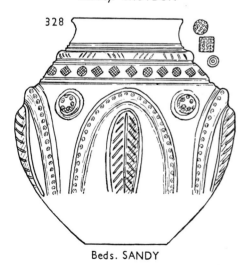

328

Beds. SANDY

1983

Beds. KEMPSTON

Fig. 25. *Urns with pedestal and footring bases*

SCALE: Pottery 1:4; Stamps 1:2

27 BERKS., FRILFORD (Ashmolean Museum 1886. 1401)
Biconical urn with low pedestal foot, rim and neck missing: thin reddish ware, burnished dark-grey. Decorated with three lines above irregularly spaced hollow bosses on the carination.

1669 NORFOLK, CAISTOR-BY-NORWICH M 48(a) (Norwich Museum)
Shoulder-boss urn, with solid flat footstand, rim missing: smoothed rough dark ware. Decorated with two grooves at the base of the neck and numerous plain vertical hollow bosses on the shoulder.

202 CAMBS., GIRTON (Cambridge Museum of Arch. and Eth.)
Sub-biconical urn with footring, and wide mouth with flaring rim: hard burnished grey/brown ware, reminiscent of Romano-British wares. Decorated with three pairs of vertical bosses on the carination.

1122 LEICS., THURMASTON 11 (Leicester Museum)
Rounded shoulder-boss urn with pedestal foot, rim missing: very well-made black ware, once polished. Decorated with one groove at the base of the neck, below which are twenty-two hollow bosses. This vessel is extremely stylish in design and execution.

428 HUNTS., WOODSTON (Peterborough Museum)
Rounded shoulder-boss urn with pedestal foot, conical neck, and short everted rim: dark-grey ware. Decorated with a band of stamps arranged in chevrons on the neck, demarcated above and below by three faint lines. Below are eight hollow long bosses, the panels between which are wholly or partly filled with faint vertical lines. One stamp is used.

2373 SURREY, WALTON-ON-THAMES[1] (Weybridge Museum)
Shouldered pot with low footring, conical neck, and everted rim: rough light-grey ware, neatly made. The body is firmly shaped into six or seven slightly concave facets with raised vertical ridges between them.

126 YORKS., DRIFFIELD (Hull Museum)
Shoulder-boss urn with footring, hollow neck, and flaring rim: very rough and mis-shapen. Decorated with grooves on the neck and a zone of random stamping above a single groove. On the shoulder are nine long bosses, the panels between which are filled with vertical grooves. One stamp is used.

2098 SUFFOLK, WALDRINGFIELD (British Museum 72 5–20. 4)
Biconical urn with footring, conical neck and short, everted rim: very highly polished black ware. Decorated on the upper part with a row of finger-tipping set between two strong grooves above and another three below. On the carination are fourteen small round hollow bosses, the panels between which are filled with three vertical lines.

1083 KENT, WESTBERE (Royal Museum, Canterbury, R.M. 6437)
Small biconical urn with high footring, conical neck, and everted rim: black ware, once polished. Decorated with four necklines between the lowest two of which is a space, and on the carination nineteen hollow long bosses running to the constriction above the foot, the panels between which are filled with four vertical lines.

1121 LEICS., THURMASTON 16 (Leicester Museum)
Biconical urn with low pedestal foot, narrow neck, and short everted rim: dark-grey ware, now rather rough, but very well made. Decorated with a raised slashed collar, demarcated above and below by three firm lines. On the carination are ten round hollow bosses, each outlined on both sides with three firm vertical lines; below are three firm horizontal lines.

[1] This pot may come from the Shepperton cemetery on the Middlesex bank of the river opposite Walton-on-Thames: information kindly supplied by Mr. Bryan Blake, lately Curator of the Weybridge Museum.

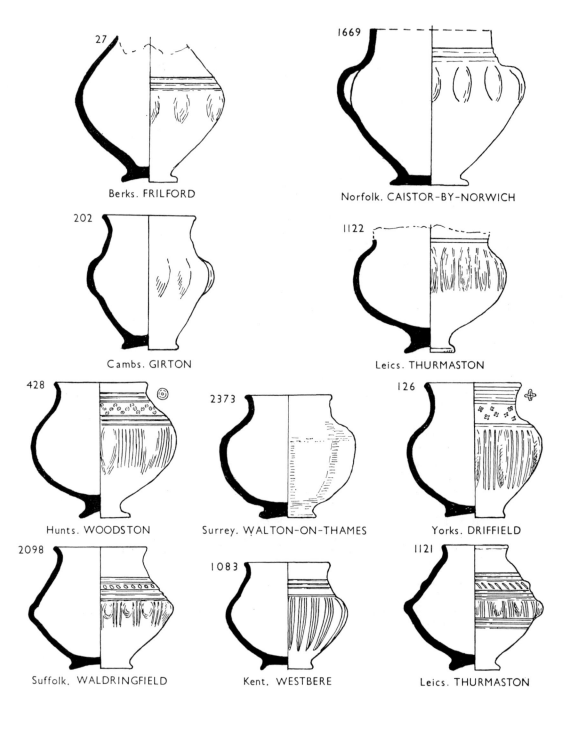

27
Berks. FRILFORD

1669
Norfolk. CAISTOR-BY-NORWICH

202
Cambs. GIRTON

1122
Leics. THURMASTON

428
Hunts. WOODSTON

2373
Surrey. WALTON-ON-THAMES

126
Yorks. DRIFFIELD

2098
Suffolk. WALDRINGFIELD

1083
Kent. WESTBERE

1121
Leics. THURMASTON

Fig. 26. *Rectangular linear designs*

SCALE 1:4

522 LINCS., ANCASTER (Grantham Museum)
Shouldered urn with conical neck and slightly everted rim: well-made burnished brown/dark-grey ware.
Decorated with seven close-set necklines above continuous vertical lines on the shoulder.

1582 NORFOLK, CAISTOR-BY-NORWICH N 21 (Norwich Museum)
Shouldered urn with hollow neck and upright rim: well-made smooth dark ware, probably once burnished black.
Decorated with six sharply tooled necklines above vertical grooves making continuous corrugation on the shoulder interrupted in four places by vertical panels of feather-pattern grooves.

2103 near OXFORD (British Museum 68 7-9. 77)
Sub-biconical urn with sagging base, tall, hollow neck, and slightly everted rim: rough grey ware.
Decorated with five broad shallow grooves on the neck above alternate panels of three vertical grooves and two grooves in the form of a cross.

143 YORKS., SANCTON 12 (Hull Museum)
Wide-mouthed shouldered urn with upright neck and slightly everted rim: burnished dark-brown/black ware.
Decorated with three deeply tooled grooves on the neck above groups of three vertical grooves on the shoulder.

1017 SUFFOLK, INGHAM (Society of Antiquaries)
Shouldered urn with slightly sagging base, tall conical neck and everted rim: well-made thick black ware.
Decorated with two wide grooves at the base of the neck above groups of three or four vertical grooves, the panels between which are mostly filled with three diagonal grooves pointing in opposite directions: one panel is left empty.

717 NORFOLK, NORTH ELMHAM (Lincoln Museum)
Biconical urn with short everted rim: polished black ware.
Decorated with five strong grooves on the neck above groups of three vertical grooves, the panels between which are filled with three diagonal grooves.

581 LINCS., LOVEDEN HILL NE 28 (Lincoln Museum)
Large sub-biconical urn with sagging profile, rim missing: thick red ware.
Decorated with at least eight deeply grooved necklines above alternate panels of seven vertical and seven horizontal lines.

1411 LINCS., LOVEDEN HILL B. 34/296 (Lincoln Museum)
Sub-biconical urn with everted rim: brown ware.
Decorated with three wide, firm necklines, above a continuous zone of diagonal grooves on the maximum diameter.

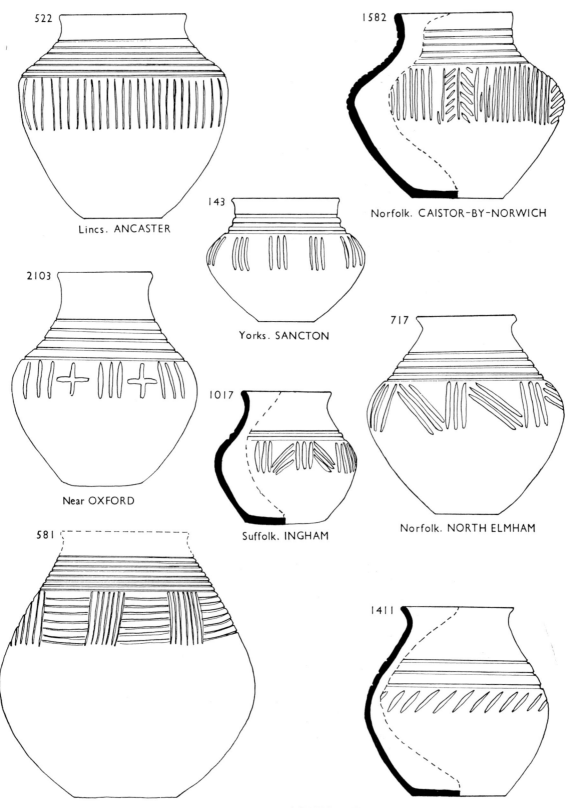

522   Lincs. ANCASTER

1582   Norfolk. CAISTOR-BY-NORWICH

143   Yorks. SANCTON

2103   Near OXFORD

1017   Suffolk. INGHAM

717   Norfolk. NORTH ELMHAM

581   1411   Lincs. LOVEDEN HILL

Fig. 27. *Rectangular panel-style with bosses*

165 CAMBS., GIRTON (Cambridge Museum of Arch. and Eth. S. 13)
Shoulder-boss urn with low footring, upright neck, and slightly everted rim: smooth dark-grey/brown ware.
Decorated with two horizontal rows of stamps demarcated above and below by two necklines, and separated by one. On the shoulder are four oval hollow bosses, bordered on each side by three vertical lines. Two stamps are used.

324 CAMBS., LITTLE WILBRAHAM (British Museum)
Biconical bossed urn, rim missing: smooth dark-grey ware.
Decorated with a row of stamps on the neck demarcated above by three and below by four lines. On the maximum diameter are four or five vertical hollow bosses, bordered on each side by three vertical lines. The panels contain a horizontal row of stamps from the centre of which a vertical row of stamps rises to the lowest neckline. One stamp is used.

283 CAMBS., ST. JOHN'S (Cambridge Museum of Arch. and Eth.)
Biconical bossed urn with upright rim: hard grey ware.
Decorated with a row of stamps on the neck demarcated above and below by three firm lines. On the maximum diameter are vertical bosses, the panels between which are filled with vertical lines. One stamp is used.

771 NORTHANTS., KETTERING (Northampton Museum D 334/ 1954-5)
Small biconical bossed urn with everted rim: smooth brown ware.
Decorated with a row of stamps on the neck demarcated above and below by three firm lines. On the maximum diameter are seven slashed solid bosses, bordered on each side by four vertical lines, with a vertical row of stamps down the centre of each panel. Two stamps are used.

147 YORKS., SANCTON 13 (Hull Museum)
Ovoid shoulder-boss urn with short hollow neck and slightly everted rim.
Decorated with two necklines above rounded bosses on the shoulder, the panels between which are filled with three horizontal rows of stamps. One stamp is used.

255 CAMBS., GIRTON (Cambridge Museum of Arch. and Eth.)
Shoulder-boss urn with upright neck, rim missing: bright-red/brown ware, well made.
Decorated with a plain raised collar, demarcated above and below by a single deeply incised line. On the shoulder are seven narrow vertical slashed bosses bordered on either side by two vertical lines. The panels are filled with random stamping. One stamp is used.

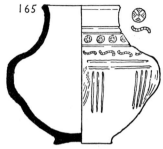

Cambs. GIRTON

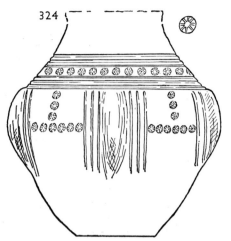

Cambs. LITTLE WILBRAHAM

Cambs. ST. JOHN'S

Northants. KETTERING

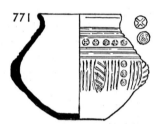

Cambs. GIRTON

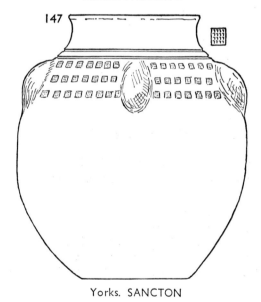

Yorks. SANCTON

Fig. 28. *Triangular and chevron linear designs*

SCALE 1:4

63 YORKS., SANCTON (Ashmolean Museum 1886–1301)
Wide-mouthed bowl with hollow conical neck and everted rim: smooth dark ware.
Decorated with eight shallow close-set grooves on the neck forming continuous corrugation above three-line chevrons in similar wide grooves.

1612 NORFOLK, CAISTOR-BY-NORWICH N 102 (Norwich Museum)
Shouldered urn with tall conical neck, rim missing: well-made smooth dark ware, once burnished black.
Decorated with at least six deep grooves on the neck forming continuous corrugation above a low raised collar bearing a row of large dots: below are three more grooves above a zone of diagonal corrugation in chevron panels set at right angles to each other, giving a basketry effect. At one point the pattern is broken by a confused jumble of vertical and diagonal lines.

540 LINCS., LOVEDEN HILL (Lincoln Museum 73 L.H.)
Sub-biconical urn with everted rim: leathery dark-grey/brown ware.
Decorated with five light necklines above a zone of four-line chevrons outlined on each side with a row of stamps. One stamp is used.

1234 LINCS., LOVEDEN HILL 56/7 (Lincoln Museum)
Wide-mouthed sub-biconical urn with upright neck and slightly everted rim.
Decorated with two horizontal grooves on the neck above a zone of chevrons made up of irregular groups of lines and rows of stamps following no consistent pattern. One stamp is used.

754 NORTHANTS., KETTERING (Kettering Museum 6)
Small shouldered urn with upright neck, rim missing: rough grey ware.
Decorated with a line of dots on the neck between two pairs of firm lines above a zone of three-line pendent triangles each containing three dots; a single dot is set at the top of the space between them.

2101 PETERBOROUGH (British Museum 73 6–2. 123)
Shouldered urn with tall hollow neck and everted rim: smooth grey ware, once burnished black.
Decorated with nine close-set fine lines at the base of the neck, between the third and fourth of which is a flat slashed collar. On the shoulder are three-line chevrons, in the spaces above and below which are three stamps. One stamp is used.

789 NORTHANTS., BRIXWORTH (Northampton Museum D 298/1954–5)
Sub-biconical urn with short slightly everted rim: burnished hard grey ware.
Decorated with five close-set grooves on the neck above two-line pendent triangles each containing a horizontal row of stamps along the upper edge and a diagonal row of stamps bordered on each side by a line across the centre. A single stamp is set at the lowest point of each triangle. One stamp is used.

468 LEICS., near MELTON MOWBRAY (Leicester Museum)
Sub-biconical bowl with everted rim: brown/grey ware.
Decorated with a row of stamps on the neck, demarcated on each side by three sharp lines. Below are pendent triangles filled with stamps, and in the spaces between them are three stamps. Three stamps are used.

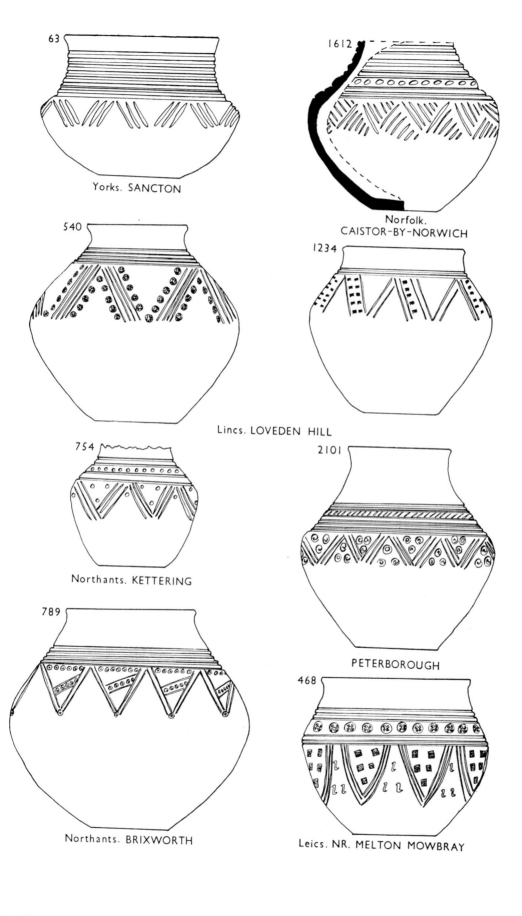

63 Yorks. SANCTON

1612 Norfolk. CAISTOR-BY-NORWICH

540 Lincs. LOVEDEN HILL

1234

754 Northants. KETTERING

2101 PETERBOROUGH

789 Northants. BRIXWORTH

468 Leics. NR. MELTON MOWBRAY

Fig. 29. *Triangular panel-style*

SCALE: Pottery 1:4; Stamps 1:2; Brooch 1:2

774   NORTHANTS., KETTERING (Northampton Museum D 331/1954–5)
Shoulder-boss urn with tall conical neck, rim missing: smooth dark ware.
Decorated with at least three rows of stamps on the neck, each demarcated with four firm lines; there are five lines below the lowest row of stamps. On the shoulder are five vertical hollow bosses each carrying three vertical lines; they are contained in two-line pendent triangles and two two-line pendent triangles fill the panels between them. The design is somewhat irregular. At least two stamps are used.

2452   WAR., BAGINTON (in private possession)
Shoulder-boss urn with tall conical neck, rim missing: smooth dark ware.
Decorated with at least one row of stamps on the neck, demarcated above and below by two horizontal lines. On the shoulder are five vertical hollow bosses, the panels between which contain one-line pendent triangles filled with stamps. One stamp is used.

1825   NORFOLK, CAISTOR-BY-NORWICH X 7 (Norwich Museum)
Shoulder-boss urn with tall conical neck and swollen rim: hard smooth grey ware.
Decorated immediately below the rim with two firm lines above three rows of stamps each demarcated by two lines. On the shoulder is a double line of stamps interrupted by six small hollow bosses. The panels between them contain two-line pendent triangles filled with stamps. Five stamps are used.

288   CAMBS., ST. JOHN'S (Cambridge Museum of Arch. and Eth.)
Shoulder-boss urn with hollow neck and everted rim: hard grey ware.
Decorated with two light necklines above two rows of stamps each demarcated by two lines. On the shoulder are six bosses, the panels between which contain two-line pendent triangles filled with stamps. Five stamps are used.

290   CAMBS., ST. JOHN'S (Cambridge Museum of Arch. and Eth.)
Small shoulder-boss urn with short upright rim: rough sandy pinkish-orange ware.
Decorated with one sharp neckline above a row of stamps. On the shoulder are five narrow vertical bosses, between which are rows of stamps arranged roughly as pendent triangles. Two stamps are used.

371a   WAR., BAGINTON (Coventry Museum A/1014/2)
Globular urn with upright neck and everted rim: smooth brown/red/black ware.
Decorated with two rows of stamps on the neck each demarcated above and below by two lines. Below are two-line pendent triangles filled with stamps. Three stamps are used.
In this urn was a burnt bronze saucer brooch decorated with an elevenfold running spiral pattern.

230   CAMBS., GIRTON (Girton College)
Ovoid urn with tall upright neck, rim missing: rough coarse brown ware.
Decorated with two horizontal rows of stamps on the neck, above rows of stamps forming pendent triangles without guiding lines. One stamp is used.

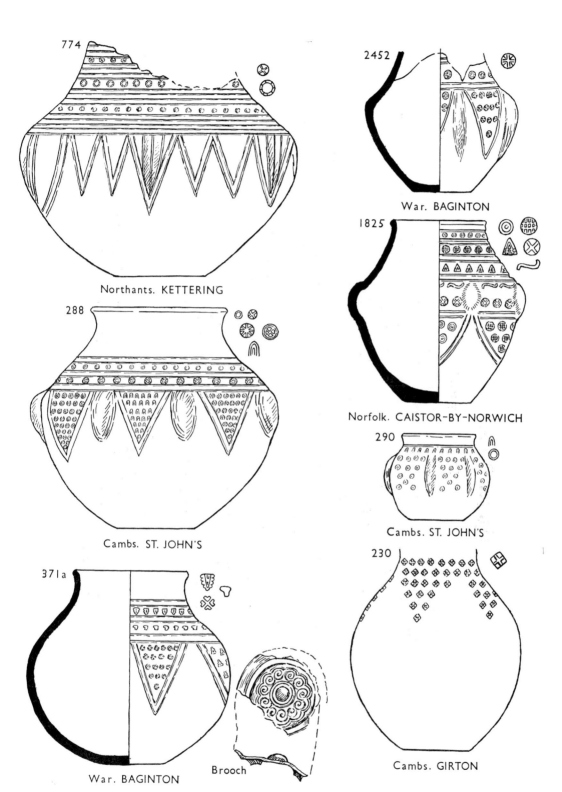

774

Northants. KETTERING

288

Cambs. ST. JOHN'S

371a

War. BAGINTON

Brooch

2452

War. BAGINTON

1825

Norfolk. CAISTOR-BY-NORWICH

290

Cambs. ST. JOHN'S

230

Cambs. GIRTON

Fig. 30. Panel-style with stamped swags

SCALE: Pottery 1:4; Stamps 1:2

151 YORKS., SALTBURN (Middlesbrough Museum)
Upper part of beaker-shaped vessel with short flaring rim: smooth dark-grey ware.
Decorated with a row of stamps on the neck, demarcated above and below by a light line. Below
are deep two-line swags filled with stamps. One stamp is used.

121 YORKS., ROBIN HOOD'S BAY (Yorkshire Museum, York)
Wide-mouthed jar with upright neck and rim: rough, dark-brown ware with smoothed surface.
Decorated with a row of finger-tipping on the neck demarcated above and below by two lines.
Below are five deep two-line swags filled with stamps. One stamp is used.

1263 LINCS., LOVEDEN HILL 57/36(b) (Lincoln Museum)
Bag-shaped urn with tall neck, rim and base missing.
Decorated with six fine close-set necklines above deep four-line swags filled with stamps. One
stamp is used.

149 YORKS., SANCTON 9 (Hull Museum)
Sub-biconical urn with upright neck and slightly everted rim: smooth dark-grey ware.
Decorated with three horizontal rows of stamps on the neck each demarcated above and below by
three fine lines. Below is a complex arrangement of interlacing three-line swags, all filled with
stamps. Five stamps are used.

2299 YORKS., SANCTON 108b (Hull Museum)
Biconical urn with short everted rim.
Decorated with a row of large dots on the neck demarcated above by three and below by two lines.
Below are single-line swags each containing a vertical line of stamps outlined by a row of dots.
One stamp is used.

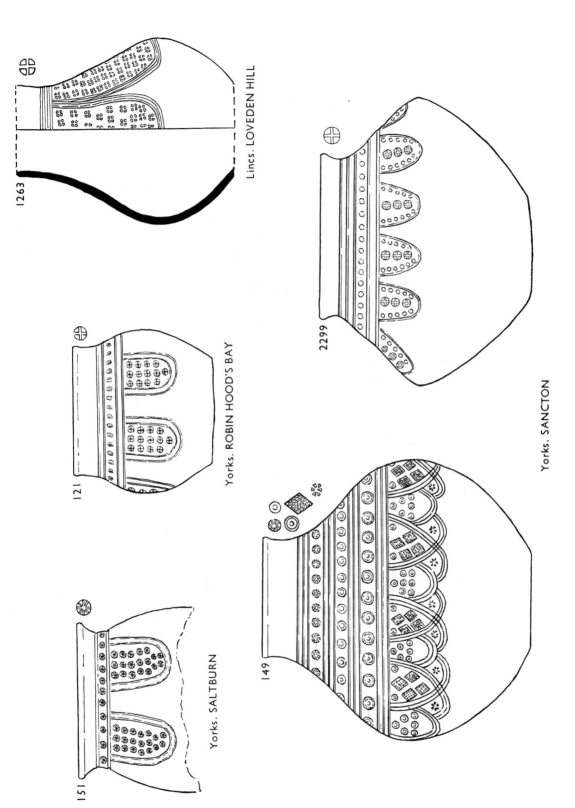

1263

Lincs. LOVEDEN HILL

2299

Yorks. SANCTON

121

Yorks. ROBIN HOOD'S BAY

151

Yorks. SALTBURN

149

Fig. 31. *Urns from Caistor-by-Norwich related to Plettke's Types A3-A6 and C*

SCALE: Pottery 1:4; Tweezers 1:2

E5 Heavily made shouldered urn with short hollow neck, wide mouth, and well-moulded rim: red ware, burnished black.
Decorated with four deeply grooved necklines above two-line pendent triangles in deep grooves: at one point a diagonal cross is substituted for a triangle, and at two points one and two finger-tips respectively are set between the triangles.

N52 Wide-mouthed urn with sloping shoulder, upright neck, and slightly everted rim: smooth dark-red/brown ware, once burnished.
Decorated with four lightly tooled necklines above faint three-line pendent triangles.

X35 Heavily made shouldered urn with wide mouth and slightly everted rim: smooth dark ware, once burnished.
Decorated with three grooved necklines from which depend seven groups of three/four vertical grooves extending below the shoulder.

P23 Shouldered urn with wide mouth and everted rim: smooth dark-grey/brown ware.
Decorated with three faintly grooved necklines above long three-line chevrons, one of which is replaced by a diagonal cross.

P53 Sub-biconical urn with tall neck and heavily moulded rim: thick smooth dark-brown ware.
Decorated on the neck with a continuous arcade of dots above four broadly tooled lines: below are six/ten-line chevrons mostly bordered above and below by lines of dots.

K7 Wide-mouthed bowl with tall neck and slightly everted rim: dark-brown/grey ware.
Decorated with three necklines from which depend widely spaced groups of three vertical lines.
This urn contained a well-preserved pair of bronze tweezers of late Roman type suspended from a bronze loop.

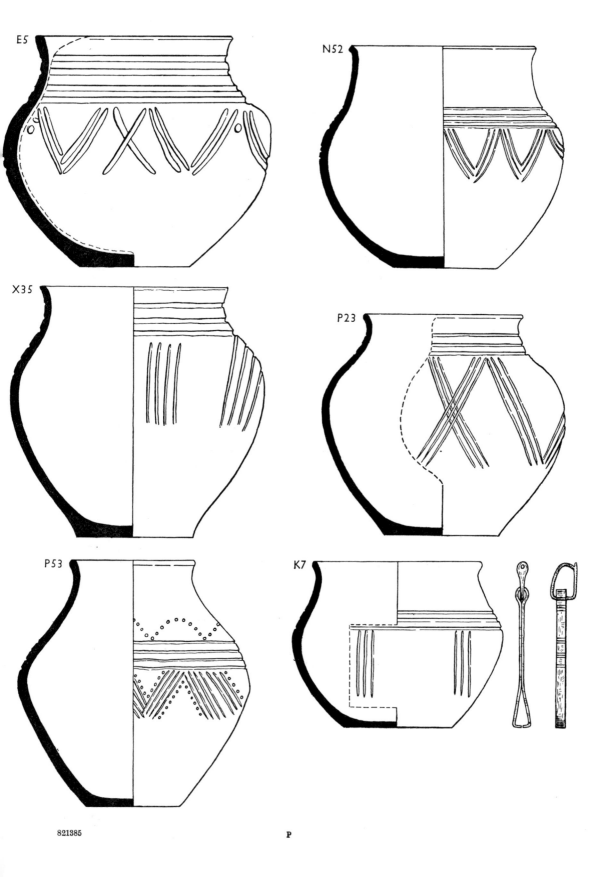

P

Fig. 32. *Urns related to Plettke's Type A6*

SCALE 1:4

93 YORKS., HEWORTH 23 (Yorkshire Museum, York)
Large globular urn with tall neck and flaring rim: brown/grey ware, once burnished.
Decorated with three broad shallow grooves at the base of the neck, above three-line chevrons.

163 CAMBS., GIRTON (Cambridge Museum of Arch. and Eth.)
Large shouldered urn with tall neck and flaring rim: soft sandy-buff ware.
Decorated with two faintly tooled lines at the base of the neck above a raised slashed band on the shoulder. Below are three-line pendent triangles.

880 SUFFOLK, LACKFORD HB 02 (Cambridge Museum of Arch. and Eth. 49. 15)
Sub-biconical urn with tall neck and everted rim: burnished dark-brown ware.
Decorated with four horizontal lines low on the neck above four-line chevrons.

1407 LINCS., LOVEDEN HILL C. 4/301 (Lincoln Museum)
Large globular urn with short neck and everted rim: dark-brown ware.
Decorated with a plain raised collar above five necklines. Below are three/seven-line pendent triangles with convex sides.

685 LINCS., ELKINGTON 161 (Lincoln Museum)
Large shouldered urn with tall upright neck and slightly everted rim: dark-brown ware.
Decorated with two lines at the base of the neck above a flat collar carrying groups of diagonal lines forming chevrons. Below are irregular three/four-line chevrons.

467 LEICS., near MELTON MOWBRAY (Leicester Museum)
Large globular urn with hollow neck and everted rim: smooth dark-grey/black ware.
Decorated on the neck with a flat collar carrying two-line chevrons, demarcated above by two and below by three firm lines. Below are two-line chevrons.

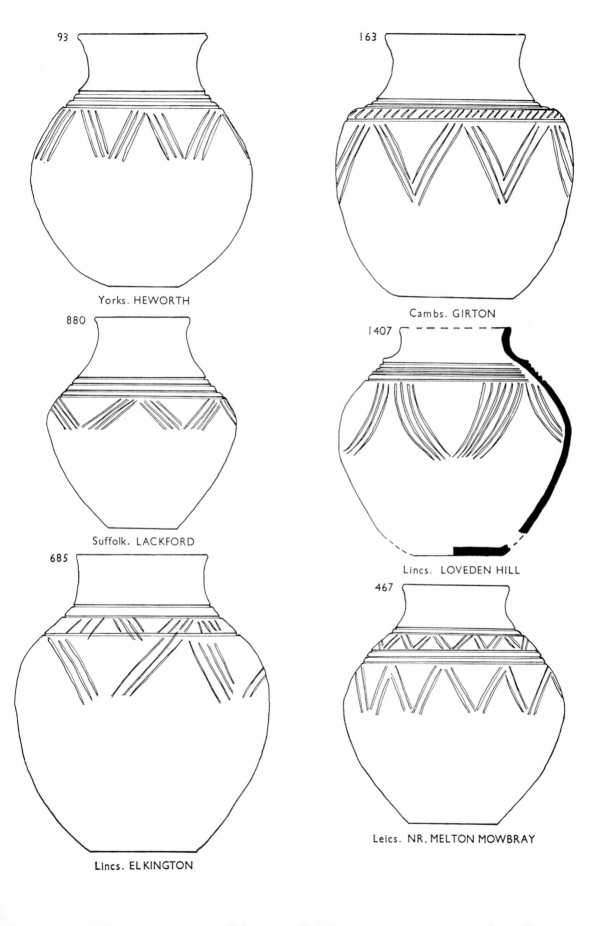

93   Yorks. HEWORTH

163   Cambs. GIRTON

880   Suffolk. LACKFORD

1407   Lincs. LOVEDEN HILL

685   Lincs. ELKINGTON

467   Leics. NR. MELTON MOWBRAY

Fig. 33. *Chevron-and-dot designs*

SCALE 1:4

320 CAMBRIDGE (Cambridge Museum of Arch. and Eth. Z. 14810)
Sub-biconical urn with swollen everted rim: smooth polished black ware. Decorated on the shoulder with three wide grooves forming continuous rippling above two-line chevrons, with a single finger-tip in each triangle.

765 NORTHANTS., KETTERING (Northampton Museum D. 340/ 1954-5)
Large shouldered urn with hollow conical neck and everted rim: smooth brown ware.
Decorated at the base of the neck with three firm lines above three-line chevrons, with a single oval finger-tip in each triangle.

869 SUFFOLK, LACKFORD (Cambridge Museum of Arch. and Eth. 49. 585)
Globular urn with conical neck, rim missing.
Decorated at the base of the neck with three strong grooves above three-line chevrons, in the upper triangles of which are single large circular impressions.

627 LINCS., ELKINGTON 33 (Lincoln Museum)
Sub-biconical urn with upright neck and everted rim: smooth dark ware. Decorated with two groups of three fine necklines above three/four-line chevrons, with a single vertical finger-tip in each triangle.

2295 YORKS., SANCTON 103 (Hull Museum)
Biconical urn with flaring rim.
Decorated low on the neck with a collar carrying a row of dots demarcated above by two and below by one line. Below are groups of three diagonal lines, forming irregular chevrons.

1166 NORFOLK, CASTLE ACRE (King's Lynn Museum)
Globular urn with upright neck, rim missing: smooth buff/brown ware. Decorated with five firm necklines above three-line chevrons, the upper triangles of which contain three faint vertical finger-tips arranged as a triangle, the lower triangles contain a vertical line of three similar finger-tips.

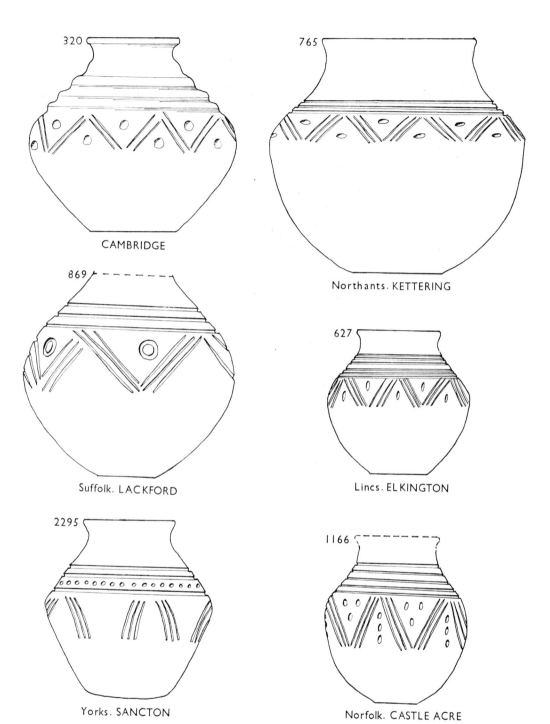

320 CAMBRIDGE

765 Northants. KETTERING

869 Suffolk. LACKFORD

627 Lincs. ELKINGTON

2295 Yorks. SANCTON

1166 Norfolk. CASTLE ACRE

(214)

Fig. 34. *Dated Continental pieces for comparison with Fig. 33*

SCALE: Pottery 1:4; Brooches, etc. 1:3 (Westerwanna 1:4)

BORGSTEDT, Kr. Eckernförde, 156 (Genrich (1954), Tafel 8F)
Sub-biconical urn with upright rim: light-brown ware.
Decorated with three strong grooves on the neck, above continuous one-line chevrons, with a single finger-tip at the top of each triangle.
Contents: bronze pincers of late Roman type and other objects.

STENDERUP, Kr. Haderslev, 1 (Genrich (1954), Tafel 25C)
Rounded accessory with tall upright neck and everted rim: burnished dark-brown ware.
Decorated with a raised slashed collar above two plain collars, below which are continuous three-line chevrons.
In the same grave were two cross-bow brooches and other objects.

WESTERWANNA, Kr. Land Hadeln, 174 (*Westerwanna* i, Tafel 24)
Rounded urn with tall upright neck and slightly flaring rim: ware not recorded.
Decorated with a raised slashed collar above two strong grooves, below which are continuous chevrons in line-and-groove with a single finger-tip in each triangle.
Contents: spring of a *tutulus* brooch and other objects.

WESTERWANNA, Kr. Land Hadeln, 1122 (*Westerwanna* i, Tafel 139)
Rounded urn with tall hollow neck and slightly flaring rim: ware not recorded.
Decorated with two grooves at the base of the neck above continuous two-line chevrons with a single finger-tip in each lower triangle.
Contents: iron cross-bow brooch and parts of three others.

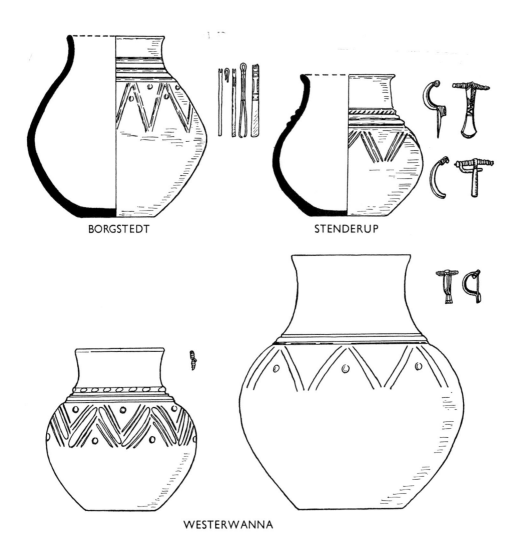

BORGSTEDT

STENDERUP

WESTERWANNA

Fig. 35. *Small bowls with linear ornament*

SCALE: Pottery 1:4; Brooch 1:4

433 HUNTS., WOODSTON (Wyman Abbott Colln. Peterborough Museum)
Small wide-mouthed vessel with tall hollow neck and everted rim: rough red/grey/brown ware.
Decorated with nine strong close-set grooves on the hollow neck.

537 LINCS., SLEAFORD (British Museum 83 4–1. 604)
Small wide-mouthed vessel with hollow neck and upright rim: rough grey ware, heavily made.
Decorated with nine sharp close-set lines on the neck above irregular groups of three/six sharp diagonal lines arranged as chevrons.

386 BEDS., KEMPSTON (Bedford Museum D3. 3777)
Small biconical vessel with everted rim: smooth hard brown ware, well made.
Decorated with four strong close-set grooves on the neck above continuous diagonal lines on the carination.

520 ?LINCS., STAMFORD (bought there by the late V. B. Crowther Beynon)
Small wide-mouthed bowl with swollen rim: smooth grey ware, well made.
Decorated with three firm grooves on the neck above continuous faint vertical lines on the carination.

784 NORTHANTS., site unknown (Northampton Museum D. 307/1954–5)
Small biconical bowl with everted rim: smooth corky grey/brown ware.
Decorated with four firm lines on the neck above three-line pendent triangles broken at the lowest point.

809 NORTHANTS., CRANFORD (Northampton Museum D. 303/1954–5)
Small wide-mouthed bowl with slightly everted rim: rough red/brown ware.
Decorated with three light grooves on the neck above two-line pendent triangles within each of which is a central vertical line.

410 ESSEX, FEERING (Colchester Museum 170)
Small biconical bowl with everted rim: dark-grey/brown ware, once burnished.
Decorated with three light lines on the neck, above three-line chevrons, with two sharp vertical jabs in each triangle.
In the same grave was a bronze penannular brooch decorated with chevron-and-dot pattern.

1241 LINCS., LOVEDEN HILL 56/2 (Lincoln Museum)
Small biconical vessel with tall neck and slightly everted rim; lower part incomplete.
Decorated with three horizontal lines on and above the carination, below which are widely spaced diagonal lines cutting the lowest horizontal line.

405 CAMBS., WHITTLESEY (Wyman Abbott Colln. Peterborough Museum)
Small shoulder-boss bowl with tall hollow neck and slightly flaring rim: dark-grey ware.
Decorated with four strong grooves on the neck and eight small bosses on the shoulder, the panels between which are filled with four vertical lines.

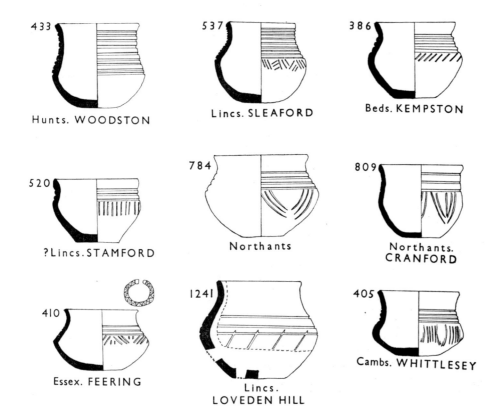

433 Hunts. WOODSTON

537 Lincs. SLEAFORD

386 Beds. KEMPSTON

520 ?Lincs. STAMFORD

784 Northants

809 Northants. CRANFORD

410 Essex. FEERING

1241 Lincs. LOVEDEN HILL

405 Cambs. WHITTLESEY

Fig. 36. *Small bowls with line-and-dot ornament and restrained use of stamps*

SCALE: Pottery 1:4; Brooches 1:4

1467 **ESSEX, LITTLE OAKLEY** (in private possession)
Part of a small carinated bowl with hollow neck, rim and base missing: fine hard burnished light-grey ware.
Decorated with five strong lines on the neck, below which, and resting on the carination, are flat single-line *stehende Bogen*, each covering a horizontal line; in each spandrel is one stamp.

817 **OXON., EWELME** (Ashmolean Museum 1911–505)
Small sub-biconical vessel with wide mouth and everted rim: dark-grey ware, once smoothed.
Decorated on the neck with two firm lines between which is a row of dots. Depending from this are widely spaced vertical lines of four dots, and below are two further horizontal lines above the maximum diameter with a row of dots between them.

804 **NORTHANTS., DUSTON** (Northampton Museum D. 308/1954–5)
Small rounded bowl with wide mouth and slightly everted rim: smooth grey ware.
Decorated with one light horizontal line on the neck from which hang single-line pendent triangles containing groups of sharp diamond-shaped jabs. On the maximum diameter is a zone of short diagonal lines demarcated above and below by a single line.

41 **BERKS., ABINGDON B24** (Ashmolean Museum)
Small biconical vessel with everted rim: reddish ware.
Decorated with a zone of short two-line chevrons having a single dot in each triangle, demarcated above by three and below by two lines, the latter resting on the carination.

812 **NORTHANTS., WELTON** (Northampton Museum D. 301/1954–5)
Small biconical vessel with everted rim: rather rough dark-grey ware.
Decorated with a zone of single-line chevrons demarcated above and below by two fine lines. Above the chevrons runs a row of dots, and there is one dot in each of the upper triangles of the chevron. On the carination is continuous short diagonal slashing.
In the same grave were two bronze short/long brooches of different design.

530 **LINCS., SLEAFORD** (British Museum 83 4–1. 602)
Small shouldered vessel with hollow neck, upright rim, and slightly hollowed base: rough corky grey ware.
Decorated close under the rim with three necklines above a row of small circular stamps, below which is a single horizontal line above continuous single-line chevrons.

1465 **NORTHANTS., BARTON SEAGRAVE** (British Museum 1936 5–4)
Small wide-mouthed biconical bowl with swollen everted rim: rather rough dark-grey ware.
Decorated with two firm necklines above a single row of stamps below which are two more lines and a row of firm vertical jabs on the carination. One stamp is used.

16 **BERKS., EAST SHEFFORD Grave No. III** (Newbury Museum)
Small biconical bowl with wide mouth and everted rim: rough dark-grey ware.
Decorated with a zone containing small diagonal jabs set as chevrons, demarcated above and below by three firm lines. On the carination are widely spaced groups of four vertical jabs.

1008 **SUFFOLK, near BURY** (Ashmolean Museum 1909–439)
Small biconical bowl with slightly flaring rim and heavy base: soft black ware, once burnished.
Decorated with a row of irregularly applied stamps, demarcated above and below by two firm lines. Below the carination are continuous single-line chevrons. One stamp is used.

1467 Essex. LITTLE OAKLEY

817 Oxon. EWELME

804 Northants. DUSTON

41 Berks. ABINGDON

812 Northants. WELTON

530 Lincs. SLEAFORD

1465 Northants. BARTON SEAGRAVE

16 Berks. EAST SHEFFORD

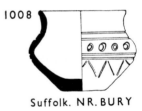

1008 Suffolk. NR. BURY

Fig. 37. *Vessels with facetted carination*

SCALE 1:4

1127 RUTLAND, NORTH LUFFENHAM (Leicester Museum 722 1954)
Small sub-biconical bowl with wide mouth and slightly flaring rim: rough red/brown ware.
Decorated with nine sharp close-set necklines above a slightly facetted carination.

5 SUSSEX, HIGH DOWN (Worthing Museum)
Carinated bowl with hollow neck, widely flaring rim, and hollowed base: smooth sandy
dark-grey ware.
Decorated on the neck with a row of faint dots demarcated above and below by two faint
lines. The carination is strongly facetted.

11 SUSSEX, ALFRISTON (Barbican House, Lewes)
Small carinated bowl with flaring rim: dark-brown ware.
Decorated with a strongly facetted carination, giving the appearance of a row of twenty-one
small bosses.

401 CAMBS., HASLINGFIELD (Ashmolean Museum 1886–1361)
Small sharply carinated bowl with tall hollow neck and everted rim: smooth dark-grey ware.
Decorated with two firm necklines above a broad groove and another firm line. There is
continuous facetting on the carination.

2035 BERKS., ABINGDON B. III (Ashmolean Museum 1935–57)
Small sharply carinated bowl with hollow neck and slightly everted rim: smooth dark ware,
well made.
Decorated on the neck with a flat slashed collar between two fine lines. There is continuous
facetting on the carination.

49 GLOS., FAIRFORD (Ashmolean Museum 1961–14)
Small wide-mouthed bowl with hollow neck and slightly everted rim: smooth dark ware.
Decorated with four deep grooves on the neck, above a heavily facetted carination.

154 SURREY, GUILDOWN 206 (Guildford Museum 857)
Small sub-biconical bowl with everted rim: brown ware, once burnished.
Decorated with three deeply incised necklines. On the carination are thirteen depressions
each containing a stamp. Below are two-line hanging swags. One stamp is used.

2072 CAMBS., BARRINGTON (British Museum 76 2–12. 67)
Sharply carinated biconical bowl with everted rim: smooth black ware, well made.
Decorated with three firm necklines above a row of stamps demarcated below by a single
line. On the carination is widely spaced facetting with a single stamp set above the intervening spaces. One stamp is used.

391 BERKS., EAST SHEFFORD (Ashmolean Museum 1955–360)
Biconical vessel with hollow neck and slightly everted rim: smooth grey ware.
Decorated with three faint necklines above two rows of stamps, each demarcated below
by a single horizontal line. The carination is faintly facetted.

27

Rutland.
NORTH LUFFENHAM

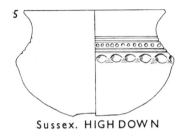

5

Sussex. HIGH DOWN

11

Sussex. ALFRISTON

401

Cambs. HASLINGFIELD

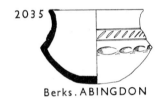

2035

Berks. ABINGDON

49

Glos. FAIRFORD

54

Surrey. GUILDOWN

2072

Cambs. BARRINGTON

391

Berks. EAST SHEFFORD

Fig. 38. *The long-boss style I*

377 BERKS., WALLINGFORD Gr. II (Ashmolean Museum 1938–1211)
Biconical bossed urn with tall neck, wide mouth, and everted rim: smooth brown/grey ware.
Decorated with four close-set necklines above a zone of stamps arranged in pendent triangles. From the carination nine long bosses reach the base, each carrying four or five vertical lines. One stamp is used.

35 BERKS., ABINGDON C. 8 (Abingdon Museum)
Biconical bossed urn with sharply everted rim.
Decorated with a row of stamps on the neck, demarcated above and below by two lines. Below is a zone of three-line chevrons and two further lines. From the carination five slight undecorated long bosses reach the base. One stamp is used.

1994 BERKS., LONG WITTENHAM (British Museum 75 3–10. 14)
Sub-biconical bossed vessel with wide mouth, everted rim, and slightly omphaloid base: smoothed dark-grey/brown ware.
Decorated with three necklines above a slightly raised collar carrying widely spaced groups of nicks. Below is a row of stamps demarcated above and below by a single line, below which is a flat collar also carrying widely spaced groups of nicks. From the maximum diameter five long bosses reach the base, each carrying a vertical line of nicks set between groups of vertical lines. One stamp is used.
In the same grave was a zoomorphic buckle of Type III(B). See pp. 91–4.

29 BERKS., FRILFORD (Ashmolean Museum 1886–1402)
Sub-biconical bowl with everted rim: buff-surfaced dark-grey ware.
Decorated with a row of stamps demarcated above by three and below by one horizontal line. From the maximum diameter long bosses reach the base, the panels between them being filled with a vertical line of stamps demarcated on each side with two vertical lines. Two stamps are used.

52 OXON., BRIGHTHAMPTON 43 Urn 3 (Ashmolean Museum 1966–94)
Sub-biconical bowl with upright rim, and markedly omphaloid base: gritty black/red ware.
Decorated with five fine necklines below which numerous long narrow hollow bosses reach the base, demarcated on each side by two vertical lines.

53 OXON., BRIGHTHAMPTON 24 Urn 1 (Ashmolean Museum 1966–68)
Sub-biconical bowl with upright rim, and markedly omphaloid base: burnished dark-buff ware.
Decorated with four fine necklines below which numerous long narrow flat-topped hollow bosses run to the base, each carrying a vertical line of stamps. The panels between the bosses are filled by irregularly spaced vertical lines. One stamp is used.

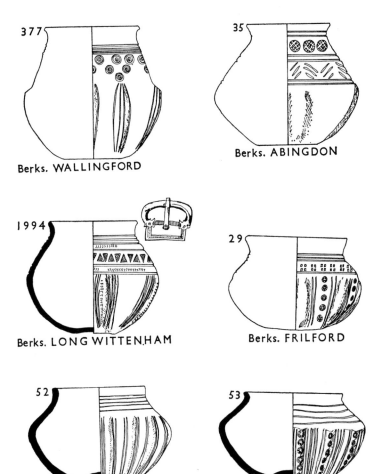

377 Berks. WALLINGFORD

35 Berks. ABINGDON

1994 Berks. LONG WITTENHAM

29 Berks. FRILFORD

52

53

Oxon. BRIGHTHAMPTON

Fig. 39. *The long-boss style II*

SCALE: Pottery 1:4; Brooches 1:4

1993 BERKS., LONG WITTENHAM (British Museum 62 6–13. 109)
Small sub-biconical vessel, the rim broken in antiquity and pared down to the neck: rough dark ware, much worn.
Decorated with a zone of chevron jabs, made by a six-point comb, demarcated above by at least one neckline and by two below. From the carination six long bosses outlined by two lines on each side reach the base, the intervening panels being filled with stamps. One stamp is used.

28 BERKS., FRILFORD (Ashmolean Museum 1920–266)
Small sharply carinated bowl with wide mouth and everted rim: smooth dark-brown ware.
Decorated with a row of stamps demarcated above by one neckline and by three below. From the carination twelve slight bosses reach the base, the intervening panels containing one vertical line each.

1984 BERKS., EAST SHEFFORD (British Museum 93 7–16. 27)
Small carinated bowl with hollow neck, wide mouth, and everted rim: smooth dark-grey ware, well made, probably once burnished.
Decorated with two sharp necklines above a horizontal row of stamps alternating with jabs. Below is another line and a zone of diagonal slashing on the carination. From the carination seven groups of four/five sharp vertical lines reach the base. One stamp is used.

23 BERKS., READING (Reading Museum)
Small carinated bowl with hollow neck and flaring rim: very roughly made grey ware.
Decorated with eight close-set necklines between the rim and the carination. Below, slight long bosses reach the base, the panels between which are filled with groups of three vertical lines.

378 BERKS., WALLINGFORD (Ashmolean Museum 1938–1211)
Small biconical bowl with well-made thickened base, wide mouth, and slightly everted rim: rough buff/brown ware, coarsely made.
Decorated with a row of jabs demarcated above and below by two light necklines. Below, wide grooves bordered on each side by two vertical lines reach the base.
In the same grave were two small/long brooches of different design.

1993
Berks.
LONG WITTENHAM

28
Berks. FRILFORD

1984
Berks. EAST SHEFFORD

23
Berks. READING

378
Berks. WALLINGFORD

Fig. 40. *Jutish pottery in the south-east*

2269 KENT, FAVERSHAM (British Museum 1389 70)
Squat shouldered urn with tall neck, everted rim, and angled base: smooth dark ware.
Decorated on the neck with a raised slashed collar, demarcated above and below by a line and a groove. From shoulder to base run groups of two vertical grooves bordered and divided by a vertical line. Each panel contains a diagonal and a curved group of line-and-groove, forming an irregular pendent triangle.

1088 KENT, WESTBERE (Canterbury R.M. 6440)
Globular round-bottomed urn with tall hollow neck and flaring rim: burnished dark-grey ware.
Decorated with two broad grooves at the base of the neck above continuous three/five-line chevrons.

451 KENT, HOWLETTS (British Museum 1936 5–11. 136)
Globular round-bottomed vessel with hollow neck and flaring rim: grey ware, once burnished.
Decorated with two grooves at the base of the neck above groups of two vertical grooves. In the panels are pairs of curving diagonal lines pointing alternately in opposite directions.

355 KENT, SARRE (Maidstone Museum)
Round-bottomed bowl with hollow neck and everted rim: dark-grey ware, once burnished.
Decorated on the neck with a broad groove demarcated above and below by a sharp line, above vertical bands of line-and-groove running to the base. The panels contain curvilinear designs in line-and-groove.

1100 MIDDX., HANWELL (London Museum)
Small round-bottomed bowl with everted rim, base missing: fine polished black ware.
Decorated with a plain raised collar demarcated above by one and below by two lines. Below are flat chevrons composed of diagonal groups of line-and-groove. There are further groups of diagonal line-and-groove below the chevrons.

1085 KENT, WESTBERE (Canterbury R.M. 6434)
Small round-bottomed bowl with hollow neck and everted rim: rough grey ware.
Decorated with two broad grooves on the neck above irregular three/five-line chevrons.

2269

Kent. FAVERSHAM

1088

Kent. WESTBERE

451

Kent. HOWLETTS

355

Kent. SARRE

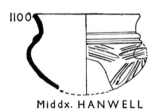

1100

Middx. HANWELL

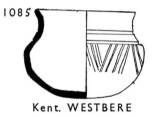

1085

Kent. WESTBERE

Fig. 41. *Accessory vessels with stamps*

519 LINCS., STAMFORD (Lincoln Museum)
Small hollow-necked biconical bowl with flaring rim and rounded base: smooth red/grey ware. There is a small glass window in the base.
Decorated with two strong necklines above a row of stamps. One stamp is used.

327 CAMBS., HASLINGFIELD (Cambridge Museum of Arch. and Eth.)
Wide-mouthed sub-biconical bowl with everted rim and rounded base: polished gritty black ware. There is a small glass window in the base.
Decorated with a row of stamps, demarcated above and below by three sharp lines. One stamp is used.

176 CAMBS., GIRTON (Cambridge Museum of Arch. and Eth.)
Wide-mouthed biconical vessel with everted rim: rather rough grey ware.
Decorated with a row of very poorly applied stamps, demarcated above by three and below by two lines. One stamp appears to have been used.

1090 OXON., CASSINGTON (Ashmolean Museum)
Small biconical bowl, rim missing: hard smooth grey ware.
Decorated with at least two strong necklines above a row of deeply impressed stamps, set just above the sharp carination. One stamp is used.

796 NORTHANTS., ISLIP (Northampton Museum D. 349/1954-4)
Small hollow-necked bowl with flaring rim and rounded base: smooth dark-grey/brown ware.
Decorated with a row of stamps, demarcated above and below by two fine lines.

14 BERKS., EAST SHEFFORD Grave XX (Newbury Museum)
Biconical bowl with sharply everted rim: roughish dark-grey ware.
Decorated with a row of stamps, demarcated above and below by three lines. Below is a line of zigzag rouletting above three more lines on the carination. One stamp is used.

403 CAMBRIDGE (Ashmolean Museum 1886-1378)
Sub-biconical vessel with slightly everted rim: smooth brown ware.
Decorated with two rows of stamps, separated and demarcated above and below by a single line. Below is a continuous chevron line forming pendent triangles each filled with three stamps. One stamp is used.

155 SURREY, GUILDOWN (Guildford Museum 185)
Biconical vessel with everted rim: burnished black ware.
Decorated with a row of stamps, demarcated above and below by two lines. On the carination is another row of stamps. Two stamps are used.

452 KENT, HOWLETTS (British Museum 30 5-11. 45)
Small hollow-necked biconical bowl with everted rim: smooth grey ware, probably once burnished.
Decorated with a row of stamps on the carination, demarcated above and below by a single line. One stamp is used.

400 CAMBS., HASLINGFIELD (Ashmolean Museum 1874-2810)
Small biconical vessel with everted rim: red ware, surfaced brown.
Decorated with a row of stamps, demarcated above by three and below by two firm lines. Below the carination are two rows of stamps. Two stamps are used, which on the lower part are arranged to suggest a chevron pattern.

305 CAMBS., ST. JOHN'S (Cambridge Museum of Arch. and Eth.)
Biconical bowl with everted rim: hard leathery grey/black ware.
Decorated with two rows of stamps separated by three strong lines and demarcated above by four and below by two more lines. One stamp is used.

187 CAMBS., GIRTON (Cambridge Museum of Arch. and Eth.)
Wide-mouthed sub-biconical bowl with slightly everted rim: grey/brown ware.
Decorated with a row of stamps, demarcated above by three and below by two light lines. Below are diagonal lines of four points arranged in chevrons, and produced either by rouletting or a small comb. One stamp is used.

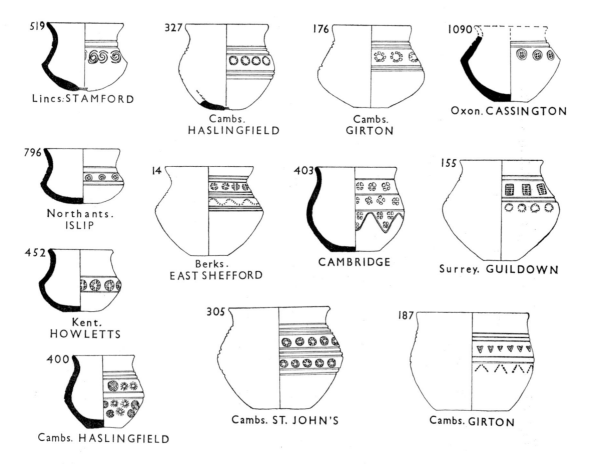

519 Lincs: STAMFORD

327 Cambs. HASLINGFIELD

176 Cambs. GIRTON

1090 Oxon. CASSINGTON

796 Northants. ISLIP

14 Berks. EAST SHEFFORD

403 CAMBRIDGE

155 Surrey. GUILDOWN

452 Kent. HOWLETTS

400 Cambs. HASLINGFIELD

305 Cambs. ST. JOHN'S

187 Cambs. GIRTON

Fig. 42. *Hand-made biconi from Sancton, Yorks.*

SCALE: Pottery 1:4; Stamps 1:1

2294 YORKS., SANCTON 99 (Hull Museum)
Wide-mouthed biconical bowl with sharply everted rim.
Decorated with three sharp necklines above a zigzag line of five jabs, as if made by a small comb. Above the carination are two more lines, and below it a similar zigzag line of jabs.

2285 YORKS., SANCTON 124a (Hull Museum)
Wide-mouthed biconical urn with everted rim.
Decorated with five necklines above a row of stamps and two more lines. Below is a zigzag line of jabs similar to those on 2294. Resting on the carination are three more lines below which is another zigzag line of jabs.

2298 YORKS., SANCTON 107 (Hull Museum)
Wide-mouthed biconical bowl with everted rim.
Decorated with a row of the same stamp as that on 2285, though impressed diagonally, demarcated above by four and below by two lines above the carination. Below is a zigzag line of five jabs similar to those on 2294.

2278 YORKS., SANCTON 108a (Hull Museum)
Wide-mouthed biconical urn with upright rim.
Decorated with four necklines above a zone composed of two interlacing pairs of zigzag lines, enclosing irregular spaces. In the centre of each space are two vertical lines, to the left of which are three impressions of the same stamp as that on 2285 and 2298. A zigzag line of five jabs runs along the bottom of the zone, interrupted by the decoration. The zone is demarcated below by two lines on the carination, above a further zigzag line of five jabs.

2293 YORKS., SANCTON 98b (Hull Museum)
Sub-biconical urn with upright rim.
Decorated with three necklines from which hang rectangular two-line panels filled with stamps similar to those on 2285. Between the panels are short diagonal lines. Below the maximum diameter is a zigzag line of five jabs.

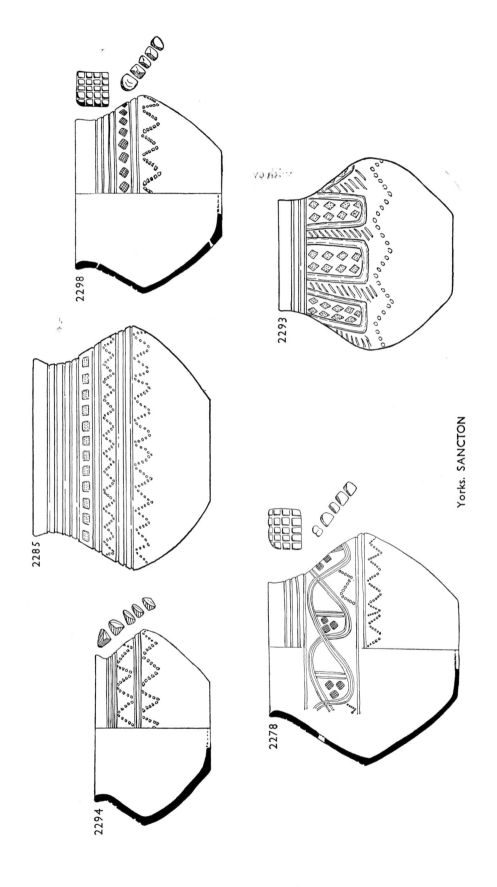

2298

2293

2285

2294

2278

Yorks. SANCTON

Fig. 43. *The Kettering long-boss potter*

SCALE: Pottery 1:4; Stamps 1:2

747 NORTHANTS., KETTERING (Kettering Museum 81)
Large biconical bossed urn with everted rim: grey ware, probably smoothed. Decorated with two rows of stamps and one of double dots set alternately, separated from one another and demarcated above and below by three lines. On the carination are seven hollow bosses, every alternate boss continuing upwards through the decoration to the top three necklines. These long bosses carry a vertical row of nicks demarcated on each side by two vertical lines. The intervening bosses carry three vertical lines and separate panels with two-line pendent triangles, each containing a double row of dots, three horizontal lines, another double row of dots, and four more lines. There are some irregularities in carrying out this decorative scheme. One stamp is used.

758 NORTHANTS., KETTERING (Northampton Museum D 309/ 1954–5)
Large biconical bossed urn, rim missing: smooth grey/brown ware.
Decorated with at least three alternate rows of stamps and double dots on the neck, separated from one another and demarcated below by two or three lines. On the carination are four hollow bosses, of which the alternate ones continue upwards through the decoration. These long bosses carry three vertical lines. Between the bosses are two-line pendent triangles outlined with various arrangements of stamps. Two stamps are used, one of which is on 747.

746 NORTHANTS., KETTERING (Kettering Museum 80)
Large sub-biconical bossed urn with flaring rim: smooth red/brown ware. Decorated similarly to 747, but with four rows of stamps or double dots. On the carination are nine hollow bosses, the alternate ones continuing upwards through the decoration to the top necklines and carrying three vertical lines. Between the bosses are two-line pendent triangles, containing an inner line of dots, double along the top edge, and with a vertical row of dots down the centre. The arrangement is somewhat irregular. One stamp is used.

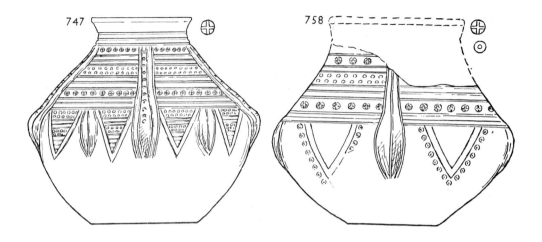

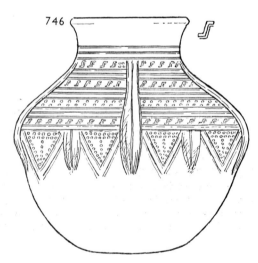

Northants. KETTERING

Fig. 44. *Cambridge and Northamptonshire potters*

SCALE: Pottery 1:4; Stamps 1:2

748 NORTHANTS., KETTERING (Kettering Museum 2)
Small stamped *Buckelurne* of Group V with everted rim: rather rough dark-grey ware, once burnished.
Decorated with two lines of stamps on the neck, each demarcated below by a single line. On the shoulder are four vertical hollow bosses between which are slashed diagonal hollow bosses. Each boss is outlined with a single line and the spaces between them are filled with stamps. Three stamps are used.

734 NORTHANTS., BARTON SEAGRAVE (British Museum 91 3-19. 1)
Wide-mouthed sub-biconical urn with hollow neck and everted rim: smooth dark ware.
Decorated with three rows of stamps on the neck, each demarcated above and below by a single line. Below is a single chevron line, outlined on both sides, and at the top, with stamps. Three stamps are used, of which two are on 748.

227 CAMBS., GIRTON (Girton College)
Globular urn with everted rim: smooth dark ware.
Decorated with three sharp necklines, below which is a zone of three-line chevrons, demarcated below by two horizontal lines between which is a row of stamps. One stamp is used.

810 NORTHANTS., LITTLE WELDON (Northampton Museum D 310/1954–5)
Wide-mouthed biconical bowl with sharply everted rim: rough corky grey/brown ware.
Decorated with three sharp necklines, below which is a zone of three-line chevrons, above a row of stamps demarcated on the carination by two more lines. One stamp is used, similar to that on 227.

196 CAMBS., GIRTON (Cambridge Museum of Arch. and Eth.)
Sharply biconical shoulder-boss urn, rim missing: smooth buff/brown ware.
Decorated with at least four necklines, below which is a zone of three-line chevrons, the spaces filled irregularly with stamps, and demarcated below by a single line. On the carination are four groups of three bosses and one of four, each boss outlined by two lines. The panels between the groups of bosses are filled with one or two single-line *stehende Bogen*, sometimes interlaced. One stamp is used.

742 NORTHANTS., NEWTON-IN-THE-WILLOWS (Kettering Museum 130)
Large sub-biconical bossed urn with everted rim: polished black ware, well made.
Decorated with three fine necklines, below which are triangular groups of stamps arranged to fill the spaces between chevron lines which have not been drawn. Below are twenty-two long hollow bosses, each outlined by a single line. One stamp is used, similar to that on 196.

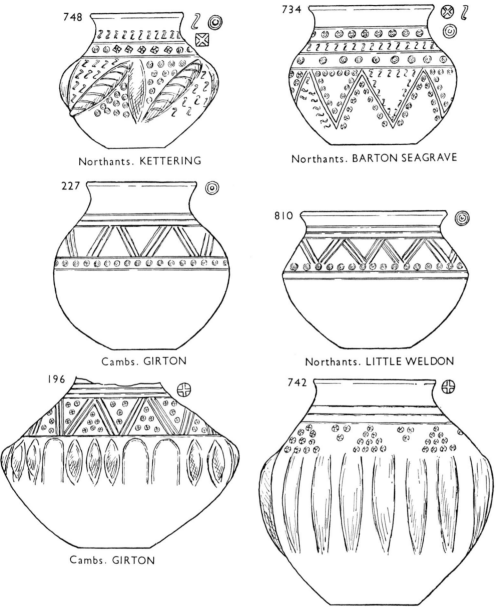

748   Northants. KETTERING

734   Northants. BARTON SEAGRAVE

227   Cambs. GIRTON

810   Northants. LITTLE WELDON

196   Cambs. GIRTON

742   Northants. NEWTON-IN-THE-WILLOWS

Fig. 45. *The Lackford/Thurmaston potter*

SCALE: Pottery 1:4; Stamps 1:2

996 SUFFOLK, LACKFORD (Cambridge Museum of Arch. and Eth. 50. 33)

Large stamped *Buckelurne* of Group V with upright neck and rim.

Decorated with three necklines above three rows of stamps each demarcated by a slight line. Below are large vertical bosses outlined by a single line, and carrying a central vertical line with a vertical row of stamps on each side. The bosses are surrounded on each side by a row of stamps. The spaces between the bosses contain small round bosses encircled by stamps which form a further line between them. Five stamps are used.

1112 LEICS., THURMASTON 88 (Leicester Museum)

Large stamped *Buckelurne* of Group V with upright neck and slightly everted rim: smooth dark-grey ware.

Decorated with four strong necklines above five large diagonal feathered zoomorphic bosses with stamps for eyes. To the right of the head of each boss is a large rosette stamp, and the area between the bosses and the necklines is filled with irregular rows of stamps. Four stamps are used, three of which are the same as those on 996.

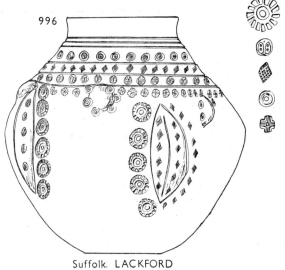

996

Suffolk. LACKFORD

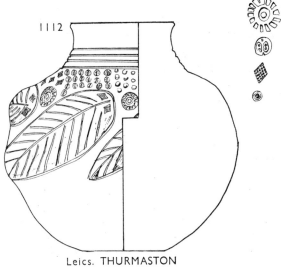

1112

Leics. THURMASTON

Fig. 46. *The Sancton/Elkington potter*

SCALE: Pottery 1:4; Stamps 1:2

129 YORKS., SANCTON 18 (Hull Museum)
Sub-biconical *Buckelurne* of Group II, with narrow neck and everted rim: dull black ware. Decorated with nine necklines above four vertical slashed bosses, the panels between which contain a triangle of small round bosses, one at the top and two on the maximum diameter. The panels are filled with freehand designs, one containing two large three-line swastikas, another continuous chevrons, a third one swastika and a B reversed, and the fourth two rows of diagonal lines set in opposite directions.

2275 YORKS., SANCTON 9a (Hull Museum)
Large biconical *Buckelurne* of Group II, with narrow neck and everted rim.
Decorated with four necklines above a number of small, round bosses. On the carination is another row of small round bosses. The spaces are partly divided by groups of three vertical lines forming panels containing freehand designs which include an S reversed, three-line surrounds to some of the bosses, and three-line *stehende Bogen*.

130 YORKS., SANCTON W1 (Hull Museum)
Small sub-biconical *Buckelurne* of Group II, rim missing: rough brown ware, very lopsided, but with burnished surface.
The upper part is restored but probably had necklines. Below are four vertical slashed bosses, the panels between which contain small round bosses arranged as on 129. The panels are filled with freehand designs, one containing at least six swastikas, another four groups of concentric semi-circles facing inwards, a third an arrangement of diagonal lines, the fourth a curvilinear motif, now restored, probably originally an S reversed.

2025 YORKS., SANCTON (Ashmolean Museum)
Sharply biconical *Buckelurne* of Group IV with narrow neck and everted rim: smooth mottled black/red/fawn ware.
Decorated with six necklines above four vertical slashed bosses, the panels between which contain small round bosses arranged as on 129 and 130. The panels are filled with freehand designs, one containing two reversed S surrounded by stamps, between which is a small swastika with a stamp in each quadrant: in two panels are continuous rows of chevron lines, and in the fourth, two swastikas. One stamp is used, and in one panel only.

2276 YORKS., SANCTON 95 (Hull Museum)
Sub-biconical bossed urn with narrow neck and everted rim, base missing.
Decorated with four necklines and a row of small round bosses on the maximum diameter, above which is a random arrangement of vertical rows of diagonal lines and of single chevrons set one above the other. In one place are two vertical lines, as though to divide the space into panels, but the design does not appear to have been completed.

660 LINCS., ELKINGTON 110 (Lincoln Museum)
Sub-biconical *Buckelurne* of Group II with narrow neck and everted rim: grey/brown ware.
Decorated with four necklines above five vertical slashed bosses, the panels between which contain small round bosses arranged as on 129, 130, and 2025. The panels are filled with groups of diagonal and curving horizontal lines.

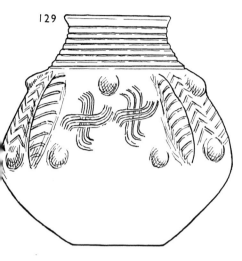

129

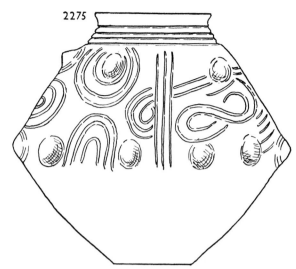

2275

Yorks. SANCTON

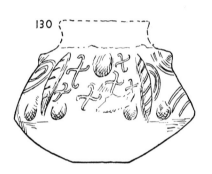

130

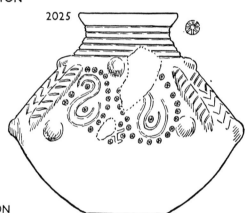

2025

Yorks. SANCTON

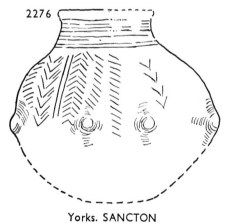

2276

Yorks. SANCTON

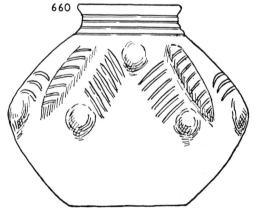

660

Lincs. ELKINGTON

Fig. 47. *Stylistic links between Yorkshire and Lincolnshire*

SCALE: Pottery 1:4; Stamps 1:2

2300 YORKS., SANCTON 111a (Hull Museum)
Wide-mouthed biconical urn with sharply everted rim.
Decorated with two rows of stamps separated and demarcated above and below by a wide groove.
Below is a zone of two-line chevrons. One stamp is used.

83 YORKS., HEWORTH 10 (Yorkshire Museum, York)
Shouldered urn with tall upright neck and rim: hard rough dark-grey/black ware.
Decorated with two groups of three deeply incised necklines between which is a row of stamps.
Below is a zone of three-line chevrons. One stamp is used, similar to that on 2300.

1145 LINCS., WEST KEAL (Lincoln Museum 18–54)
Wide-mouthed biconical urn with sharply everted rim: smooth brown ware.
Decorated with two groups of four necklines between which is a row of stamps. Below is a zone
of two/three-line chevrons. One stamp is used, similar to that on 2300 and 83.

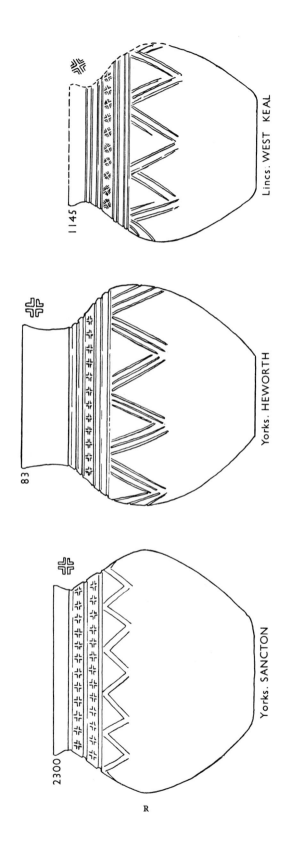

1145

Lincs. WEST KEAL

83

Yorks. HEWORTH

2300

Yorks. SANCTON

Fig. 48. The Illington/Lackford potter

SCALE: Pottery 1:4; Stamps 1:2

2144 NORFOLK, ILLINGTON 147 B (Norwich Museum)
Globular urn with short neck and everted rim: smooth dark-brown ware.
Decorated with ten close-set necklines above a line of stamps, four more lines, another line of stamps and four more lines. Two stamps are used.

930 SUFFOLK, LACKFORD (Cambridge Museum of Arch. and Eth. 48. 2478)
Globular urn with short neck and slightly everted rim: smooth dark-brown ware, burnished.
Decorated with seven close-set necklines above a line of stamps, three more lines, a zone of three-line chevrons and three more lines. One stamp is used.

2060 SUFFOLK, WEST STOW HEATH (Ashmolean Museum 1909-435)
Globular urn with short neck and slightly everted rim: smooth dark ware, burnished.
Decorated with nine close-set necklines above a line of stamps and four more lines: below are two-line pendent triangles filled with stamps. Two stamps are used.

2625 CAMBS., LITTLE WILBRAHAM (Cambridge Museum of Arch. and Eth. 48. 1266)
Globular urn with short neck and slightly everted rim: grey ware.
Decorated with twelve close-set necklines above a line of stamps and four more lines: below are two-line pendent triangles filled with stamps. Two stamps are used.

286 CAMBS., ST. JOHN'S (Cambridge Museum of Arch. and Eth.)
Large globular urn with short conical neck and straight rim: smooth grey/black ware.
Decorated with eight close-set necklines above a raised slashed collar, four more lines and a line of stamps, another four lines and another line of stamps. On the maximum diameter are ten narrow vertical slashed bosses, separating two-line pendent panels containing a line of stamps demarcated above and below by four close-set lines, then a zone of triangular groups of dots set two-and-one above three more lines. The lower parts of the panels are pendent swags filled with stamps. Four stamps are used (identical with those on 931).

931 SUFFOLK, LACKFORD (Cambridge Museum of Arch. and Eth. 48. 2475)
Large globular urn with short neck and everted rim: smooth brown ware, once burnished.
Decorated with five close-set necklines above a raised slashed collar, four more lines, a line of stamps, six more lines, and another raised collar, partly slashed and partly dotted. From this collar depend about nine narrow vertical bosses, carrying close-set vertical lines and separating panels containing large raised swastikas alternately slashed and dotted, demarcated above by four and below by five/six close-set lines, and with lines of stamps between the arms. Below the bosses and panels is a further horizontal line of stamps above three more lines. Four stamps are used (identical with those on 286).

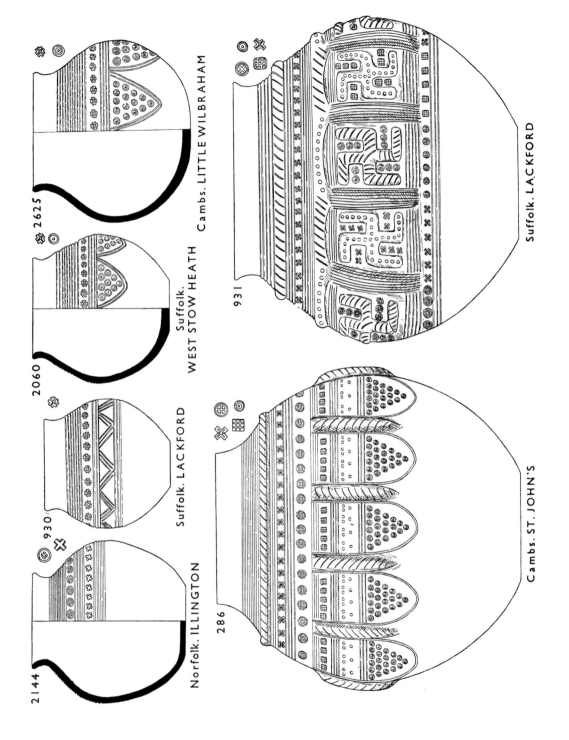

2625   Cambs. LITTLE WILBRAHAM

2060   Suffolk.
        WEST STOW HEATH

930   Suffolk. LACKFORD

2144   Norfolk. ILLINGTON

931   Suffolk. LACKFORD

286   Cambs. ST. JOHN'S

(244)

Fig. 49. 'Wyrm' designs

SCALE 1:4

74 YORKS., SANCTON (Ashmolean Museum 1886–1334)
Globular urn with hollow neck and swollen rim: pitted dark ware.
Decorated with three shallow tooled necklines above free-hand curvilinear designs of which one is partly missing, another is a large upright cross, and the third and largest a complex pattern of running curves probably intended to represent 'wyrm'-like figures.

1539 NORFOLK, CAISTOR-BY-NORWICH N 69 (Norwich Museum)
Large wide-mouthed bowl with tall concave neck and flaring rim: very well-made hard dark ware with high black burnish.
Decorated with four strong neck grooves above two series of free-hand interlocking reversed S- curves in three strong grooves, each forming a procession of 'wyrm'-like figures. At each end the two processions meet at a group of three-line *stehende Bogen* set between three vertical grooves, possibly intended to indicate fenced grave-mounds.

511 LINCS., WEST KEAL (Lincoln Museum 13–54)
Shouldered urn with tall hollow neck and everted rim: polished grey/brown ware.
Decorated with a raised slashed collar at the base of the neck, below which is a zone containing groups of three diagonal lines irregularly arranged, between some of which is a single stamp. The zone is demarcated above and below by a horizontal groove, below which are irregular three-line chevrons. Between some of these is a single stamp, and in one place a two-line reversed S-curve representing a 'wyrm'. One stamp is used.

779 NORTHANTS., KETTERING (Northampton Museum D 325/54–5)
Shoulder-boss urn with tall conical neck and slightly everted rim (restored): hard burnished dark ware.
Decorated with four strong necklines above a zone of interlocking two-line zoomorphic curves, each with a finger-tip to represent an eye at one end. On the shoulder are four bosses, each outlined with three lines and carrying a large finger-tip above a triangle of three dots. The intervening panels contain a line of dots and three-line pendent triangles with three dots in each.

2279 YORKS., SANCTON 112a (Hull Museum)
Wide-mouthed biconical urn with everted rim.
Decorated with three necklines, below which is a broad zone containing two-line interlocking reversed S-curves above three more lines on the carination. The triangular areas above the curves are filled with stamps. One stamp is used.

66 YORKS., SANCTON (Ashmolean Museum 1886–1306)
Large shouldered urn, rim missing: pitted dark ware.
Decorated with a row of stamps, demarcated above and below by two necklines. Below is a zone containing two-line interlocking reversed S-curves above three more lines. The triangular areas above the curves are filled with stamps. Below are two-line hanging swags. One stamp is used, different from that on 2279, though the two urns clearly come from the same workshop.

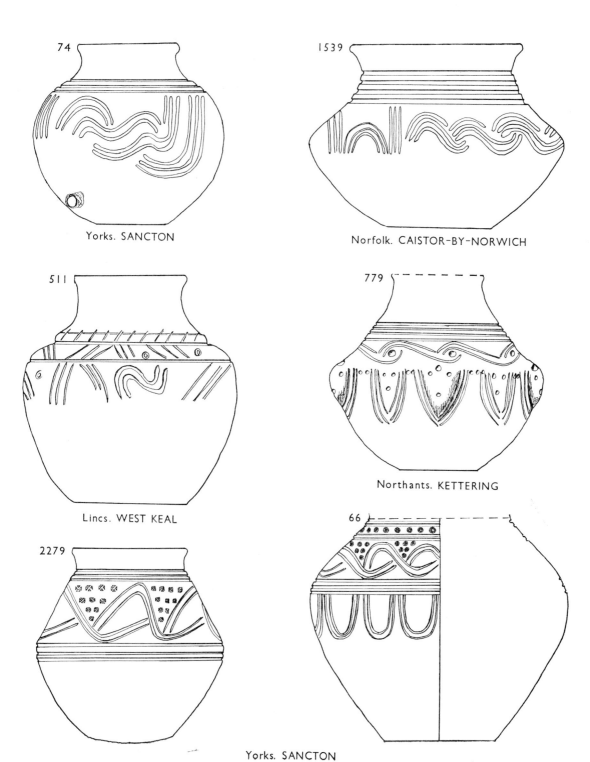

74   Yorks. SANCTON

1539   Norfolk. CAISTOR-BY-NORWICH

511   Lincs. WEST KEAL

779   Northants. KETTERING

2279

66   Yorks. SANCTON

Fig. 50. *Urns carrying runes or rune-like signs I*

SCALE: Pottery 1:4; Stamps 1:1

1653 NORFOLK, CAISTOR-BY-NORWICH R 13 (Norwich Museum)
Sub-biconical urn with slightly everted rim: smooth black ware, once burnished.
Decorated on the neck with five strong lines, below which are seven '↑' runes drawn free-hand, two of these being separated by one group of four diagonal lines.

N104 NORFOLK, CAISTOR-BY-NORWICH N 104 (Norwich Museum)
Upper part of a shoulder-boss urn: thick smoothed brown ware.
Decorated on the neck with three lines above groups of at least two shoulder-bosses: between the bosses of each group are three firm vertical lines, and in the panels between the groups are large firmly drawn two-line chevrons with a vertical line depending from the apex, which may be intended for '↑' runes.

1853 NORFOLK, CAISTOR-BY-NORWICH P 36(c) (Norwich Museum)
Part of a shouldered urn, rim and base missing: smooth dark ware, well made.
Decorated on the neck with at least two lines of stamps below each of which are three lines. On the shoulder are three-line pendent swags containing two groups of three vertical lines. Two stamps appear, of which that filling the lower line is circular and contains a raised '↑' rune.

M5(b) NORFOLK, CAISTOR-BY-NORWICH M 5(b) (Norwich Museum)
Small part of a shouldered or globular urn, rim and base missing: smooth brown ware.
Decorated apparently with random stamping without lines. One stamp appears, and there are also two scratched '↑' runes.

1711 NORFOLK, CAISTOR-BY-NORWICH M 33 (Norwich Museum)
Large shouldered urn, rim missing: smooth brown ware.
Decorated on the neck with two strong lines above large two-line chevrons, from the points of at least some of which depend two vertical lines, thus producing what may be intended for '↑' runes.
This urn was found in fragments in a group that had probably been disturbed by later Anglo-Saxon grave-diggers. In doubtful association with it was part of a bronze cruciform brooch, too distorted by fire for its type to be ascertainable.

1701 NORFOLK, CAISTOR-BY-NORWICH W 51 (Norwich Museum)
Part of a globular urn with conical neck, rim and base missing: smooth dark ware.
Decorated with at least six close-set necklines above irregular free-hand designs separated by groups of vertical lines below a line of dots and a short horizontal line. The designs include a large two-line diagonal cross, and a two-line 'V' bisected by a single vertical line which continues below it. There is a horizontal line of dots between the upper points of each of these figures. They may be intended for the 'X' and 'Y' runes respectively.

1703 NORFOLK, CAISTOR-BY-NORWICH P 7 (Norwich Museum)
Globular urn with short conical neck and everted rim: smoothed red/brown ware.
Decorated with four necklines between the third and fourth of which there is a widely spaced line of dots. Below are groups of three/four diagonal or vertical lines, in each panel between which is a short horizontal groove above a deep circular depression. Below this are linear designs which could be intended for the 'Y', 'Λ' and 'ᛉ' runes, the last being on its side as 'W'.

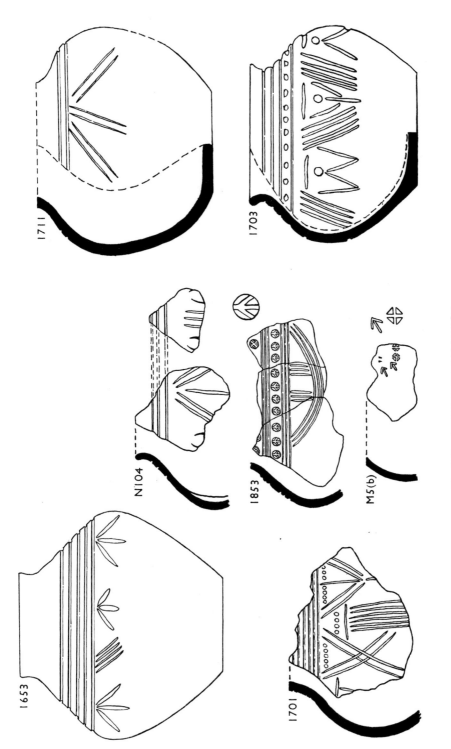

1711

1703

N104

1853

M5(b)

1653

1701

Norfolk. CAISTOR-BY-NORWICH

Fig. 51. *Urns carrying runes or rune-like signs II*

SCALE: Pottery 1:4

1675 NORFOLK, CAISTOR-BY-NORWICH N 25 (Norwich Museum)
Shoulder-boss urn with conical neck and upright rim: smooth brown ware, well made
and once burnished.
Decorated low on the neck with six close-set fine lines above seven hollow vertical shoulder-
bosses, separating panels outlined on each side with three fine vertical lines and filled
with linear designs which may be intended for the 'X' rune (three times), the '✳' rune
(twice upside down as '⅄'), and the '⋈' rune (twice upside down as '⋈').

2987 SUFFOLK, LACKFORD (Cambridge Museum of Arch. and Eth. 50. 101)
Part of a shoulder-boss urn, neck, rim and base missing: brown ware, burnished.
Decorated low on the neck with at least two close-set lines above at least seven hollow
vertical shoulder-bosses, separating panels outlined on each side with two vertical lines
and filled with linear designs which may be intended for the 'X' rune, the '⋈' rune (twice),
the '⋈' rune (upside down as '⋈'), and possibly the '✳' rune (once as '✶', and once as
'⋏').
1675 and 2987 (Caistor-by-Norwich N 25 and Lackford 50. 101) are similar in form,
fabric, and design, and may well be products of the same workshop.

718 NORFOLK, NORTH ELMHAM (formerly Trollope and V. B. Crowther
Beynon collections: see drawing by R. Elwes at the Society of Antiquaries in J. Hawkes
Early Britain (1945), 45).
Shoulder-boss urn with conical neck, rim missing: smooth grey ware, probably once
burnished.
Decorated low on the neck with six close-set light lines, above (?) nine hollow vertical
shoulder-bosses, slashed horizontally and outlined on each side by a single vertical line.
The three surviving panels contain linear designs apparently intended for the '⌇' rune
(twice on its side as 'W'), and the '⋈' rune (once on its side as 'xx').

1038 SUFFOLK, INGHAM (Society of Antiquaries C 2)
Shoulder-boss urn with conical neck and everted rim: hard black ware, burnished.
Decorated on the neck with a line of stamps demarcated above and below by four strong
lines. On the shoulder are four hollow oval bosses separating panels demarcated on each
side and divided centrally by three/four strong lines. The spaces between these grouped
lines contain linear designs apparently intended for the '⌇' rune (once), the 'ß' rune
(twice), and the 'R' rune (five times).
The general similarity of design between 718 and 1038 (North Elmham and Ingham)
makes it possible that they are products of the same workshop.

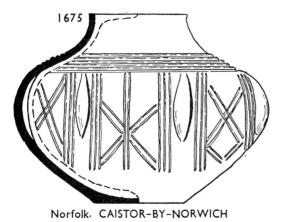

Norfolk. CAISTOR-BY-NORWICH

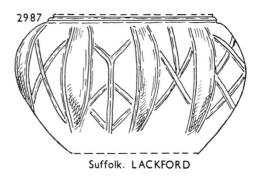

Suffolk. LACKFORD

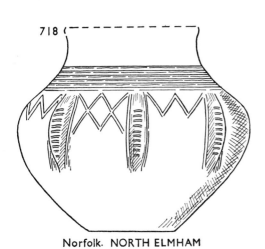

Norfolk. NORTH ELMHAM

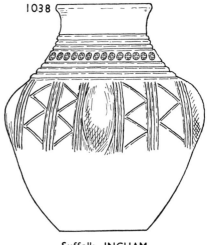

Suffolk. INGHAM

INDEX

PLATE 1

a. Y36

b. P15

c. A11

d. X2

EARLY URNS FROM CAISTOR-BY-NORWICH. Scale 1:3

PLATE 2

b. Kirton Lindsey

d. Long Wittenham Gr. 57

a. Mitcham Gr. 205

c. Reading Gr. 13

PEDESTAL AND LONG-BOSS POTTERY. Scale 1 : 2

PLATE 3

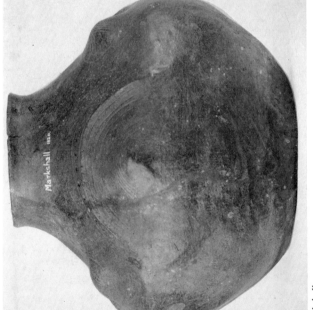

b. Abingdon Cro

d. Kettering

a. Markshall

c. Newton-in-the-Willows

BUCKELURNEN OF GROUPS II–V. Scale 1:3

PLATE 4

a

b

c

d

URNS FROM KETTERING WITH BICONICAL DECORATION. Scale 1:4

a and *b*. Simple types
c and *d*. Combined with bossed panel-style

PLATE 5

a

b

c

d

SHOULDER-BOSS URNS FROM KETTERING WITH RECTANGULAR
PANEL-STYLE DECORATION. Scale 1:3

PLATE 6

d. Drakelow

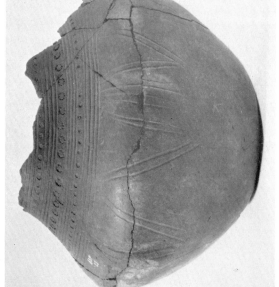

b, Newton-in-the-Willows

a. Kettering

c. Barton Seagrave

URNS WITH TRIANGULAR PANEL-STYLE DECORATION. Scale 3 : 10

PLATE 7

b

a

d

c

TWO KETTERING POTTERS. Scale 3 : 10

PLATE 8

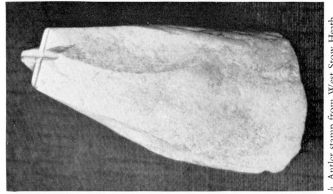

b. Antler stamp from West Stow Heath

a. Detail of stamped decoration on urns from Lackford

THE ILLINGTON/LACKFORD POTTER. Scale 1 : 1